THE CONTEMPORARY IRISH NOVEL

Related titles from Palgrave Macmillan

James Acheson (ed.), *The British and Irish Novel since 1960*

Liam Harte and Michael Parker (eds), *Contemporary Irish Fiction: Themes, Tropes, Theories*

Jennifer M. Jeffers, *The Irish Novel at the End of the Twentieth Century: Gender, Bodies, Power*

Christina Hunt Mahoney, *Contemporary Irish Literature: Transforming Tradition*

The Contemporary Irish Novel

Critical Readings

Linden Peach

First published 2004 by
PALGRAVE MACMILLAN
Houndmills, Basingstoke, Hampshire RG21 6XS and
175 Fifth Avenue, New York, N.Y. 10010
Companies and representatives throughout the world

PALGRAVE MACMILLAN is the global academic imprint of
the Palgrave Macmillan division of St. Martin's Press, LLC and of
Palgrave Macmillan Ltd. Macmillan® is a registered trademark in the
United States, United Kingdom and other countries. Palgrave is a
registered trademark in the European Union and other countries.

ISBN 0–333–94892–0 hardback
ISBN 0–333–94893–9 paperback

This book is printed on paper suitable for recycling and made from fully
managed and sustained forest sources.

A catalogue record for this book is available from the British Library.

Library of Congress Cataloging-in-Publication Data
    Peach, Linden, 1951–
    The contemporary Irish novel : critical readings / Linden Peach.
        p. cm.
    Includes bibliographical references and index.
    ISBN 0–333–94892–0 — ISBN 0–333–94893–9 (pbk.)
        1. English fiction – Irish authors – History and criticism.
    2. English fiction – 20th century – History and criticism.
    3. Ireland – Intellectual life – 20th century. 4 Northern
    Ireland – Intellectual life. 5. Northern Ireland – In literature.
    6. Ireland – In literature. I. Title.

PR8803.I43 2004
823'.910   2003054925

10 9   8   7   6   5   4   3   2   1
13 12 11 10 09 08 07 06 05 04

Printed in China

For Angela, Hedley and Cynthia

Contents

Preface

This book offers the reader a discussion of selected contemporary novels, the majority of which were published in the late 1980s and early 1990s that make or have made a significant contribution to the literature of Ireland and Northern Ireland, and to the development of the novel in English. (I have tried throughout to use 'Ireland' to refer to the Republic, rather than the island as a whole, and terms such as 'Irish literature' and the 'Irish novel' to refer to both the Republic and Northern Ireland.) Established writers who began publishing in the 1960s and the 1970s but have still produced distinctive and original work in the 1990s – William Trevor (*Felicia's Journey*), John Banville (*Birchwood*) and Brian Moore (*The Magician's Wife*) – are represented alongside some of the important figures that have emerged since the 1980s such as Dermot Bolger (*Emily's Shoes, Father's Music*), Roddy Doyle (*The Snapper, The Woman Who Walked Into Doors*), Emma Donoghue (*Stir-fry, Slammerkin*), Patrick McCabe (*The Butcher Boy*), Mary Morrissy (*Mother of Pearl*) and Robert McLiam Wilson (*Eureka Street*).

Up to a point, the selection of texts is intended to be representative – for example, in terms of style, gender, geography and religion – rather than definitive. It is intended to make a contribution to the wider, fast developing scholarship on Irish writing and, most importantly, contribute to the reader's on-going engagement with Irish literature and the novel generally. I hope that readers will take from this book some ideas that might be developed or might provoke thought and debate. The subjects raised by the discussion of the texts include the mother figure, parent–child relations, domestic violence, child abuse, self-harm, fetishism, modernity and postmodernity. Ostensibly different texts are read in relation to each other and recommended as a way of casting new light even on familiar novels. The selection is intended to reflect the richness and diversity of the contemporary Irish novel, ranging from urban realism, to modern or late modern gothic and speculative narrative.

The critical frameworks within which the novels are discussed are equally eclectic. I draw on work by key European

philosophers, cultural critics, psychoanalysts and linguistic theorists – such as Homi Bhabha, Jean Baudrillard, Jacques Derrida,
Michel Foucault, Melanie Klein and Julia Kristeva – as well as figures, such as the psychoanalyst Dusty Miller, who are less well
known outside their discipline. Hopefully the reader will feel that
their work has been selected as a starting point for criticism or as
providing a framework within which to pursue particular lines of
argument because it is relevant and appropriate to the novels
under discussion. But the book has sought to avoid a rigid distinction between 'literature' and 'theory' in the belief that the
novel, especially at its most philosophical and speculative, makes
its own contribution to theoretical discussion. Directly or indirectly, the Irish novel may be seen as extending our understanding of some of the issues with which theorists such as Kristeva
and postcolonial critics such as Bhabha are concerned. But how
far European theory, even allowing for Ireland and Northern
Ireland's contribution to European letters and the former's participation in European culture(s) and politics, is appropriate to
the writing and culture of Ireland and Northern Ireland is kept in
mind throughout. Moreover, not only is the diversity of Irish
culture and writing stressed throughout the book but also the
blurred boundaries between Ireland and Northern Ireland and
the symbiotic cultural relationships between, for example, Britain
and Northern Ireland and between Ireland and America. Many of
the novels have been selected for the contribution they make in
moving us beyond traditional representations of, for example, the
urban and the rural and for enlarging our perspective of the conflicts and antagonisms within, and centred on, Ireland and
Northern Ireland.

The first three chapters introduce some of the principal themes
and perspectives that underpin the book. Chapter 1 argues that
the contemporary Irish novel occupies an especially complex cultural and intellectual space where there is a strong sense of both
continuity and disruption. This space is similar to that which one
of our leading postcolonial critics, Homi Bhabha, identifies as the
'in-between' space or 'timelag' which those who have been
previously marginalized or silenced enter before they find their
new identities. It argues that the contemporary novel in Ireland
and Northern Ireland, without eliding their different though
interleaved histories and cultures, reflect how there are many
groups of people who have found a voice that has been long

denied them. These groups, and many of the writers featured in this book, because they are giving a voice to what was once concealed or denied, find themselves in spaces that are not only new to them but also marked by uncertainty. The chapter asks, what has this done, is doing, to the wider national identity? It also asks, what has been the effect on Ireland, and in different ways, on Northern Ireland's perception of themselves as part of the late modern or postmodern world? These questions are addressed with reference to some important texts about Northern Ireland in Chapter 2. The focus of that chapter is the extent to which notions of 'modernity' and 'postmodernity' prove problematic when translated into the complexity of Northern Ireland and Ireland. Drawing on the French cultural philosopher Jean Baudrillard's ideas, it explores how some key texts engage with, and at the same time resist, postmodernity. 'Modernity' and 'postmodernity' are seen as concepts at once appropriate and inappropriate to Belfast.

Chapter 3 further develops Bhabha's concept of an 'in-between' space when applied to Ireland and Northern Ireland because, often, what has been previously marginalized or silenced in Irish history has also been shrouded with secrecy. Secrecy has been such a feature of Irish cultural life on a national, local and even domestic level that even Bhabha's vision of the nation state as marked in general by 'internal difference', most obviously applicable to Northern Ireland and Ireland, has to be refocused to take this into account. Moreover, it needs revisioning to acknowledge that in Ireland the previously inarticulate, or unarticulated, challenges our understanding of 'modern', especially in cultural contexts where narratives, too, habitually conceal as much as they reveal. Many of the texts discussed in this book involve protagonists who find themselves in an 'in-between' space, inevitably located between what Bhabha calls 'relocation' and 'reinscription'. The chapter introduces a framework in which to discuss the key protagonists in this respect, and what they are analogous of, provided by the psychoanalyst Sigmund Freud. It argues that Freud's concept of Nachträglichkeit helps us to understand the self-divided nature of a lot of the cultural discourse in contemporary Ireland and Northern Ireland. For the individual, Nachträglichkeit marks the failure of the normal processes of memory in which what is too painful to remember is concealed. The chapter explores ways in which this is analogous of how the nation might discover its own protective shield of memorializing failing.

The three principal texts of Chapter 4 are linked in their preoccupation with 'mimicry' and its role, paradoxically, in both the maintenance and the secret subversion of authority. In each of these texts, these two principal preoccupations are closely interleaved because in each history is read through the interconnection of power, mimicry, authority and subversion. Again, the chapter draws on ideas from the postcolonial critic Homi Bhabha. But it is argued that, although Bhabha writes primarily with the colonial and postcolonial experience in mind, the relationship between power and mimicry enters more generally into contexts that are dependent upon the maintenance of dominant and subordinate relations. The texts in this chapter recognize, like Bhabha and the critic Edward Said upon whose work he draws, that mimicry is an ironic, secretive interface between the dominant authority, and its panoptical vision of identity and status, and the subordinate subject.

The first four chapters of the book argue for the significance for contemporary Irish fiction of Bhabha's ideas about what happens when the previously silenced or marginalized emerge from the margins. Chapter 5, focusing upon secret and forbidden desires in the work of some interesting women writers, explores how this is particularly relevant to work by women writers which demonstrate the truth of his thesis that previously marginalized voices confront and contradict the dominant discourses that have been directly or indirectly responsible for their silence and marginalization. Bhabha's arguments prompt us to examine the consequences for the Irish novel of it occupying an in-between space from where it questions not only the discourses but also the frames of reference that they employ.

Chapter 6 is a development from the previous chapter in that its texts deal with themes that have not been the subject of serious fiction in Ireland and Northern Ireland previously: self-harm and shoe fetishism. They explore activities which are linked in different ways to maintaining a kind of emotional control and which are shrouded with secrecy. Each of these novels also examines the subject of absence, and, what might be called, the fetishization of absence.

The two novels discussed in Chapter 7 develop the way in which women's writing, in emerging from the margins, confront and contradict the discourses that have sought to silence them. The subject of this chapter, though, is how the female and the maternal body have been idealized but also rendered abject in western culture. The extent to which female desire is not only located within metaphor but determined and confined by the available discourses in which it is, and can be, articulated is pursued in relation to what has been described by some critics as a 'new realist' or 'dirty realist' novel and to a text, indebted to Susan Sontag's thinking about metaphor, which ultimately rereads the representation of women from the Bible, and revisions some of the concepts of the Virgin Mary, from feminist perspectives.

Chapter 8 examines novels concerned with violence to women – domestic violence, the murder of a woman who is also a mother by a disturbed child, and a serial killer's pursuit of a young woman who becomes an agent in bringing about his suicide. At one level, in giving a voice to previously concealed or half-admitted subjects, these novels, between them, present a critique of contemporary Ireland and Northern Ireland; of post-industrial society in Britain as much as Ireland; and of Americanization and globalization. However, the chapter also discusses how there is an element in these novels which both attracts and repels the reader, especially in the exposition of sexually related violence. In other words, these texts situate the reader in an in-between position, uncertain, for a while at least, of what to make of them. This aspect of our reading experience is anchored not only in the subject matter of these books, but also in their interest in pushing these kind of subjects to the limit. This is explored with reference to ideas provided by the French cultural historian Michel Foucault.

Although the two novels discussed in Chapter 9 explore, in their different ways, the return of what has been shrouded in secrecy or suppressed, what separates their engagement with Nachträlichkeit, the Freudian concept introduced in Chapter 3, is their emphasis upon examining the possibility of transcendence. While many of the novels that we have looked at so far involve the movement out of silence, the first of the novels examined here moves into, and redefines, silence as an important stage in bringing a female voice and consciousness out of the silence to which they have been confined by patriarchal discourses and cultural practices. Many of the texts discussed up to this final chapter, too, have explored the possibility of moving out of an in-between location, as well as examining what it means to occupy such a physical or temporal space within different specific political and historical contexts. The other text discussed here enters a philosophical space that is in-between conventional representations of good and evil and temporal spaces that are outside of linear, and even cyclical, notions of time. Both novels share a rediscovery of the feminine and what is associated with the maternal and the female body.

Acknowledgements

References to the principal works discussed in the book are to the following editions. Page numbers are given in parentheses in the text.

Linda Anderson, *To Stay Alive* (London: The Bodley Head, 1984).
John Banville, *Birchwood* (1973; London: Picador, 1998).
Dermot Bolger, *The Journey Home* (1990; London: Penguin, 1991).
——, *Emily's Shoes* (1992; London: Penguin, 1993).
——, *A Second Life* (1994; London: Penguin, 1995).
——, *Father's Music* (1997; London: Flamingo, 1998).
Seamus Deane, *Reading in the Dark* (1996; London: Vintage, 1997).
Emma Donoghue, *Stir-fry* (1994; Harmondsworth: Penguin, 1995).
——, *Slammerkin* (2000; London: Virago, 2001).
Roddy Doyle, *The Snapper* (1990; London: Minerva, 1993).
——, *The Van* (1991; London: Minerva, 1996).
——, *The Woman Who Walked Into Doors* (London: Minerva, 1996).
Kathleen Ferguson, *The Maid's Tale* (1994; Northern Ireland: Poolbeg Press, 1995).
Jennifer Johnston, *The Railway Station Man* (1984; London: Penguin, 1989).
——, *Fool's Sanctuary* (1987; London: Penguin, 1988).
Bernard MacLaverty, *Grace Notes* (London: Jonathan Cape, 1997).
Patrick McCabe, *Carn* (1989; London: Picador, 1993).
——, *The Butcher Boy* (1992; London: Pan, 1993).
——, *The Dead School* (1995; London: Picador, 1996).
John McGahern, *Amongst Women* (1990; London: Faber and Faber, 1991).
Brian Moore, *The Magician's Wife* (1997; London: Flamingo, 1998).
Mary Morrissy, *Mother of Pearl* (London: Jonathan Cape, 1996)
Joseph O'Connor, *Cowboys and Indians* (1991; Flamingo, 1992).
Joseph O'Connor, *The Salesman* (1998; London: Vintage, 1999).
Glenn Patterson, *Fat Lad* (1992; London: Minerva, 1993).
William Trevor, *Felicia's Journey* (1994; London: Penguin, 1995).
Robert McLiam Wilson, *Eureka Street* (London: Secker and Warburg, 1996).

Virginia Woolf, *A Room of One's Own. Three Guineas* (Oxford:
  Oxford University Press, 1992).

I should like to thank my friends and colleagues for their advice
and support, and especially the students in my seminars at
Loughborough University for lively discussions that have helped
me in writing this book. I should like to acknowledge the specific
suggestions of Professor Bob Welch, when this book was no more
than an idea, Michael Parker and Siobhán Holland. Most of all,
I would like to thank Angela, as always, for her encouragement.
With immense gratitude, I would like to acknowledge the careful
work of Mukesh and colleagues at Newgen Imaging Systems,
Thiruvanmiyur, India, in the editing and production processes for
this book.

1

Interruptive Narratives

Emergent Voices and Haunted Presents

The contemporary Irish novel occupies an especially complex cultural and intellectual space where there is a strong sense of both continuity and disruption. It is a space that is similar to that which one of our leading postcolonial critics, Homi Bhabha, identifies as the 'in-between' space or 'timelag' which those who have been previously marginalized or silenced enter before they find their new identities. Of course, Irish literature itself has occupied a central position in, for example, the development of European modernism in the early twentieth century. But within Ireland and Northern Ireland, there are many groups of people who have been denied a voice and new writers who believe they speak on their behalf. In finding a voice after so long, these groups and writers find themselves in a space which is not only new to them but marked by uncertainty – an 'in-between' space indeed. Moreover, the subject matter of late twentieth-century Irish literature has, and is, changing despite its, sometimes self-conscious, affinity with the past. Not only are there new topics, opinions and perspectives but also much of what was once implied, at best a covert subtext, is now more overtly articulated. Two of many important questions for us to ask are: What has this done, is doing, to the wider national identity? And what is its effect on Ireland, and in different ways, Northern Ireland's perception of themselves as part of the late modern or postmodern world? In exploring the significance of the 'timelag' for, and in, Irish fiction, I am especially interested in the way this concept at the end of the twentieth century has empowered a number of women writers.

There has not been the sense of anxiety about the future of the novel in Ireland and Northern Ireland as there has been in England. This may be because Ireland and Northern Ireland have not had the same affiliation with the realist novel as is to be found in English culture. As Gerry Smyth, the author of the first, book-length overview of the late twentieth-century Irish novel, observes:

> Many Irish cultural nationalists felt that the novel … was inadequate to the task of representing the nation. The novel, it was felt, was a form that had emerged specifically from the concerns of British cultural history and the existence of its leisured middle class …. At the same time, it seemed to many that Irish society was too 'thin', not subtle or developed or large enough to sustain a novelistic tradition, and when prose fiction did emerge as a form it was the short story – with its roots in the Gaelic story-telling tradition and the moral-didactic tales of the first part of the nineteenth century – rather than the novel which drew the Irish prose writer.   (1997: 25–6)

Thus, the Irish novel in the second half of the twentieth century is not overshadowed as it is for some English writers by anxiety about the form itself. Post-Second World War critics in England saw 'realism' as integral to the novel and argued that a crisis in realism betokened a crisis of the novel as a form. As scholars such as Andrzej Gąsiorek have pointed out, because these critics further believed that liberal ideology underpinned realism, it was a short and inevitable step to believing that a crisis in the realist novel, in turn, betokened a crisis in liberalism. Thus, the novel in England, as Gąsiorek says, equated first with realism and then with liberalism, was perceived as fracturing under aesthetic and social pressures into disparate narrative modes (1995: 6).

If the Irish writer feels any deep affinity with the novel as a verbal art form, it may be when, as Gerry Smyth says, it is 'parodied, mimicked, [and] overlain with other forms of narrative' (1997: 26). Indeed, as Smyth goes on to say, it may be that the Irish writer has not experienced the same sense of anxiety over the realist novel as their English counterpart because it is when the novel employs parody, pastiche and fabulation that it appears to be in least collusion with what he calls 'the colonialist *status quo*'. Thus, although the realist novel has thrived in Ireland and Northern Ireland, there has been a greater readiness to recognize that the mimetic is only a part of the novel along with, for example, parody and fabulation. Perhaps, it is only in the last few decades that English critics have acquired confidence in the

capacity of the novel to adapt and survive in a variety of cultural
contexts – largely as a result of postcolonial criticism's recognition
that the novel, despite being an essentially European art form, has
flourished in a wide variety of postcolonial cultures and aesthetic
situations.

There are aspects of the novel as a genre that appear to lend
themselves to the 'in-between' intellectual, cultural and emotional spaces in which writers dealing with subject matter that
has been hidden or eschewed altogether find themselves. In
Ireland and Northern Ireland, there has always been a strong
sense of the novel as a mutable and transgressive form. But it is
also an appropriate vehicle for the ideological debates and conflicts that constitute so much of Irish social and political history.
Many critics, in and outside Ireland and Northern Ireland, interested in this aspect of the novel and in its appropriateness as a
genre in which to explore the nature of nationhood and national
identity, have made use of the work of the Russian theorist
Mikhail Bakhtin. Smyth is no exception. Drawing broadly on
Bakhtin's work, he suggests that it is possible to see the novel as
'developed to introduce heteroglossia into monologic national
discourse' (1997: 29). Readers unfamiliar with Bakhtin's writings
might be baffled by the terminology here. Smyth is acknowledging that a nation is a product of, and dependent upon, a historical narrative which reflects the voice of the dominant group. But,
if we look beneath any national voice there are many voices –
what Bakhtin calls 'heteroglossia' or 'many tongueness' – some
of which, at least, are suppressed or marginalized by the dominant discourse. Bakhtin (1984) argued that the novel as an art
form has the capacity to give simultaneous expression to a variety of voices, and competing ideologies, and, thereby, to under-
mine the language of hegemonic, or 'centralising' groups and
forces. But, Bhabha's concept of the in-between adds another
dimension to this argument that is relevant to the Irish novel.
While the novel, because of what Bakhtin sees as its innate 'many
tongueness', has the potential to bring hitherto marginalized
voices to the fore, these voices, and indeed often the topics with
which they are concerned, enter a 'timelag' in the Bhabha sense
of the concept.

The extent to which Ireland and Northern Ireland have
contributed to the development of European art and aesthetics cannot be gainsaid. (Here I don't want to elide Ireland and Northern

Ireland as if they did not have their own histories and important cultural differences, despite the interconnections between them.) Yet it is worth asking how applicable some European cultural or aesthetic theory is to Ireland or Northern Ireland. Bakhtin's now very familiar thesis that any linguistic community consists of multiple social languages (1981: 325–6) has an obvious appropriateness for Ireland and Northern Ireland as generally perceived in fiction, and certainly the British mass media, in the 1980s and 1990s. The concomitant 'heteroglossia' within the novel as a genre, as contemporary critics such as David Lloyd have argued, has enabled Irish fiction to contribute to the awareness of this diversity. But it is difficult to ignore the peculiarly fluid and complex nature of the diversity within contemporary Ireland and Northern Ireland. The persistence of tradition and customary affiliations (however they may be redefined in modern Ireland), the presence of freshly emerging voices, the absent presence of voices that are still occluded and the shifting balances and alliances in spheres of cultural and socio-economic influence in Ireland and Northern Ireland constitute a context in which Bakhtin's ideas are implicitly rewritten.

Realism and Non-realist Fiction

It is difficult to study literature without coming across the opposition that some critics create between 'realist' and 'non-realist' fiction. The differences between the two are complex. Realist fiction is generally associated with an assumption that what one sees as one looks out on the world is 'real'. Its window on to the world is a sheet of clear, transparent glass whereas, for others, recognizing, for example, partiality, subjectivity, cultural influences and the unreliability of perception, the window on to the world is more like a piece of stained glass. The apparent confidence in its world view that characterizes many realist novels is matched by equal faith in the central, authoritative voice that shapes and determines the nature of the text, the selection of its dilemmas and issues, the resolutions and how the text itself is brought to a satisfying closure. What happens to the style and organization of a text when the author begins to entertain the complexity of human perception and the random nature of perception and memory is evident if we turn to James Joyce's *Ulysses* or compare his English contemporary Virginia Woolf's *Mrs Dalloway* with what she regarded as her earlier 'traditional' work. She was, of course, influenced in writing *Mrs Dalloway* by *Ulysses* – both novels are concerned with events that occur on a single day and invest much in trying to represent perception and thought in ways that are faithful to their partiality, randomness and selectivity.

Joyce's influence upon one of England's foremost writers of what has been generally regarded as 'non-realist' fiction is important to my argument. Joyce's determining presence makes it difficult to think of a linear development from the early to the late twentieth century. But it also means that it is not as natural and inevitable in Ireland and Northern Irealnd as in England to think in terms of a 'singular realism'. In both Ireland and Northern Ireland, the concept of a single authoritative world view has inevitably seemed hollow. After the 1937 Constitution which sought to shape the Republic according to Catholic values, which privileged the rural bourgeoisie over their urban counterparts and hardly favoured women at all, other than as wives and home-makers, no one in mid-twentieth-century Ireland could but be aware of what Bakhtin calls a 'monological national discourse'. But such an uncompromising national discourse drew attention to the almost suppressed heterogeneity of Ireland. What the monological national discourse sought to eschew found expression, especially in rural Ireland, in ways that became shrouded with secrecy. For example, in her novel *Stir-fry*, discussed in Chapter 5, Emma Donoghue describes the heightened secrecy with which women read the new feminist texts of the 1960s.

The diversity in Irish fiction, however, is based, at least in part, on recognition that realism is a much more open concept than English critics after the Second World War were willing to acknowledge. The novel that employed different narrative modes, and addressed different aesthetic and political convictions, was not viewed with the same degree of alarm and despondency as in England because Irish fiction had always responded in different ways to different socio-historic contexts. I am not, however, suggesting that the Irish novel is inevitably more sophisticated than the English novel. Only that the sophistry of the English novel generally went unrecognized by post-War English critics who tended to assign a naiveté to realism that in practice it never really possessed.

Thus, the binarism of realist and non-realist writing has never haunted Irish literary criticism as it has English literary scholarship, and, in fact, it would not be a very useful distinction to make in relation to Irish fiction. Joseph McMinn reminds us that it is 'a drastic over-simplification of the genre, its complex Irish manifestations, and the dynamic relation between realistic and non-realistic styles of writing' (2000: 80, 81). In trying to understand what the Irish writer and critic have seen in realism that has prevented the kind of anxieties about the novel that for several decades dogged English literary criticism, it may be useful to call upon the work of a European literary theorist, Paul Ricoeur, who, like Bakhtin, has made an important contribution to our understanding of the nature of concepts such as 'realism' and 'mimesis'.

In 'Mimesis and Representation', Ricoeur argues that 'mimesis' is double edged. 'Reality' is not configured but reconfigured in the 'realist' text. In other words, for Ricoeur, there is more active agency in realist novels than we sometimes care to admit and much more engagement with the nature of realism, perception and consciousness, which are generally seen as the territory of non-realistic fiction. Thus, realist novelists, Ricoeur suggests, are more self-consciously concerned with the nature of their art and not as accepting of the apparent transparency of the windows through which they look as the binarism of 'realistic' and 'non-realistic' might suggest. Realistic writing, Ricoeur, usefully stresses, is a 'productive' and not a 'mirror' referencing (1991: 137).

Moving from Ricoeur's work in the latter part of the twentieth century to the beginning of the twenty-first century, scepticism about realism as a 'mirror' referencing is prevalent in literary, social and cultural criticism. It is the given from which we now often start to argue rather than the point that has to be made. Interest in the 'productive', or we might say 'creative', nature of referencing is the product of wider thinking about representation that has many ramifications for Irish literary culture. What we see in the contemporary Irish novel is the influence on artists and writers of a wider, international transformation in how representation is regarded and the legacy of Irish modernists such as James Joyce. In the Irish, and the Anglo-American and European novel, for example, this is evident in its 'metafiction', that is fiction's self-conscious awareness of its role in the process of reconfiguration and its capacity to asks questions about representation. However, metafiction is not entirely a contemporary phenomenon. What we are probably witnessing is a more conscious emphasis upon metafiction, and upon what Ricoeur sees as the double edge of mimesis, than has existed in the past.

The newfound emphasis upon heterogeneity, and upon representation as reconfiguration as much as configuration, brings together contemporary art, culture, history and politics in a shared concern with the limits and the nature of individual and collective identity in Ireland and Northern Ireland, often in comparable but also different ways. It is easy to reduce Irish history to overt, frequently covert, ongoing struggles. As I suggested earlier, Bakhtin's concept of 'many togueness' has an obvious relevance to Ireland and Northern Ireland. But even more so is Homi Bhabha's perception, indirectly if not directly indebted to Bakhtin's concept of 'many tongueness', of a nation as 'internally marked by cultural difference, the heterogeneous histories of contending peoples, antagonistic authorities, and tense cultural locations' (1990: 299). It hardly needs pointing out that different groups have forged cohesive often antagonistic identities in Ireland and Northern Ireland, and that understanding them requires a knowledge of these different identities including, of course, denominational histories. The importance of different traditions and histories is never gainsaid in contemporary Irish fiction, even in works, some of which are discussed in the next chapter, which go out of their way to stress the late modern – or even the postmodern – in Irish culture. Yet Ireland and Northern Ireland must not be thought of solely in terms of the traditional antagonistic identities.

Generally speaking, recent critical work on Irish fiction, as much as the writing itself, is sensitive to the complexity of its historical and cultural contexts, and to how much in Ireland and Northern Ireland, albeit in radically different ways at times, has been invented and reinvented to serve competing internal and external ideological, cultural and socio-economic interests. It is not hard to find Irish novels from the 1980s and 1990s concerned with the relentless socio-economic and cultural changes that have further complicated and confused what it means to be 'Irish'. Contemporary Irish fiction has offered new interpretations of Irish history. It has also provided radical insights into the diversity and complexity of Ireland, as well as Northern Ireland. The contemporary novel has given a voice to what was previously unarticulated. As far as Irish history is concerned, in common with former colonies generally, Bhabha's thesis needs to be further qualified to take into account the secrecy that not only surrounded the voices of opposition but also was necessary for their very survival. In Chapter 4, I discuss 'mimicry', one example

of the presence of covert subversion even within overt displays of
obedience to imposed monological discourse. But, talking of a
'national discourse' in relation to Ireland is itself complicated, of
course, because one has to ask, whose national discourse do we
mean? This is especially true for post-1937 Ireland, when, as I main-
tained earlier, the obverse of the monological national discourse
was a culture marked as much by covert as overt opposition and, in
some respects, by secrecy and concealment.

Thus, when applied to Ireland and Northern Ireland, the internal differences of which Bhabha writes are more complicated and
fluid than might be supposed. The conflicts and antagonisms
within Ireland and Northern Ireland, of which we hear so much,
are themselves internally marked by changing perspectives and
shifting alliances and coalitions. One finds further layers of secret
opposition and disagreement even within the principal covert
communities and organizations themselves. Like a Russian doll,
there are secrets within the secret while the dominant discourses
are often contradictory and frequently change to accommodate
new and emergent perspectives. Within this wider, complex and
fluid environment what constitutes the perceived centres and
margins is unstable, and is further rocked as what is previously
silenced or marginalized acquires or is given a voice. Thus, we
must go even further than Bhabha's emphasis upon 'internal difference' and his concept of 'in-between' space as he has developed them, and consider what Bhabha has to say about what is
involved when the previously inarticulate or marginalized
achieves self-expression in the light of how Irish history(ies) and
cultures are marked by covert activity, concealment and secrecy.

As I suggested in the Preface, the subject matter that had previously been unarticulated, or at best cryptically expressed,
which enters contemporary Irish fiction more overtly than in the
past may also be conceived of as occupying an in-between space.
Such topics would include child abuse which figures in a number
of texts including Patrick McCabe's *The Butcher Boy* (1992) and
William Trevor's *Felicia's Journey* (1994), discussed in Chapter 8;
domestic violence which is the principal concern of Roddy
Doyle's *The Woman Who Walked into Doors* (1996); self-harm
which is a salient trope in Dermot Bolger's *Father's Music* (1997);
'coming out', the subject of Emma Donoghue's *Stir-fry* (1994); and
shoe fetishism which Dermot Bolger explores in *Emily's Shoes*
(1992). When such suppressed subjects and issues first come to

the fore in the wider public consciousness, there is often a lack of clarity not only in how they should be responded to but in how they are to be conceptualized.

What Bhabha has to say about the emergence of previously marginalized voices can provide us with a framework in which to discuss this phenomenon. Moreover, as Bhabha says of the emergence of socially marginalized groups, once what was formerly acknowledged only in secret surfaces in the public domain, it becomes a significant 'other' within the dominant discourse. One has only to think of the impact of the cases of child abuse by Catholic priests upon the image and public perception of the Catholic Church, to see how these subjects in themselves, as well as the previously silenced groups associated with them such as the victims of violence and abuse, have the capacity to bring about a revisioning of the nation's sense of itself.

Bhabha (1983) argues that when those who have previously been silenced acquire a voice, when the socially marginalized emerge from the margins, a spatial shift occurs. This spatial movement can be envisaged in geographical, social and even metaphorical terms. For the socially marginalized are not only labelled as different by the kind of spaces they occupy and their perceived status in the dominant society but 'othered' by the dominant discourse through the way in which they are represented. That is to say, the socially marginalized occupy a position at the intersection of the geographical, the cultural and the figurative. Consequently, when socially marginalized groups begin to achieve recognition for themselves they do not immediately cast off the stigmatization to which they have been subjected. This is acknowledged in many of the contemporary novels exploring, for example, domestic violence and abuse. But they also pursue how the voices of previously unacknowledged victims do become a more significant 'other' within the dominant discourse; how previously marginalized groups, albeit not entirely free of their marginalized social, physical and cultural status, bring about a revisioning of the nation's map in terms of margins and centres. The nature of concealment and of the impact of what is hidden upon individual and collective sense of identities is something that will be discussed in more detail in Chapter 3. For the moment, it is important to note that concealment, and the kind of local and national cultures it creates, complicates our understanding with reference to the Irish novel of what we mean by the 'previously silenced' voices.

Timelags

Bhabha's concept of a 'timelag' provides us with a concept that usefully fuses the diversity and recalcitrance of many contemporary Irish novels with the emergent, contemporary Ireland and Northern Ireland since both may be seen as based upon the emergence of the previously silenced or socially marginalized. Typically, Eugene O'Brien, in a recent study of Seamus Heaney's poetry, points out: 'We are more open, more multicultural and far more confident in our ability to compete on equal terms with the rest of Europe and the world' (2002: 157). He envisages these changes in spatial terms. Ireland, in his view, has been relocated in terms of the world map and reinscribed geographically, socially and economically. This is reflected, he implies, in the newfound 'centring' of Irish writers:

> Culturally, our writers and artists can justly claim to be at the forefront of the world stage. Poets, novelists, playwrights and filmmakers have achieved great success over the past twenty years, and Irish cultural entertainment has never been more popular, or more central in terms of its importance. No longer relegated to a sub-genre of Anglo-Irish writing, Irish writing has now assumed centre stage. The corollary of this process is that Irish writing, while still occupied with Irish themes, has assumed a more Eurocentric perspective, looking towards European and world literature to provide images, analogues and a broader outlook on those themes.   (157)

It is not only Ireland we are talking about. Whilst not wishing to conflate Ireland and Northern Ireland in any easy sense, Northern Ireland texts, too, as Laura Pelaschiar points out, project a 'new sense of Northern Ireland, this new feeling of its life and especially of its cityscapes as normal and modern, places which are no longer "apart" but rather a part of 1990s Europe' (1998: 105).

O'Brien's observations, though, need to be further complicated because it is not simply that Ireland is more centred in European if not world affairs than it used to be. Within contemporary Ireland itself, there are numerous examples of classes and subjects that have a more prominent voice. This is the product of dialectic between dominant and marginalized discourses of which the 'contemporary' in this respect is itself a product. It hardly needs pointing out now that nationalism, initially finding expression in covert communities, organization and activities, became a homogenizing discourse to which other subject identities based on class, gender, sexuality or race were subordinate. The consequences of this included not only the privileging of certain groups over others, but the marginalization, if not silencing, of many aspects of lived experience. This has implications for how 'contemporary' in Ireland is to be defined if we think of contemporary as embracing the late twentieth century. It hardly needs to be said that few writing about Northern Ireland would exclude the peace process from an account of 1990s Northern Ireland. As Christine St. Peter said, in describing a return visit to Belfast: 'In 1995, for the first time in my 20 years of visits to that region, a superficially peaceful Belfast wore giddy holiday colours under a blazing sun' (100). Yet what is characteristic of cultural criticism and fiction in the 1980s and 1990s in Ireland and Northern Ireland is a readiness in most areas of life to be sceptical about what has been achieved, and a tendency to go beyond socio-cultural analysis and, in submitting the whole concept of modernization to scrutiny, to take a philosophical mirror as well as a critical scalpel to modern Ireland and Northern Ireland. It is impossible to separate all of this from the presence of what was previously at best an absent presence, and from what has come forth not simply from marginalized but concealed spaces. But it also means that in Ireland previously marginalized voices and silenced issues come to the fore in a public mind in which the notions of 'modern' and 'modernity' are crowded with uncertainties.

How Modern is Modern?

In contemporary scholarship, it is not difficult to find earlier interpretations of Irish cultural history criticized for their neat polarities, such as the dislocation between the urban and rural, or between tradition and modernity. Up to a point, the preoccupation with the modernization of Ireland in contemporary fiction has drawn upon discourses critical of tradition and the legacy of cultural nationalism. However, the contemporary novel, broadly speaking, has challenged the easy association of contemporary Ireland with modernization, and the ease with which the development of the mass media is linked with a generation of new, progressive ideas.

Joe Cleary argues: 'For a variety of reasons, the conception of modernization that currently prevails in contemporary Irish society is a quite restricted and impoverished one' (2000: 109). Thus, what has to be recognized more widely in Irish society, and culture, is that interrupting the continuum of the past and the present involves reclaiming and revisioning rather than rejecting tradition. This can be seen in many contemporary novels where identity for the central protagonist is a matter of fantasy arising from their sense of dispossession. But, increasingly in the late twentieth-century Irish novel, characters are not defined in relation to themselves and their own bodies but to images generated by the consumer-oriented, mass media society. That the internalization of socially conceived images should be a determining force in the construction of individual identities is not, however, a late nineteenth or even twentieth-century phenomenon. As we shall discover in Chapter 4, Emma Donoghue's *Slammerkin*, set in the eighteenth century, provides a critique of how female identity, especially, was becoming increasingly commodified in the early modern metropolis. This has implications for how we conceive of the concept of 'modern', and, of course, Donoghue's reader cannot but be aware that, in writing of the eighteenth century, Donoghue is indirectly offering a feminist critique of late twentieth-century, capitalist–society. 'Modernism' in her novel is a phenomenon ushered in with a complicated relation between openness and closure. That her critique is of early modern, consumer society suggests that the contradictions within it are innate to it.

Thus, despite the historical specificity of *Slammerkin*, its criticisms of modernity have much in common with novels written by contemporaries still living in 'modern' or 'late modern' Ireland or Northern Ireland. But in writing of eighteenth-century England and the Welsh/English borders, Donoghue is able to avoid how 'tradition' and 'modern' in Ireland and Northern Ireland are complicated by the way that modern has been associated with a nationalism which paradoxically looked, almost romantically, to the past. For example, *The Dead School* (1995), by Patrick McCabe whose earlier novel *The Butcher Boy* (1992) is the subject of extended discussion in Chapter 8, compares two generations of teachers. At one point, nationalism invokes an idealized view of the past and of Ireland itself, stemming from the legacy of the Easter Rising (1916) and the War of Independence (1919–21). It is in the description of the love affair between the ostensibly pure-of-heart teacher Raphael Bell, the older teacher, and his wife-to-be, Nessa:

> Yes, the happiest days that were ever known were lived by Raphael and his beautiful wife way back when the sun shone on the garden, the little boys sang for Jesus and each and every other night they offered up the rosary for the conversion of Russia and all the pagan peoples of the world and then repaired to bed to join together in a pure and wholesome union which they prayed to Jesus would result in a special gift being granted to them; a little boy called Maolseachlainn perhaps, whose tumbling golden curls would be the envy of all to whom his daddy would tell stories of the hated Black and Tans and the Eucharistic Congress and a day in Belfast with the gentlest creature in the world.   (125)

The overt sentimentality and coyness signify the spirit behind the Irish Constitution – which, as I stressed earlier, Ireland's first President hoped would usher in a monological national discourse. It was intended to be the foundation stone of a highly moral, Christian, rural and largely isolationist Republic. In the passage above, the romanticism is undermined by the hint of real, unresolved anger and grief; Raphael's father had been killed in his presence by the Black and Tans. (The reader unfamiliar with the term 'Black and Tans' may wish to refer to the appendix at this point.)

The in-between position from which McCabe writes is especially evident in *The Dead School* which contrasts the radio with its conventional fare, especially programmes of traditional music and sentimental ballads, enjoyed by the conservative Raphael Bell and Father Stokes, with the popular Terry Krash Show in 1965:

> One woman said to Terry 'You're shocking!' but you could tell that she didn't mean it. What she really meant was that he was great fun. And Terry knew it. That was why he said more cheeky things. The topic tonight was ladies' underwear. The sort they would wear for their boyfriends or husbands.   (138)

Although the word 'bra' has an immediate impact upon Raphael, the text is configuring a contrast between the cultural psychologies of the opening decades of the twentieth century and the 1960s:

> That night in bed, he lay awake for hours. He thought of his mother, the lovely Evelyn, now interred in a lonely Cork grave-yard, and he thought of his father lying dead in a field as his Black and Tan murderer wiped blood off his hands with a rag. (139)

The reference to underwear has a specific cultural resonance – the presenter of *The Late Late Show*, Gay Byrne, famously asking a woman what she wore on her wedding night to which she replied 'nothing'. (The century opened with a national scandal caused when Synge's *The Playboy of the Western World* (1907) placed Irish females on stage in their underwear.) But *The Dead School* is not simply saying that what has replaced the outmoded values in the traditional radio programme is not much better. It is concerned with the relationship between text and context; how each style of programme espouses values through which the present is mediated and which are to an extent created by a particular present.

The difficulties involved in using the term 'modern' in the context of mid-twentieth-century Ireland is exemplified also in William Trevor's *Felicia's Journey* (1994), to which, as I said earlier, I will return in Chapter 8. Trevor's novel is a version of the exile narrative; much of the plot concerns a young woman's search for the father of her unborn child in post-industrial, post-Thatcherite Britain. Thus, it is concerned with a subject that was concealed in most Irish families and certainly in traditional Irish communities, although both remained haunted by what it tried to keep secret, a topic to which I will return in more detail in Chapter 3. But the subject matter of Trevor's novel also brings to the fore the confusion around the concept of 'modern' in Ireland. Sex outside of marriage, abortion and the rights of a woman's control over her own body anchor notions of progress, implicitly conflating 'progress' and 'modern'. They also underline the importance of rupture to the definition of what is modern. However, viewed from another perspective, these issues, especially abortion, can be perceived as challenging too easy an elision of progress and modern, creating a space in which the concept of 'modern' morality itself comes under scrutiny.

The attitude towards the past and the modern in *Felicia's Journey* is complex. Although the novel is primarily focused on the serial killer Hilditch who ostensibly befriends Felicia but seeks to entrap her, as he did his previous victims, her past in Ireland is recalled fragmentarily, interrupting the main plot. At one point, Trevor explicitly draws on the romantic view of Ireland enshrined in the 1937 constitution:

> The wallpaper scrapbooks, Felicia's father believed were a monument to the nation ... Among peeping flowers were the hallowed sentiments of Eamon de Valera:
>
> *The Ireland which we have dreamed of would be the home of a people who valued material wealth only as the basis of right living, of a people who were satisfied with frugal comfort and devoted their leisure to the things of the spirit; a land whose countryside would be bright with cosy homesteads, whose fields would be joyous with the sounds of industry, with the romping of sturdy children, the contests of athletic youths, the laughter of comely maidens; whose firesides would be forums for the wisdom of old age. It would, in a word, be the home of a people living the life that God desires men should live.* (26–7)

Here, as in McCabe's novel, the past and present continuum is interrupted by uncertainty about inscribing the 'modern'. In fact, in this text the past is interrupted and revisioned by the unresolved uncertainties of modernity. The novel contrasts the post-industrial English Midlands, which is posited on the present/future trajectory, with small town Ireland posited on the past. An idealized sense of community, in contact with a more organic life, is displaced in both. In the former it is undermined by spiritual meanness and the oppression of women. Felicia's father is secretly

> relieved [Felicia] hadn't been qualified for the opening at Maguire Pigs. Some little part-time arrangement would get her off the dole and allow her to continue to do the housework, and the cooking for himself and her remaining brothers. A full-time job would mean having to pay Mrs Quigly for looking after the old woman in the middle of the day, as the job at

the Slieve Bloom had. He'd worked it out; he had probably discussed it with the nuns.   (28)

In the English Midlands, it is displaced by post-industrialism:

The industrial estate is an endless repetition of nondescript commercial buildings, each with a forecourt for parking ... The concrete roads of the estate are long and straight. Nobody casually walks them for the pleasure of doing so. No dogs meet other dogs. Business is in all directions, buying and selling, disposal and acquisition, discount for cash.   (14)

It almost goes without saying that nationalist narratives have been constructed around moments of history such as the Great Famine 1845–9, the Fenian Rising 1867, the Manchester Martyrs and the Easter Rising 1916. Again this is exemplified in Felicia's father's scrapbooks in Trevor's novel:

Felicia's father honoured the bloodshed on his own: regularly in the evenings he sat with his scrapbooks of those revolutionary times ... At the heart of the statement they made – the anchor of the whole collection, her father had many times repeated to her – was the combined obituary of the three local patriots ... Next in importance came a handwritten copy of Patrick Pearse's proclamation of a provisional government, dated 24 April 1916, its seven signatories recorded in the same clerkly calligraphy. Columns of newsprint told of the firing of the General Post Office, and the events at Boland's Mills, of Roger Casement's landing from a German U-boat on Banna Strand, of the shelling of Liberty Hall.   (25–6)

At one level, the scrapbook is ironically becoming part of an almost secret horde of memories. But what is interesting in the concern with conflicting narratives in these texts is that each focuses upon the way that contemporary Irish culture is still moored to the struggle for independence 'as *the* definitive zone of memory for an understanding of Irish society today' (Cleary, 108). Jennifer Johnston, whose work is discussed in Chapter 5, for example, tends to approach the contemporary 'troubles' through the period just after the First World War. In this, to employ Cleary's words, there is 'a sense of Irish history as trauma' which in turn discloses 'a need to recreate a history in which an overwhelming event could not be fully assimilated at the time of its occurrence, and which must therefore belatedly be compulsively repossessed'. Here the language is decidedly psychoanalytic, conflating historicist and psychoanalytic narrative. In talking of trauma, incomplete assimilation and compulsive repossession, Cleary implicitly fuses the history of the nation, dispossessed communities and estranged individuals.

Cleary is right to argue that 'as the distance between the present and that past widens, the social ills that obsess these works – clerical dogmatism, domestic tyranny and oppression, sexual repression, poverty of opportunity or whatever – will themselves increasingly come to be identified with the past, with a particular time and not with a social system that subtends both past and present' (114). But the point has also to be made in relation to Ireland that some of these social ills were shrouded with such secrecy that Cleary's 'definitive zone of memory for an understanding of Irish society today' inevitably involves not only confronting concealment but the nature of concealment, and its wider consequences for the culture in which it is concealed.

Cleary is dependent upon what Lyotard has characterized as a distinctly 'modern' approach to the past which is interested in assessing its 'errors' and 'crimes' and ultimately revisioning it (2000: 35–8). To a great extent this is true of the contemporary novel which at one level seeks to repossess the past, but at a deeper level conceives of subjects exposed to the shock of what was hidden for so long, and the subsequent interruption not only of the past and present continuum but the nature of the past preserved in the public consciousness and the State's institutions. This interruption is itself traumatic because the subject finds her or himself confronted with the 'in-between' temporality of which Bhabha writes: the subject cannot be integrated into the present while the past has never been fully experienced. In other words, the present may be seen as disarming the past rather than influenced by it, which also leaves the present in a state of uncertainty because it is no longer the product of a memorializing process that forgets and distorts in the construction of, what are to the dominant groups, comfortable narratives. Thus, the contemporary Irish novel is marked by its concern, and direct engagement, with a divided temporality where the previously accepted past and present are undone by the interruption of

what has been hitherto silenced or marginalized, in turn complicated by the levels of secrecy in which it was located.

Some cultural critics offer an alternative, broader view of modernization from a Marxist–cultural materialist perspective. Whilst
capitalist modernization points to positive benefits, it also leads,
as Marxist thinkers such as Marshall Berman and David Harvey
have pointed out, to

> negative concomitant features such as the destruction of older
> forms of social arrangement, the uprooting of whole rural com-
> munities because of the mechanisation of agriculture, the
> resultant creation of an army of workers with nothing to sell
> but their labour-power, the powerful surge of migration from
> rural to urban areas, overcrowding in cities, the process of reifi-
> cation (where relationships between human beings are
> reduced to the logic of cash exchange).   (McCarthy, 2000: 19)

This kind of critique is to be found in a number of contemporary
novels. For example, in Roddy Doyle's *The Van* (1991), set deliberately in the triumphalist summer of 1990 when Ireland reached
the quarter finals of the soccer world cup in Italy, casts a critical
eye over the way in which multinational capital in Ireland is
changing, and has changed, the nature of employment and examines the impact that global modernization is having, and has had,
on the Irish economy. In particular, the text focuses upon the way
in which traditional notions of masculinity and work are being
revised as the employment patterns that people have been used
to, especially the notion of a job for life and the value accorded
traditional skills, have been revised. Not least, this is because of
the way in which dominant, heterosexual assumptions about
masculinity are sustained within the public realm of work:

> Only, it was easier to cope if you didn't think things like that,
> getting work. You just continued on, like this was normal; you
> filled your day … Sometimes he made up things to tell [his
> wife], little adventures … He felt like a right prick when he was
> telling her but he kind of had to, he didn't know why; to let her
> know he was getting on fine.   (67–8)

Here the divided temporality that is important to Cleary's
argument is evident in the secrecy into which Jimmy is forced.

Jimmy's internal crisis is analogous of the wider crisis of direction that contemporary Ireland might be enduring. But through Jimmy's eyes, it does not seem like it: '[Town] had changed a lot; pubs he'd known and even streets were gone. It looked good, though, he thought. He could tell one thing; there was money in this town.' But, of course, it is the capital that enfranchises one group of people but disenfranchises the unemployed like him. His sense of a loss of identity is underscored by the disappearance of the physical locations that he has known all his life and has become part of himself, of how his sense of himself has developed. It makes a spectre, a mirage, of his personal past.

The first part of Patrick McCabe's *Carn* (1993) is set around the time that the Irish Government introduced its policies on the modernization of Ireland, perceived by cultural critics such as Jo Cleary as a watershed:

> For the political or constitutional historian, 1948 represents a landmark in modern Irish history, the moment when the Irish Free State severed its residual ties with Britain ... For the economic historian, however, 1958 – the moment when Sean Lemass and T. K. Whittaker launched the First programme for Economic Expansion that abandoned the protectionist policies of the previous generation and opened the country to foreign investment and multinational capital – will seem the more decisive watershed. (2000: 106–7)

But it highlights how at this time people were being forced to leave Ireland by the boatful because the country failed to fully embrace capitalism and its concomitant economic development, especially ironic given what happens to Doyle's Jimmy years later. The novel opens with an account of the period between the closure of the railway in the 1950s and the opening of the Carn Meat Processing Plant:

> After that, all talk of the railway began to gradually recede and after a while it was as if it had never existed. The place went to rack and ruin. Within a matter of weeks, the town plummeted from aristocrat to derelict. Under cover of darkness, rocks were hurled through the windows of the depot. Sleepers were torn up and used to make garden fences, or simply left to rot on waste ground. Paint peeled off doors. Many of the workers

emigrated to England and America, standing with their suit cases on The Diamond, waiting for the bus to take them to the ferry terminals of Dublin and Belfast. Those who remained loitered at the street corners, dividing their time between the bookmaker's and the public house. They turned away sourly from each other and looked up and down the deserted main street. It got to the stage where no one expected anything good to happen ever again.   (12)

Those who 'loiter' and the street corners are analogous of the 'timelag' in which parts of Ireland find themselves. McCabe's timelag is not the energetic space that Bhabha describes, but one of disillusionment, anger and frustration. In the preceding passage from *Carn*, there are a number of familiar motifs suggesting scepticism over Ireland's integration with a wider, modern world: surreptitious rebellion, tense antagonisms, emigration and the emasculation of the Irish male. But McCabe is wary also of the new conservatism that can emerge from such scepticism, evident in Ireland in the rising tide of Catholic conservatism and its disassociation from a broader, middle ground of opinion.

Thus, when applied to cultural criticism and fiction in Ireland and Northern Ireland, Bhabha's concepts of 'relocation' and 'reinscription' are far from acceptable as givens. Nevertheless, Bhabha's work is useful in reading the Irish novel because it foregrounds the shifting nature of the heteroglossic reality of linguistic communities which Bakhtin describes, even though the Irish context challenges some of Bhabha's assumptions. Taken together, Bhabha and Bakhtin help us to define the 'in-between state', or timelag, that must inevitably accompany this process of 'centring' that Eugene O'Brien describes. For Bhabha, as for many Irish novelists, it is an 'interrogative space', allowing for a process of exploration, experiment and re-vision. But it also involves reclamation of tradition in ways that make it peculiarly unhelpful to talk of contemporary Irish fiction, as one might more easily of British fiction, in terms of 'experimental' and 'traditional' writing.

Previously marginalized and silenced voices, emerging from and in turn determining the spatio-cultural shift in a nation's ideas of itself, confront and contradict the dominant discourses that have been directly or indirectly responsible for their silence and marginalization. But Bhabha goes further and argues that they also question the frames of reference that inform the nation's narrative about itself. It hardly needs stating that the contemporary Irish novel confronts and contradicts the discourses defining, for example, Irishness, nation, home, belonging, exile, sexuality, desire, religion and spirituality. But Bhabha's essay prompts us to ponder further the consequences for the novel of it occupying an in-between space from where it questions not only the discourses but also the frames of reference that they employ. Second, contemporary Irish fiction can be seen as occupying, to build on Bhabha's notion of an 'interrogative space', a space of 'radical openness', while at the same time straddling traditional representation and 'unrepresentability', in that it explores what was once concealed, together with the nature of concealment and its wider consequences.

However, an important distinction has to be made between the recalcitrance and questioning which characterizes many contemporary Irish novels and the 'postmodernism' that constitutes a dominant strain in late twentieth-century British and American contemporary fiction. For example, much of what is said above about the interrogative nature of the contemporary Irish novel would be applicable to the works of Angela Carter. But Carter's fiction is much more committed than many contemporary Irish novels to an all-pervading scepticism as to whether representation can ever be anything more than the product of, and the disseminator of, preconceptions. Even at its most radical, representation in Carter's work is perceived as offering the exchange of one set of conventions for another. As soon as a Carter novel seems to pin something down, it appears to run away with the pin. Carter's fiction is playful and mischievous but also wary of the whole process of defining and labelling. It is on the side of relocation, perhaps at times endlessly so, rather than reinscription. More often than not it is the reverse that is true of the Irish novel. But, as we shall see in the next chapter, a number of Irish novels confront the unreliability of narratives, symbols and definitions and challenge the seduction of postmodernity.

2
Posting the Present

Modernity and Modernization in Glenn
Patterson's *Fat Lad* (1992) and Robert McLiam
Wilson's *Eureka Street* (1996)

In the previous chapter, I argued for the usefulness of Homi
Bhabha's concept of the 'timelag' in discussing the intellectual
and cultural space which young writers, some of the subjects to
which they gave voice and even Ireland and Northern Ireland
themselves have come to occupy. But the notion of the in-between
space which they enter, have entered, requires further development of Bhabha's thesis because what has been previously marginalized or silenced in Irish history has also been shrouded with
secrecy. Secrecy has been such a feature of Irish cultural life on a
national, local and domestic level that even Bhabha's vision of the
nation state in general marked by 'internal difference', most obviously applicable to Ireland, has to be refocused to take it into
account. What Bhabha has to say about a 'timelag' is also useful
in that what has been previously marginalized or concealed challenges the very mapping of the nation. But even here it needs
revisioning to acknowledge that in Ireland and Northern Ireland
the previously inarticulate or unarticulated challenges our
understanding of 'modern'. Narratives, too, habitually conceal as
much as they reveal.

The way that what is previously hidden or eschewed challenges established notions of the nation is complicated because
the concept of the 'modern' is itself embroiled with disruption.
Glenn Patterson's *Fat Lad* (1992) is an appropriate novel to consider in this respect. It concerns the return of the young Protestant
Drew Linden, who works for a chain of English bookstores, to
Belfast to open a branch there. He finds himself in a thriving
metropolis which has emerged from the city which he had left

dying on its feet years earlier and which is trying to redefine itself as a European cosmopolitan centre. It is a city occupying Homi Bhabha's timelag. Both Drew and his new environs are in a period, to invoke Bhabha's terms, between 'relocation' and 'reinscription'. But narratives of a vibrant metropolis seem to conceal the fact that there are other sides to Belfast and to deny something of its past. Thus, Drew finds himself thinking about his parents and grandparents' lives and how this late modern or postmodern Belfast developed from the one that they knew. His return to Belfast is an encounter with a newness that interrupts the continuum of the past and present. As Bhabha suggests, this act of interruption involves rejecting notions of the present as evolving from the past.

The past and the present exist in a more complicated relation to each other than a cause–effect narrative allows. This is encapsulated in the complicated structure of the novel itself, which interleaves different narratives, different voices and different periods of history in a way that ostensibly readers might find confusing. Drew's initial assumption that, as a Protestant born in Northern Ireland, he is doomed to dissect endlessly his sense of self is displaced by an awareness of how his ancestors, like himself, must have been confronted by an emergent sense of the modern. The history of Northern Ireland, which is given us through Drew's account of his family, is one that consists of 'interruption' and 'disruption', encapsulated in the perspectives of his sister, father and grandmother.

The French cultural theorist Jean Baudrillard envisages the concepts of 'old' and 'new' as the products of interruption rather than development in the past and present continuum. As such, his work complements Bhabha's ideas about the encounter with 'newness' and is pertinent to the co-existence of the tradition and the innovative in many contemporary Irish novels. Baudrillard argues that the 'traditional' and the 'modern' are defined by 'a schema of rupture, progress and innovation':

> Tradition is no longer the pre-eminence of the old over the new: it is unaware of either – modernity itself invents them both at once, at a single stroke, it is always and at the same time 'neo' and '*rétro*', modern and anachronistic. The dialectic of rupture very quickly becomes the dynamics of the amalgam and recycling.   (1993; 89–90)

Baudrillard shifts the focus away from the conventional idea of the traditional giving way to the modern, stressing that what is deemed 'modern' and 'traditional' is always being reinvented.

Baudrillard argues that a new generation of signs emerged with the industrial revolution, which from the outset were '*products* on a gigantic scale' and which had 'meaning only within the dimension of the industrial simulacrum' (55). This has a particular resonance for Belfast, which, initially through its linen and cotton factories and then through its shipbuilding yards, overtook Derry as the principal urban centre of Northern Ireland. But the history of Belfast, especially the way in which it is implicated in Northern Ireland's sectarianism, cannot be easily gainsaid. What different writers handle differently is the way Belfast, as a successful industrial city built upon bog land, is associated with the Protestant settler class and almost seen as the Protestant miracle, and the way in which it remained an alien environment for the influx of Catholic workers from the rural areas.

Drew and his lover Kay link the prosperity of contemporary Belfast very clearly to its industrial past. This is especially the case when she shows Drew's boss from England a strong prosperous city in which she and Drew take an obvious, if blinkered, pride. However, in her emphasis upon a city based upon 'destruction and construction', she unwittingly stresses Baudrillard's thesis that the modern is an invention of, and dependent upon, 'rupta'. In the course of her narrative to Drew's boss, it becomes clear that Kay not only signs up to, but also actually lives, this Baudrillardian way of looking at the relation of the past and present. Not only does she elide herself with the struggle of her ancestors to create what was then a modern industrial city but also in her day-to-day life enacts the rhythm of 'destruction and construction'.

Kay's narrative is an example of the novel's concern as much with what is eschewed as expressed. Thus her voice, and somewhat blinkered account of Belfast, provides only one perspective in this novel which contrasts the present of the Belfast to which Linden returns with Ulster's shipbuilding past in which the *Titanic* was launched. The sinking of the *Titanic* is symbolic of the end of the Industrial age and, of course, of Ulster itself. But if we follow Baudrillard's thesis, it also marks the shift from what Baudrillard sees as one order of signs to another. By this I mean his argument that the symbolic order associated with the Industrial Revolution gave way to a different kind of symbolism associated with the post-industrial and postmodern. Drew's 'Bookstore' signifies the order that Baudrillard sees as having displaced the industrial simulacrum. The serial reproducibility of the Industrial Revolution, the *Titanic* is one of a series of heavy ships, is replaced by simulacra in which signs do not acquire meaning from an external referent but other references. Ironically, if we read Kay's enthusiastic exposition of industrial Belfast through Baudrillard's thesis, we can see that her views are more post-industrial than she realizes. She does not simply describe the history of Belfast but creates a narrative in which the different elements of history derive more meaning from the ways in which they are linked to one another within the narrative than from the real or supposed events to which she is referring. At one point, she confuses the Biblical and Darwinian accounts of creation, stressing the way Belfast was created out of mud and water and the importance of naming.

The novel's preoccupation with the postmodern sign as a defining feature of the contemporary is reinforced in the way in which the *Titanic*'s fate becomes a refrain in the text. In other words, a great man-made product, a symbol of the industrial past, passes into a universe of signs and simulacra. Its original meaning becomes lost in a series where there is no social finality and simulacra prevail over history. Drew's chain store is a symbol in Baudrillard's terms of both 'neo' and 'rétro':

> Many people in many different towns took them for a local firm; some were even prepared to swear (market research had proved it) that their family had always bought books there, though the first shop was opened as recently as 1977 and the majority had appeared within the last five years. (11)

Clearly the bookshop, which Drew opens in Belfast, is a 'rupta' which invents itself as modern and which, in the process, invents a tradition. While here we are made aware of the importance of tradition to Northern Ireland cultures, we are also provided with a sense of how these cultures are themselves 'neo' and 'rétro'.

Encountering the City

Glenn Patterson presents us with a Belfast not so very different in many respects from that described by another Northern Irish

novelist, Robert McLiam Wilson, in *Eureka Street* which is structured around the parallel love stories of two central characters,
the Catholic Jake Jackson from West Belfast, one of the most dangerous parts of the city, and the Protestant Chuckie Lurgan. At the
centre of the novel is a deep-rooted ambivalence about modernity
and the prosperity of the contemporary city exemplified in
Patterson's novel in the bars, restaurants and takeaways that line
the so-called Golden Mile and the chain stores – Next, Body Shop,
Tie Rack, Principles – that fill the shopping streets:

> Belfast is a city that has lost its heart. A shipbuilding, rope-
> making, linen-weaving town. It builds no ships, makes no rope
> and weaves no linen. Those trades died. A city can't survive
> without something to do with itself.   (215)

Jake Jackson exemplifies the wider dilemma in which the city in
which he lives finds itself. He lives on Poetry Street to which he
had moved with his English girlfriend who is covering the
Troubles for a London newspaper, in what Wilson depicts as leafy
Belfast – the city hidden by the mass media:

> This was bourgeois Belfast, leafier and more prosperous than
> you might imagine. Sarah had found this place and moved us
> in to lead our leafy kind of life in our leafy kind of area. When
> her English friends or family had visited us there they had
> always been disappointed by the lack of burnt-out cars or foot
> patrols on our wide, tree-lined avenue.   (12–13)

Jake has been relocated. But he inhabits a space between his former life and the life into which his girlfriend moves him. Like the
encroaching embourgeoisement of Belfast itself, Sarah has 'ironed
out' his tastes (12). But his confrontation with the new, with Poetry
Street, breaks the past and present continuum that he had taken
for granted in West Belfast. It is a rupture which, as Baudrillard
suggests in his theory of the 'modern', defamiliarizes the past:

> From my upstairs window, however, I could see the West; the
> famous, hushed West. That's where I'd been born: West Belfast,
> the bold, the true, the extremely rough. I used to send Sarah's
> visitors up there. There were plenty of those local details up
> West.   (13)

Jake finds a different way of imagining Belfast emerging out of this 'rupta'. Whereas Patterson's Drew Linden thinks of a cycle of encounters with newness throughout history, Wilson suggests a way of envisaging the city that is analogous with the heteroglossia of the novel itself:

Whether in the centre itself or the places in which people put their houses, the city's streets, like lights in neighbours' houses, are stories of the done, the desired, the suffered and unforgotten.

The city's surface is thick with its living citizens. Its earth is richly sown with its many dead. The city is a repository of narratives, of stories. Present tense, past tense or future. The city is a novel.

Cities are simple things. They are conglomerations of people. Cities are complex things. They are the geographical and emotional distillations of whole nations ...

But most of all, cities are the meeting places of stories. The men and women are narratives, endlessly complex and intriguing.   (215)

This chapter opens with Jake sleeping on Poetry Street, which draws attention to the highly poetic nature of the prose. In this account of Belfast, the details of a specific city are lost, as it becomes the City. The description self-consciously deploys the principal techniques of rhetoric: repetition; the use of threes; the balancing of one phrase against another, and the use of opposites. We are encouraged to compare the rhetoric and poetry of this account with the description of America to which Chuckie has come in search of his girlfriend, Max:

After an hour [Chuckie] left the bar and walked out into damp San Diego. The sidewalks glittered, wet and marvellous. Though it was late, citizens still walked those streets. The underlit shopfronts were lined with pairs of underdressed women whom Chuckie supposed were prostitutes ... There was plenty of fight too. Every block or so, Chuckie would see a brawl erupt in some bar, on some street. Men kicked each other's heads to pulp, smashed bottles in faces, pulled and used knives ... And there were the noises of the incidents he did not see. The muted sound of war from the interiors of houses, apartments and bars. The dull shouts of angry men and the stifled screams of women.   (266–7)

Although it opens with a poetic image of the city that might have come from the former description of Belfast as 'the City' – 'The sidewalks glittered, wet and marvellous' – this passage moves swiftly and specifically into the seedier side of San Diego – the prostitution, brawls and domestic violence. This is an aspect of San Diego – and one might add contemporary Belfast – hidden from the well-heeled visitor. But within this almost secret part of San Diego, there is further concealment – the domestic violence. Like many of the novels in this chapter, it fuses the private and the public, finding here a connection between the macho violence on the streets and the violence inflicted on women in the home. The latter has often been, and is, concealed. But its emergence into greater public consciousness, even within the narrow environs of particular local communities, disrupts how more public 'macho violence', and its part in the definition of masculinity, is perceived. Chuckie is forced to make a comparison between the violence of this city and of Belfast:

The streets upon which he walked felt splattered with some-body's blood or somebody's semen. He had a sudden and unwelcome sense of how fragile and inappropriate all his chubby, formless Irish flesh was in the midst of all this. He longed for the comfort of familiar Belfast and the understand-ably butch and brutal Sandy Row. He longed for the safety of some terrorism, some civil war.   (267–8)

Whereas Chuckie makes distinctions between Belfast and San Diego, there are aspects of San Diego that are redolent of Belfast – the streets 'splattered with somebody's blood'. The killings in Belfast seem less random by comparison and, of course, republican and loyalist discourses incorporate them into particular histories of struggle and sacrifice.

What frightens Chuckie is the destabilizing effect of the possibility of randomized violent crime. As he discovers, it is something that Americans learn to live with by carrying phoney wallets – a signifier of how they have to make an identity, ghosts of themselves, to negotiate the city streets. There are rules that American urban dwellers have to follow, rules which assailants can learn and adapt their *modus operandi* accordingly. Thus, the novel asks, how random is random? To an extent, moving around San Diego is about how much risk you are prepared to take.

Later in the novel, we might recall Chuckie's words when we are forced to witness a bomb explosion, described in more detail than we normally encounter in contemporary Irish and Northern Irish fiction. One might easily think of this detail as what has been hidden in Irish verbal culture. About two-thirds of the way into the story, we are suddenly introduced to a new character, Rosemary Daye, mirroring the way in which the city involves us criss-crossing with all sorts of people we do not know and with whom our encounters, however significant or insignificant they may seem at the time, are temporary. In other words, the appearance of Rosemary Daye signifies the randomness of city life, its rhythm of bringing together and separating, and its exhilarating anonymity: 'Rosemary crossed the street, smiling at a man who hadn't noticed her. He looked at her then, gratified and puzzled by the width and warmth of her smile' (220). But just as there is a negative side to all this energy – the possibility of alienation, indifference and loneliness – the sense of a chance meeting has its darker side, too. In the account of the bomb explosion that kills Rosemary, Wilson again asks, how 'random' is random. The detonation of the bomb is 'in short, an intricate, say, some, mix of history, politics, circumstance and ordnance' (225). But for a schoolboy who happened to be in the wrong place at the wrong time – to be sitting on a bench in the line of the street bin sent flying by the explosion – and is never able to walk properly again, it is a matter of chance.

However, the text is concerned less with the randomness as the response to it. At one level, this is evident in the account of how the emergency services cope with crises by following a blueprint, even though the blueprint is not enough, as those involved come up against the 'newness' of the slaughter and the injuries. But the focus is even more on the timelag that occurs as 'an everyday, entirely forgettable, urban situation' is changed into a 'slaughter-house': 'The living took a few seconds to understand, to start their screams' (226). This is analogous of the wider timelag in which this event is inscribed and reinscribed. Indeed, this has come to be so much a part of the experience of this kind of sudden violence that the timelag is eroded, and those who put some space between

the bomb and the inscription of what has happened are perceived
as failing:

> There was all round a lamentable lack of overview, of objec-
> tivity. Those involved refused to put the event in its proper
> context. And for some unruly souls, this was a process that
> continued for some time. Indeed, one churlish triple amputee
> actually told a newspaper some weeks later that he would
> never be able to forgive the people who had planted the
> bomb.   (227)

Posting the Truth

What emerges in both Patterson and Wilson's novels is that the
front with which late capitalism presents us, its celebration of itself
and its surface appeal, hides the truth about itself. Ostensibly
Joseph O'Connor's *Cowboys and Indians* sets out to expose the
postmodern metropolis. But its real concern is to explore the
appeal of the postmodern when its superficiality and lack of links
to anything authentic are so easily unravelled, as demonstrated in
the first few pages of the book.

The notion of change as an invention of the modern is at the
heart of O'Connor's text, which in Baudrillard's words,

> clearly and simultaneously announces the *myth* of change,
> maintaining it as the supreme value in the most everyday
> aspects, and as the structural law of change: since it is produced
> through the play of models and distinctive oppositions, and is
> therefore an order which gives no precedence to the code of the
> tradition.   (90)

The principal protagonist, Eddie Virago, ironically named after
the English feminist publishing house given his rather chauvinistic
views of women, exemplifies both the 'myth' of change and 'the
play of models and distinctive oppositions' that Baudrillard associates with what he calls the 'structural law of change':

> Eddie's hair was something else. He'd got the first mohican in
> Dublin. This was back in 1978 when hardly anyone in the city

had ever heard of The Sex Pistols or The Clash, specially not the old barber in Glasthule, who was still saying that Mick Jagger looked like a bloody girl and that nobody could write a good melody any more. Eddie used to tune into John Peel late at night, while his parents fought downstairs, imagining what it would be like to be over in London, the eye of the storm, the rotten apple, the monstrous and fetid birthplace of punk. And the rampart phoney roar of 'Anarchy in the UK' and 'Pretty Vacant' would drown out the sound of the real anarchy that raged through the kitchen below. When he swanned into Monday morning religion class with the haircut, he'd nearly been expelled on the spot.   (2)

It is quite clear that Virago's sense of himself is based around playing one set of signs off against another. In real political terms, there is something phoney about it. In this respect, he is a product of his times, characterized by the rise of an image/media-saturated society, the increasing importance of consumption and of a social geography based on consumer markets and the erosion of traditional, collective and personal identities.

In other words, Virago's milieu – or perhaps the milieu in which he would initially like to locate himself – is defined by postmodern or post-industrial society's celebration of surface over depth and of the play which can be set up between different signs once they are loosed from any mooring in the external world. This kind of society is encapsulated in the account of the London diner. Eddie from Dublin and Marion from Northern Ireland, having met on the ferry, have agreed to share a room in a hotel in London. Here, the stress is not upon the fictive world that the characters create for themselves but the 'constructed' world in which they find themselves:

> They went out to eat that night in a Mexican restaurant called Remember the Alamo. They hung their coats on a giant plastic cactus right in the middle of the floor. It was the kind of place where the menu's made of plastic and too big and they play Richard Clayderman playing Barry Manilow and the waitress tells you her name even if you don't want to know it.   (24)

Of interest here is what the surface details hide. The hyper reality, evidenced in the giant cactus and the overlarge menus, is important as part of an active recreation of the present which hides the void at its centre. The text emphasizes the solipsistic nature of this hyper reality. There is no sense of different cultures and geographies being together yet separate at the same time, where symbols such as the cactus might refer us back to an external reality valid in its own terms. Instead, the manufactured, fictive globalness is ultimately meaningless – a cultural void where cultural conflict and antagonisms are replaced by a kind of non-culture. There is nothing new in this. There are many Anglo-American, postmodern novels which assume a similar view of late capitalism. But O'Connor is primarily concerned with the way so-called postmodern hybridity actively works to conceal its own fictiveness.

In this respect, Brixton offers an interesting contrast to the postmodern consumerism exemplified by the restaurant:

> Brixton was a good place, specially in the summer, full of fruit stalls and chancers and great secondhand record shops and people trying to sell you things you didn't really want. Eddie liked just walking up and down the main street, looking in the windows, glaring at the soulboys and rockers, and beautiful girls, listening to the hip-hop that came booming out of the mini-cab offices and café's. He saw people more black than he had ever seen in his life, men and women so black that in the strong sun their skin looked not black but dark blue, like in the Irish for a black man, *fear gorm*, a blue man. (195)

The emphasis upon skin at the end of this passage is pertinent to the contrasts that this novel sets up between different places and spaces. Skin is the limit of space – of the body experienced as an internal, breathing cavity – and of the limit of the body experienced as a full entity in the environment. What cities and towns offer is social exchange based on the movements of individual bodies within social discourse. The Mexican restaurant offered opportunities for social exchange but somehow the lived space did not seem fully activated by the bodies that constituted it. The description of looking through the hotel window in the early part of the text similarly appears to deny true interaction between the inner and outer worlds: 'Eddie looked out [the hotel] window for a while, but he felt no thrill. He knew the scene so well from television and movies that it was like he had always lived here' (22). The room functions as a surrogate body, and its window is a surrogate eye. The walls of the room carry out the same function as the skin in so far as they act as the boundary between the inner and outer worlds. The window mimics the eye in so far as it lets in light. When we open our eyes after sleep, we want the light to reawaken our storehouse of memories. In other words, we want stimulus. But here the window fails to provide stimulation – there is 'no thrill' – because everything seems secondhand, having been experienced previously through the mass media.

Brixton, though, is different. It has more originality, and, as a district within London, has a somatic individuality. Its topological separateness guarantees its concentration of energy. Whereas the view from the hotel window is not 'felt' by Eddie, in the inscription of Brixton, there is a lot of emphasis upon bodily interaction. Even seeing is recognized as a physical activity that involves not simply the eyes but the body as a situated entity. Energy is contained and conveyed in the physical movement – all the time we are conscious of Eddie walking through the area – and in the movement within the passage.

The district around Euston station is removed from nature as the description of the pond suggests: 'Outside the station doors, Eddie sat on the concrete edge of the pond and tried to sus things out. Burger wrappers and cardboard boxes and newspaper pages floated in the scummy water' (20). The repetition of 'and' underscores the fragmentariness and the sense that Eddie in this location is at the end of something rather than at the beginning. The absent present is the sojourn into nature that provides an opportunity to sit in a natural environment beside a pond. The description of Brixton, however, eschews this somewhat simplistic, anti-modern, romantic binarism of the urban and nature. Brixton, in its own way is in tune with the seasons: in summer, it is 'full of fruit stalls' – a phrase that also suggests that the fruit itself is full. Yet Eddie, and ultimately the reader, is in danger of being seduced by the 'presentness' of Brixton.

There are two dominant ways of thinking about, dramatizing and ordering space in contemporary western culture. The first, which is identifiable with structuralism, reorders space along the axis of synchronicity, which is what is happening in this account of Brixton. It emphasizes the present, and how different signs and systems of signs relate to, and interact with each other. Thus, the above description of Brixton interleaves the fruit stalls, the record

shops, the mini cab offices and the cafés. The other way of dramatizing and ordering space, which is apparent in *Cowboys and
Indians* when Eddie goes with Marion to her home in Northern
Ireland, is to think in terms of the way that places have changed
over time:

> Eddie felt like a stranger in a Wild West town. That feeling was
> enhanced by the way everything in the main street seemed to
> have an American name. There was a Stars and Stripes Pizza
> Joint, a Yankee Doodle Bar and Fried Chicken, a Boston Tea
> House, a Hollywood Hairstyles, a Route 66 Grill bar, a Prairie
> Moon Burger Bar, a Miami Vice Fashions, complete with an
> enormous confederate flag in the window and a lifesize Uncle
> Sam on the pavement.   (166–7)

There are many different ways in which to read this passage in
relation to the novel as a whole. Perhaps the most obvious is the
emphasis upon the Americanization of Irish culture and the lack
of a real dialectic, in this instance, between the local and the global.
The reference to the flag of the Confederacy that failed to win its
sovereignty is somewhat ironic. The promise here is that Ireland
and Northern Ireland can buy into the American myths of glamour
and prosperity. But they hide the truth. The movement towards
Americanization is also a movement from diachronicity to synchronicity. The history of the town is becoming subordinate to the
way the various multinational elements interact with each other.
    For the new generation growing up in this town, 'reality' is the
hyper reality created by the interlinking of these different elements.
History itself has been reduced to a number of key events – the
Boston Tea party, the Wild West and the Civil War. Of concern
here is not the relative importance of these events, everything is
elided as if it is of equal value or significance, but the legitimacy
that this way of conceiving of different cultures and their histories
has acquired. All of this has an ironic link with Nationalist Irish
history that has tended to be written around a dramatizing and
reordering of key heroic events. The fact that Eddie likens the town
to the Wild West situates it as a frontier. At one level, this might be
the frontier between the local and the global, between Ireland and
America, and between 'independence' and neocolonialism.
At another level, it signifies the frontier opened up at the limit of
parent–daughter relations, as the text reveals Marion's secret.

Floating Capital

We might compare O'Connor's account of postmodern London with Patterson's Belfast in *Fat Lad*:

> The street filled with music. Fifties pop, acid house, a shriek of jazz trumpet from somewhere, a crash of metal from a jukebox somewhere else, Indian restaurant music from an Indian restaurant. Discrete yet oddly harmonious; a symphony for any city, summer 1990. (207)

'Somewhere' and 'somewhere' else are especially suggestive – this could be 'somewhere else'. But the gunshot reminds us that this cannot be 'somewhere else' – the city is Belfast with its sectarian differences that lie behind the high street shops. It also reminds us that the ongoing socio-economic development of Belfast in the late twentieth century has occurred alongside the conflict, but has, in all kinds of ways, been embroiled with it. Indeed, the emergent differences within sectarianism in Belfast are inseparable from the socio-economic changes within the city, especially the emergence of heavy industry, the demise of that age and its replacement in turn with a 'postindustrial' order.

Linden's present Belfast, like the London discovered by Eddie Virago, is becoming, in the sociologist's Mike Featherstone's words, a 'no-place space' in which traditional senses of culture are 'decontextualized, simulated, reduplicated and continually renewed and restyled' (1996: 99). More traditional Irelands and Northern Irelands haunt *Fat Lad* and *Cowboys and Indians* where there was a sense of engagement with something that, for all its faults, had identifiable, external referents. Worryingly Linden's 'Bookstore' implicates the book itself, including *Fat Lad*, in the process of cultures being relentlessly 'decontextualised, simulated, reduplicated'. For, as Featherstone wryly observes, 'the aestheticisation of reality', through the surfeit of mass media images, 'foregrounds the importance of style, which is also encouraged by the modernist market dynamic with its constant search for new fashions, new styles, new sensations and experiences' (86).

However, it is Robert McLiam Wilson's *Eureka Street* (1996) that, more than *Fat Lad*, picks up on the absurdity of the way that capital in late modernity, in its power balances and play of interdependencies, is manipulated by specific groups, classes and interest groups. The novel stresses that the city is divided along financial as well as religious lines:

> You see leafy streets and you see leafless streets. You can imagine leafy lives and leafless ones. In the plump suburbs and the concrete districts your eyes see some truths, some real difference. The scars and marks of violence reside in only one type of place. Many of the populace seem to live well. Many prosper while many suffer.   (214–15)

The sectarian violence, which from British mainland news reports might be thought to totally dominate the lived experience of all parts of Northern Ireland, becomes a dimension of a larger, financially prosperous city. In fact, its concern with financial sectarianism is an aspect of Wilson's novel developed through one of the two central characters, the Protestant Chuckie Lurgan. He realizes, perhaps thanks to his American girlfriend, that the Industrial Resources Board 'were mostly famous for giving enormous sums of British cash to American motor manufacturers who built expensive factories producing cars so ludicrous that they ended up only being sold to film companies, who used them as comic props for celebrated time-travel companies' (117). The allusion here is to the extravagant, American entrepreneur John Delorean who obtained 156 million dollars in grants and loans from the British government in return for locating his car factory in Northern Ireland. It promised to bring two thousand jobs to Northern Ireland but subsequently collapsed when Delorean was arrested in 1982 for putting up 1.8 million dollars to smuggle one hundred kilos of cocaine into the country to save the company. However, the reference to America, and the incorporation of an American girlfriend, may have further significance, as the humour, focusing on the absurd logic of late capitalism has an American/American-Irish flavour to it. Chuckie's cynical, redeemed hard-man, the Catholic Jake smacks at times of a character from the pages of J. P. Dunleavy. Chuckie wholeheartedly takes advantage of his insights into the abstract realization of capital in late modernity, dashing off 'a whole series of off-the-cuff pipe-dreams and improbabilities, inventing non-existent projects and ideas never intended or likely to exist' (118). This free-floating world of transferable capital, where money is signified by abstract figures in a bank statement, is analogous in the novel to the simulacra and the 'incorporeal': 'flat on his back with Max breathing American beside him, Chuckie came closer to the incorporeal than ever before. He felt less than light, more than airy' (117). Which means that the corporeal is analogous of the symbolic, the older, traditional Belfast:

> The houses were tiny. The street small. The microscale of the place in which he lived gave it a grandeur he could not ignore. In Eureka Street the people rattled against each other like matches in a box but there was sociability, warmth in that. Especially on evenings like this, when the sun was late to dip. When finally it did dip, there was an achromatic half-hour, when the air was free from colour and the women concluded their gossip, the husbands came home and the children were coaxed indoors from their darkening play. (46)

The novel is punctuated with brief, transitory achromatic moments, or moments when the text tries to get as close as possible to such a space: 'You should stand some night on Cable Street, letting the little wind pluck your flesh and listen, rigid and ecstatic, while the unfamous past talks to you. If you do that, the city will stick to your fingers like Sellotape' (215).

These are useful quotations with which to close this chapter. Eureka Street is the obverse of Poetry Street – in effect what it seeks to hide. The encounters with the late or postmodern in the three novels discussed in this chapter are marked by uncertainty. The novels occupy an in-between space, as do the cities in which they are set; between what Baudrillard describes as two orders of signs. There is an abiding concern with the way positive narratives of the brash, new consumer-oriented aspect of many late twentieth-century cities hide, as increasingly does their spatial organization, what challenges or undermines postmodern society's celebration of itself. The emphasis in these novels falls not upon exposing the postmodern as 'no-place spaces' but upon their capacity to seduce, to redefine and to hide the processes by which cultures are being, to employ Featherstone's terms once again, 'decontextualised, simulated [and] reduplicated'.

3
Secret Hauntings

Seamus Deane's *Reading in the Dark* (1996),
Joseph O'Connor's *The Salesman* (1998),
Jennifer Johnston's *Fool's Sanctuary* (1987),
Mary Leland's *The Killeen* (1985) and
Linda Anderson's *To Stay Alive* (1984)

Even from the few texts mentioned in the previous chapters concerning characters that find themselves in a psychological and cultural timelag, it is clear that the rewriting of lifescripts is an important subject in Irish fiction. This process of rewriting, because it arises from the way characters are inevitably located between 'relocation' and 'reinscription', in Bhabha's terms, involves a disarming of the past. This disarming of the past at the level of individual characters, as I suggested in the previous chapters, is often analogous of the wider re-examinations of history in which Ireland and Northern Ireland are themselves involved.

A framework in which to discuss the key protagonists in this respect, and what they are analogous of, is provided by the psychoanalyst Sigmund Freud, best known for his contentious essays on gender identity. Here I wish to invoke the lesser-known concept of 'Nachträglichkeit' that like all of Freud's significant writings is based on the case studies of his patients. By Nachträglichkeit, Freud means the way in which what has given rise to the trauma that has affected the patient, even though s/he may have suppressed the memory, returns to them. These memories disarm the ego, that rational part of the mind that suppresses potentially anarchic desires as well as traumatic experiences and enables the individual to live in accordance with a society's rules and conventions.

We may think of the return of what is concealed in the subconscious as analogous of the return of what has been suppressed
more generally in the populace and the culture as a whole. Freud
argued that Nachträglichkeit left individuals bereft of their normal ordering processes and defences. Again, one might see this as
analogous of the way in which the nation is deprived of its conventional narratives and ideological defences.

If the critic Joe Cleary is right that the contemporary novel has
made the struggle for independence 'the definitive zone of memory', as I said in Chapter 1, then Freud's concept of Nachträglichkeit
helps us to understand the self-divided nature of a lot of the
cultural discourse in contemporary Ireland and Northern Ireland.
For the individual, Nachträglichkeit marks the failure of the normal processes of memory which have kept the original trauma,
what Freud would call the 'primal scene', concealed. To pursue
the wider analogy from the previous paragraph, the nation, finding itself in Bhabha's 'timelag', discovers that the protective
shield of memorializing is failing. Thus, in the late twentieth century, for example, the revelation of numerous incidents of child
abuse in which Catholic priests were involved, overtly or cryptically forced the Church into a position where its cultural defences
were crumbling.

Thus, approached as a cultural rather than purely psychoanalytic phenomenon, Nachträglichkeit undermines the sense of certainty and stability that nationalism can provide. Here, though, it is
important not to see this stability as anti-modern. For some time
'nationalism' and 'modernism' in Ireland were perceived as mutu-
ally exclusive. But contemporary scholarship no longer conceives
of nationalism as necessarily 'atavistic, racialist, nostalgic and mili-
tant', recognizing that it can serve as 'a strategy, in both culture and
politics, of giving back to the individual subject or to a community,
a sense of hope and coherence, in the face of the shattering, frag-
menting experience of modernity' (McCarthy, 2000: 17). But in the
case of an individual or nation emerging from a marginalized position, to adapt Bhabha's argument, such 'a sense of hope and coherence' is inhibited by the timelag that is located, as it were, between
repositioning and redefinition. Thus, Bhabha is more inclined than
McCarthy to stress how 'the cultural temporality of the nation
inscribes a much more transitional social reality' (1990: 1–2).

The tension between the 'sense of hope and coherence' that
McCarthy identifies and the 'transitional social reality' that Bhabha

associates with the nation informs much contemporary Irish fiction. A sense of uncertainty is especially pronounced in the case of Ireland because, as McCarthy says, following Seamus Deane,

> the modernisation in Ireland and in Irish literary culture ... shows the imbrication of that modernising process with structures of power, and with a discourse that had the effect of relegating activities and practices of the Irish to the realm of the 'other', or 'tradition' *vis-à-vis* the modernising metropolis.   (2000: 15)

Here McCarthy provides an additional way of reading contemporary fiction through the concept of Nachträglichkeit, the return of what has been concealed. If one accepts Deane's view, which McCarthy relies upon at this point, that modernization in Ireland is implicated in the 'structures of power' and complicit in the 'mothering' of Irish cultural activities and practices, then one must also ask whether contemporary fiction is being written from the realization that previous Irish authors never really engaged with the past, because of what was kept hidden, marginalized or silenced, but responded instead to a representation of the past.

This is the case in *The Journey Home* (1990) by Dermot Bolger whose *Father's Music* and *Emily's Shoes* are discussed in Chapter 6. It is primarily concerned with the initiation of a young man, Hano, into the sleazy, corrupt but exhilarating life of 1980s Dublin from which he and another principal protagonist escape to an old woman's cottage. However, the text does not simply valorize traditional, rural Ireland. On a closer reading, it is evident that the novel provides a critique of the urban middle-class phenomenon of trying to re-establish their links with the rural which in turn is perceived as being based on the countryside as a kind of spectre or false consciousness. In this respect, the ghost story of the young steward who, having been accused of theft, committed suicide in the basement of the now derelict big house where Hano takes refuge is significant. He overturns the myth of a benevolent rural Protestant ascendancy, exemplifying in his life and death evils of which the Protestant former landowner's present condition of living in a caravan, ostracized on her own lands, does not entirely absolve her. It is Cait/Kate, reading from the Bible, who eventually manages to free the ghost. What she does is to free the old woman of the secrets that are kept within her and her family line. But her principal role in the novel, lapsing into the cliché of women as the saviour of men, is to exorcize Hano of the ghosts that haunt him. This she achieves at the end of the novel when Hano thinks of 'home' as a place in her arms and is restored to his father, who haunts him in the course of the text, through the child that she carries which he is convinced is his.

Even a cursory reading of Irish fiction in the 1980s and 1990s suggests that it is a 'haunted' literature. I don't mean by this that it is preoccupied with ghosts and phantoms in their conventional sense, signifying the traditional association with the limits of life and death. But rather that it is concerned with haunting, ghosts, and spectres as manifestations of what, in the cultural critic Fredric Jameson's words, 'makes the present waver: like the vibrations of a heat wave through which the massiveness of the object world – indeed of matter itself – now shimmers like a mirage' (1999: 38). Spectrality, which is inevitably a part of Nachträglichkeit, challenges our sense of what is ever fully present, our apprehension of a world based, mistakenly as it happens, upon limit, finality and closure. In much Irish fiction, the points at which the text reveals itself as possibly more cryptic than we thought, mirror the way in which our epistemological understanding of nation, locale, history and human behaviour as knowable is disrupted.

In *The Journey Home*, Bolger depicts the Dublin of housing estates as a secret withheld from those who have been on the outside:

> I remember once as a child missing the bus stop at the village and being carried up the long straight road into the Corporation estates in the West. I was terrified by the stories I had heard. I could have been a West Berliner who'd strayed across the Iron Curtain. When I was eight the new dual carriageway made the division complete, took away the woodlands we might have shared, made the only meeting point between the two halves of the village a huge arched pedestrian bridge. (27)

The notion, so obviously applicable to the Ireland created by the Treaty, of halves that are difficult to bridge becomes a central trope in the novel and turns Dublin in this text into a schizophrenic city:

> Far below, Dublin was moving towards the violent crescendo of its Friday night, taking to the twentieth century like an

aborigine to whiskey. Studded punks pissed openly on corners. Glue snuffers stumbled into each other, coats over their
arms as they tried to pick pockets. Addicts stalked rich-looking
tourists. Stolen cars zigzagged through the distant grey estates
where pensioners prayed anxiously behind bolted doors, listening for the smash of glass. In the new disco bars children
were queuing, girls of fourteen shoving their way up for the
last drinks at the bar.   (35)

The image of the aborigine taking to whiskey is an arresting one
that configures the remainder of the paragraph. It reminds us of
how the Australian settlers removed the indigenous population
from their lands which they then used for their own purposes,
introducing a 'modern' world to which the aborigines found it
hard to relate and which left many of them disenfranchised in
their own country.

The emphasis in this particular representation of contemporary
Dublin is upon exploitation – tourists become the new colonizers
and are themselves potential victims while children are exploited
by those who run the Dublin nightlife and, presumably, by adver-
tisers. But the focus is also upon disempowerment – the young are
left disenfranchised and the elderly, who no longer contribute to
the economy, are left trapped in hostile communities. Menace,
theft and violence are not simply signs of the underbelly of Dublin
but interleaved with negative aspects of capitalism: greed,
exploitation and selfishness. The novel's focus is upon the impact
this has upon those who make the discovery. Thus, Hano, a vari-
ant of the innocent abroad for much of the novel, is 'relocated' psychologically by what he discovers. He is left in a kind of no-person
land: 'And here I was lost in the city, cut off in some time warp,
high and warm above the crumbling streets' (35). At one level, it is
the stratified nature of Ireland that brings this about:

> We [Hano and Cait/Kate] grew up divided by only a few
> streets so you'd think we would share a background. Yet
> somehow we didn't. At least not then, not till later when we
> found we were equally dispossessed. *The children of limbo* was
> how Shay called us once.   (7)

But, at another level, it is the result of the void that is created inside
him by the fact that a country that he thought he knew contained

secrets within itself to which he was never party. Indeed, the impact of what is withheld from those who are intimately involved with a place, community or other family members has upon them is a recurring motif in Bolger's work. In Hano's case, the secret self within him is a product of how he feels about the humiliation of his father in the demeaning job he is given. But it also results from what he sees and becomes a part of in working for the corrupt politician Plunkett, evident in his job as a debt collector, working with a man who threatens to kill a mother's sick child in front of her.

Thus, in thinking of the contemporary Irish novel as 'haunted', we must free the concept of haunting from the literary moorings to which it is usually confined. The concept of haunting is not one that belongs only to genres associated with spectrality in the conventional sense such as the gothic because as the French philosopher Jacques Derrida points out, 'the question of spectres is … the question of life' (1997: 23). As far as Irish fiction is concerned, he might have said 'the question of spectres … is the question of the modern'. The proliferation of phantoms and spectres in contemporary Irish fiction are products of the identity of modernity. An English critic, Julian Wolfreys, in an account of haunting in Victorian writing, argues that 'it is a sign of the hauntological disturbance that, because of the various spectral traces, we can never quite end the narrative of modernity' (2). Modernity is haunted by spectres that disrupt notions of origin and closure. In fact, this is a point that is exemplified in Seamus Deane's *Reading in the Dark* to which I will turn in a moment.

If we are going to understand the close interleaving of fiction and spectrality in contemporary Ireland and Northern Ireland we have to rethink the relationship between literature, philosophy, psychoanalysis and pedagogy, and the way in which much of the fiction is engaged in doing that for us. We have to do much as Nicolas Abraham and Maria Torok did in their account of *The Wolf Man's Magic World: A Cryptonymy* (1976). Derrida's preface to this text suggests ways in which we might see much of contemporary Irish fiction as being concerned with 'cryptonymy' or 'the crypt'. Derrida recognizes that, in their revisioning of Freud's account of a patient demonstrating the symptoms of Infantile Neurosis, Abraham and Torok present us with alternatives to the conventional concept of the crypt which conventionally over relies on 'the easy metaphors of the Unconscious (hidden, secret, underground, latent, other, etc)' (xiii). He points out that 'the first hypothesis of *The Magic Word* posits a preverbal traumatic scene that would have been "encrypted" with all its libidinal forces, which, through their contradiction, through their very opposition, support the internal resistance of the vault' (xv). Here, consciously or indirectly, Derrida develops Freud's concept of Nachträglichkeit. Derrida is not as concerned as Freud with the return of the 'primal scene', the point of origin of the trauma, but its concealment – what he calls its 'encryptment'. What I want to suggest is that across a range of very different novels, Irish writers are preoccupied with haunting, spectrality and ghosts in so far as they are harbingers, manifestations, or reflections of what has been 'encrypted'.

At this point, it would be useful to introduce some of Derrida's key ideas about what is secret or hidden. Derrida suggests that the most useful route to an explanation of what is a crypt is to consider what the term implies: topoi (the grounds); atopos (death) and the mortgage (cipher). As far as understanding the significance of secrets, and how their importance is unveiled in contemporary Irish fiction, the 'topoi' is the most relevant of these terms. Derrida stresses that, as the location of the crypt, the 'topoi', the grounds in which the crypt is situated, are intended to hide at least as much as hold the crypt. In developing this emphasis, Derrida stresses that they are also intended 'to disguise the act of hiding and to hide the disguise' (xiv). This is a point made not only by *The Journey Home* but the other texts discussed in this chapter. Normally when we think of crypts or secrets, we focus upon what is hidden rather than the act of hiding and its wider consequences. In other words, the crypt has as much to do with concealing as concealment.

Moreover, the crypt involves, Derrida says, 'a place comprehended within another but rigorously separated from it' (xiv). In other words, we think of the secret and hidden as concealed by what it is also largely removed from it. Derrida's preface usefully refocuses our attention upon the close relationship between what is hidden and, as far as contemporary Irish fiction is concerned, the individual or national consciousness in which it is concealed. However, paradoxically, concealment involves, Derrida points out, not only a relationship between what is hidden and the place in which it is hidden but also a separation from it. Derrida suggests that, in the normal view of things, the crypt might be thought of as 'a secret interior within the public square' (xiv).

For him a fundamental question is whether this place is hermetically sealed. One has to answer 'yes' and 'no' according to Derrida because 'the crypt can constitute its secret only by means of its division, its fracture'.

Finally, for our purposes, Derrida draws attention to another paradox in the concept of the crypt. He maintains that the inhabitant of a crypt is always 'the living dead' (xxi). By this he means that we keep the secret within ourselves as if it were dead. As the national consciousness in Ireland and the church keep their secrets. But the process is never finished. Concealment and the affect of the act of hiding upon the 'topoi' in which the 'encrypted' is situated are ongoing processes that have no conclusion or finality.

Stories Not to Pass On

At one point in Seamus Deane's novel, *Reading in the Dark*, the narrator informs us: 'To reach the ruins of the distillery, we had only to cross Blucher Street, go along Eglinton Terrace, across the mouth of the Bogside, with the city abattoir on our left...' (35). He describes an act of tracing, or rather retracing. But most of the journeys undertaken in this novel are never tracing. The unpredictable disrupts the act of tracing. For example, Blucher Street was the place where, in 1948, a young boy was killed in front of the narrator's eyes by a reversing lorry. The streets are places where one negotiates life – the street where McLaughlin was shot – or the sense that we live 'in a world that will pass away' (25).

The narrator's accounts of making his way, almost anywhere, are characterized by spectrality; from the appearance of Una to the people who pass him on an early winter's evening like shadows. The shadowy nature of the territory through which one has to find a route is bound up with the abiding presence of what is perceived as 'foreign' oppression. Even though a child has been killed, the residents will not talk to the police, and the narrator is taken away, in a search for a gun, in police cars that appear 'to have landed like spaceships' (27). The 'real' is a place of negotiation because the child is never sure what will happen next or who can be trusted. Initially, the legends, fairy stories and lore seem to belong to the fantastic, the place where the real and the imagined interconnect. But as the novel progresses, and the boy gets older, they become analogies for the political nature of the world in which he lives. Thus, the green-eyed people who are close to the fairies, 'looking for a human child they could take away' (7), become an analogy for sectarian kidnapping, a point to which I will return later. The narrator grows up, like all children, into an awareness of death, but also into a realization that 'reality' is more sinister than he thought.

I want to introduce Deane's *Reading in the Dark* through Toni Morrison's famous novel *Beloved* published in the United States eight years previously. My justification for doing so comes from Deane's book itself: The phrase 'reading in the dark' refers to the creative activity that follows literal reading – a kind of creative re-reading: 'I'd switch off the light, get back in bed, and lie there, the book still open, re-imagining all I had read, the various ways the plot might unravel, the novel opening into the endless possibilities in the dark' (20).

At one level, Morrison's novel is very different from Deane's, although both draw on modernist techniques developed by William Faulkner and Virginia Woolf. *Beloved* is about a nineteenth-century black female slave who killed her daughter rather than have her taken into slavery. Like *Reading in the Dark*, it might be seen as a sophisticated kind of ghost story, since the murdered child returns as an older girl to haunt her mother. Both novels turn on a significant absence, or absent presence. At times, *Reading in the Dark* is based on an elaborate conceit of the family and the family's history as a 'text' determined by the trace of what is absent. And both novels revolve around the concept of a pain that arguably is too terrible to bear and perhaps should not be passed on, and yet should not be eschewed. Towards the end of her novel, Morrison suggests ambiguously, 'This is not a story to pass on.' With reference to a secret within the family, but not the principal act of betrayal with which the text is concerned, Deane virtually makes the same point:

So broken was my father's family that it felt to me like a catastrophe you could live with only if you kept it quiet, let it die down of its own accord like a dangerous fire. Eddie gone. Parents both dead within a week. Two sisters, Ena and Bernadette, treated like skivvies and boarded in a hen-house. A long, silent feud. A lost farmhouse, with rafters and books in

it, near the field of the disappeared. Silence everywhere ... I felt
we lived in an empty space with a long cry from him ramify-
ing through it. At other times, it appeared to be as cunning and
articulate as a labyrinth, closely designed, with someone sobbing at the heart of it.   (42–3)

Despite the differences between Morrison's and Deane's novel,
and the different cultural contexts from which the texts emerge,
both deal with events and secrets so appalling that maybe the only
way to live on is to keep silent about them. In doing so they focus
upon many of the aspects of 'encryptment' that Derrida stresses in
the preface I discussed earlier: maintaining that emphasis should
not be upon what is concealed but the act of concealing itself; that
what is concealed affects the location of what is hidden; and that
what is secret has a relationship with the surrounds in which it is
hidden while also being separate from what conceals it.

   In the act of writing the novels, both authors would seem to
signify that their respective secrets have to be exorcised, and the
only way of doing this is to pass them to others. The dire consequences of doing so are reflected in both novels in the subsequent
sense of fragmentation – in Beloved's body, in the form of
Morrison's novel itself, and in what happens to the family in
Reading in the Dark. Both novels share an overwhelming sense of
pain that develops throughout the text, and which is never finally
exorcised. In Morrison's novel, it is cries of the millions who died
in the Middle Passage, for Deane it is the hundreds who have
'disappeared' – a phrase with a particular resonance in Northern
Ireland referring to people who were suddenly taken and killed,
and some of whose bodies have never been located:

There was a belief that it was here that the souls of all those
from the area who had disappeared, or had never had a
Christian burial, like the fishermen who had drown and whose
bodies had never been recovered, collected three or four times
a year – on St Brigid's Day, on the festival of Samhain, on
Christmas Day – to cry like birds and look down on the fields
where they had been born. Any human who entered the field
would suffer the same fate; and any who heard their cries on
those days should cross themselves and pray out loud to
drown out the sound. You weren't supposed to hear pain like
that; just pray you would never suffer it.   (53)

Here, in the Fields of the Disappeared, the affect of the 'encrypted' upon the 'topoi', to use Derrida's terms, could not be clearer. In fact, each text deals with a cultural identity, based on an ancestry marked, in their different ways, by loss that has never permitted any sense of closure. What Derrida emphasizes when he uses the phrase, 'the living dead'. In Africa, to turn to the background of Morrison's novel for a moment, slavery meant that whole families were suddenly dissipated – their members, taken into slavery, disappeared and from the perspective of those who survived, their families 'were disappeared'. On the Middle Passage, there were many whose bodies went into the sea. The loss left a void in the lives of those who survived which is passed on without really being spoken about from generation to generation. This, in turn gives rise, as in Deane's novel, to a ghostly presence in rumour, folklore and anecdote.

The anecdotes and community stories have a destabilizing effect on identity, bringing to death and loss with which every one has to cope in their lives, the possibility of suffering that is 'beyond' the normal parameters: 'You weren't supposed to hear pain like that.' But the histories of Northern Ireland and Ireland, like African–American history, pose the question, what are the normal parameters? Ghosts and spectres abound in Deane's novel, which gives it a kind of Gothic speculativeness. Boundaries of the senses and of time are rendered permeable in ways that can be comforting but are, usually, disturbing, and, more often, demonic. Daddy Watt's ghost haunts the distillery – 'a black shape that moved like a shadow around the park, but that shape had a mouth that opened and showed a red fire raging within'– while the terrified squealing of pigs in the slaughter house is 'so human I imagined they were going to break into words, screaming for mercy' (35). At one point, the narrator imagines 'the living rats that remained, breathing their vengeance in dull miasmic unison deep underground' (80).

The affect of what is 'encrypted' upon the larger surrounds in which it is held is anchored in many of the novel's principal motifs. For example, characters in the book are struck dumb or driven mad by particularly unpleasant types of knowledge or experience that have been suppressed. The mother in the novel loses the power of her speech in October 1968 when the Troubles come. The text finishes shortly after, as if it is unable to be written beyond the mother's silence. But she is not the only character in the novel to be struck dumb. Larry who kills Eddie also loses the power of speech. Madness is a motif associated most obviously with Crazy Joe and his secret knowledge; he is said to have been driven mad by something that happened when he was a young man (81). But there is also the 'customs man' driven mad by being imprisoned in a secret passage by smugglers (58).

Of these different examples of Deane's concern with the impact of concealment, the most obvious link between his and Morrison's novel is the mother figure upon which the burden of pain is most spectacularly visited. In Deane's novel, it is obvious to her son that the mother has something for which she wants to be forgiven. But, of course, she feels that she cannot be forgiven. One of the secrets that she carries is that she knew that her father ordered the death of her husband's brother (Eddie) and that she went with the man who was responsible for betraying Eddie. But it is not only that she went out with the man who named Eddie as an informant but that she married Eddie's brother still loving him. *Beloved* is based on a house disrupted by the anguish and spirits of the dead slaves. However, Deane's novel seems all the more terrible for being located in an apparently ordinary domestic setting: 'When we came into the kitchen, my mother looked up and the whole history of his family and her family and ourselves passed over her face in one intuitive waltz of welcome and then of pain' (136). In Morrison's novel, it is a pain that Sethe is able to exorcize, but in Deane's text, the mother, who seems to encapsulate the sufferings of all woman kind, cannot expel it: 'Then, at last, the real crying began, a lethal sobbing that ran its fright through us like an epidemic' (142). At other times, the suffering of women in the novel, as in *Beloved*, becomes a kind of chorus. The narrator says of Grianan: 'I could hear the underground waters whispering; that was the women sighing' (58).

The issues raised by the relationship between art and human suffering are especially complicated in a Catholic cultural context because of the way in which religious art, through its depictions of the passion of Christ, the sufferings of the saints and the death of the martyrs might be said to 'beautify' pain and torture. This begs the question as to whether art has any business to eschew the suffering and degradation involved in some of the most brutal forms of execution. In this context, it is important to notice how many of the religious motifs in Deane's novel are usually part of the brutal reality of suffering and not some kind of transcendent compensatory symbolism. Throughout *Reading in the Dark*, religious cadences are fused with legend and superstition, and there are direct and indirect references to the Bible and to Catholic theology beyond, of course, memories of growing up as a Catholic. For example, Eddie's entombment, preceding his execution, has echoes of the burial of Christ. He is put in a secret passage inside the walls of a farmhouse, and it is sealed, as was Christ's tomb, by a stone being rolled across its entrance. This episode is redolent of the one in which the boy is shut by his friends in a secret passage at Grianan. The gunmen, who sit outside smoking and discussing what they will do, invoke in some respects the soldiers at the crucifixion. McIlhenny, the Judas in Eddie's narrative, has betrayed Eddie, as Christ was betrayed. And in a further echo of the Bible, no one who is left knows what has happened to the body. After Eddie's death, the Family is dispersed, rather like the disciples after Christ's death. Subsequently, Eddie becomes, like Christ, a spectral presence in people's lives. There is a rumour that Eddie has joined IRA in the South, and continues fighting for freedom.

Deane's narrator says that when he realized that his mother might have been in love with McIlhenny even when she married his father:

> I went upstairs and sat on the bed in the cold bedroom and looked at the picture of the Sacred Heart and thought I understood how Jesus felt, him with his breast open and the pierced blood-dripping muscle emblazoned there... A great lamentation of seagulls filled the air as a storm came up from the harbour and the room seemed to lift into the sky with their rising shadows.   (145–6)

Here the text, rightly or wrongly, gives the impression that the narrative is based on ideas that have come out of meditating on religious narratives. This is especially clear in the lines quoted earlier:

> I felt we lived in an empty space with a long cry from him ramifying through it. At other times, it appeared to be as cunning and articulate as a labyrinth, closely designed, with someone sobbing at the heart of it.   (43)

In other words, the death of Eddie and its impact upon the family create a narrative that enables the text to pursue theological/spiritual

concepts about the nature of the world. Is the centre a vast empti-
ness, as twentieth-century theories of the Big Bang or the notion of
a post-Darwinian Godless universe might suggest? Or is it, drawing
on Catholic notions that informed, for example, the conception of
the Virgin Mary as the 'Mother of Sorrows', discussed in Chapter 5,
a site of inconsolable sorrows? Is there a silence at the centre of the
universe, as some strands of modern science would seem to suggest? Or is it, after all, a well-designed labyrinth? The ways in which
the text is woven around images of secrecy, absence, sorrow and
vengeance point to a deep structure beyond the representation of a
nakedly pragmatic reality. For example, the description of the area
in which the distillery, one of many sites in the text important to
local nationalist history but also bound up with secrets and lies,
fuses the physical and the metaphysical, the prosaic and the poetic:
'The dismembered streets lay strewn all around the ruined distillery
where Uncle Eddie had fought, aching with a long, dolorous
absence' (34). The phrase 'aching with a long, dolorous absence'
defies the kind of closure that we might normally associate with
realist writing. This lack of closure is evident throughout the novel
in its quasi-religious meditation on the kind of universe in which we
live, and the nature of memory.

Deane's account of the 'Field of the Disappeared' demonstrates
how lived cultures are constituted from local superstition as well
as the practicalities of living in particular types of communities.
Here legends about the Banshee, concepts from Catholicism and
familial and community lore are conflated. What is especially
interesting in this section is the way in which contemporary identity looks back to traditional lore, and is also based on the new, on
economic and technological development:

> In the summer of 1950 we had more money because my father
> was working overtime in the dockyards. We could, therefore,
> afford a holiday – two weeks in a boarding-house in Buncrana.
> My father came down on the bus at the weekends, for he could
> not get time off during the week. The weather was hot, unbro-
> ken, bright as metal. (52)

But this chapter also stresses that identity is not only a matter of
cultural dispositions and the collision between the present and
particular pasts. The cultural material fuses with the psychological. There is an important link between the opening paragraph of

this section, which describes how work places the father outside the family – he is only able to share the family holiday at weekends – and the concluding projection of the child's inner-most anxieties regarding his father:

> And I ran to catch up with him but, as in a dream, he seemed never to get nearer and I gave up, stranded between them, Liam at the hedge paring his switch and looking at me, my father's back receding as he came to a turn in the road, the gulls' cries ringing piteously, angrily, in my ears. (55)

Deane's novel, like Morrison's, crosses the boundaries of a number of genres. *Beloved* is a slave narrative, a plantation story, a ghost story and even a romance. The two most obvious points to make about Deane's novel is that it is a 'border' work and a self-consciously modernist text. I describe it as a border work because it is set in Derry, a territory between Northern Ireland and the Republic. It also occupies a position between the rural and the traditional, albeit changing, Donegal and the modern, industrial world of Derry. It has an overtly 'modernist structure', indebted to the experimentalism of James Joyce, William Faulkner and Virginia Woolf. The influence of the modernist structures associated with Woolf's *The Waves* and Faulkner's *As I Lay Dying* is particularly evident in the way in which the text is divided up into sections allocated to specific dates. The chronology of the novel runs from February 1945 to July 1971. In generic terms, though, it crosses numerous boundaries, so, as some of the initial reviewers found, it is difficult to decide whether it is a memoir about growing up in Derry, a bildungsroman or a whodunit. Like *Beloved*, it blurs the boundary between history and fiction, between public and private and between the rational and the irrational. Certainly, in its use of anecdotes, it owes much, like Morrison's novel, to the techniques of oral story telling, and in its use of episodic tales produces a structure that, as in *Beloved*, is not defined by any straightforward linearity. Thus, as in sections such as 'Field of the Disappeared August 1950', Deane's novel frequently opens on to a myriad of different narrative possibilities, not all of which are pursued or anchored convincingly from a realist perspective.

Reading in the Dark seems to be structured around a dialectic between the precision we associate with, and expect of, realism – however illusory that may be in the end – and a vague, enigmatic presence. Although the various sections of Deane's novel have precise dates, and are located in a particular historical context, that precision and historical specificity is usually undermined by the fluid, enigmatic content and the shadowy, somewhat secretive, nature of some of the episodes. It would appear that the most appropriate words from within the text are the last words of the narrator's father: 'It's a strange world' (232).

Thus, the language of childhood is important to this novel because it is imaginative, and is open to an interest in the phantasmal nature of what the father calls this 'strange' world. However, in the course of the narrative, as the boy-narrator becomes older, the language loses some of its figurative energy and generally becomes less vivid. This parallels the change in the boy's mother; the effect of being awakened to the secret she has suppressed for so long is evident in how she becomes more severe, and acquires her father's 'Roman stoniness' (228). The knowledge the boy gains separates him from his mother, and may be from the poetic qualities of language that European feminist psychoanalysts and cultural critics like Julia Kristeva have associated with the mother figure through, for example, lullaby and the way mothers communicate with their babies through rhythmic sounds.

A new realism enters with the Troubles. Reality is mediated by the television, which, it would seem, is on all the time in people's homes. The narrator draws attention to how, in his home, 'tile surround had replaced the old range and made the threshold of the fire naked and banal' (230). This may be read as signifying how reality itself has changed and how the earlier sense of the poetic has been lost in a war which brings: 'Scrambled noises of glass breaking, petrol-bomb flashings, isolated shouts turning to prolonged baying and the drilled smashing of batons on riot shields'. However, the Troubles brings not only a new 'realism' to Northern Ireland but a revisioning of the Nationalist past, which is made clear when we think back over the novel in the light of what we have witnessed about secrets, the effect of concealment and the consequences of betrayal. In other words, when we read Deane's novel 'in the dark'.

Reading in the Dark, like Morrison's *Beloved*, may usefully be read not simply through Freud's concept of Nachträglichkeit, concerned as it is with the suppression and return of a 'primal scene' of trauma, but through Jacques Derrida's development of Nachträglichkeit. Like Derrida, Deane and Morrison, emphasize the processes and the consequences of concealment. The way what is hidden is part of yet separate from the consciousness that hides it is as important to these texts, if not more so, as what is hidden. As Derrida suggests, the haunting, spectrality and ghosts in these texts are harbingers, manifestations or reflections of what has been 'encrypted'.

A Mix of Desires

Joseph O'Connor's *The Salesman*, published only two years after *Reading in the Dark*, is a very different novel from Seamus Deane's. But they share, within a common conviction expressed in O'Connor's text, that 'every person is the sum of their choices ... each one of us is a story, a mix of desires, experiences, fantasies' (220), concern with secrets buried within the self. It is important here to remember Derrida's arguments that I described earlier. Focusing on the tensions between the private and public self, the secret self in both texts is like 'a place comprehended within another but rigorously separated from it' (xiv) and is constituted 'only by means of its division, its fracture'. In Deane's novel, the fractures and divisions within the family are emblematic of those within the self. This is also true of O'Connor's novel where the inner, secret self, as Derrida and Deane suggest, has to do with the need for protection, the necessity for shelter and the ongoing process of resisting discovery. Both Deane and O'Connor's novels, anchored in a sense of the 'crypt' which is unwittingly Derridean, provide an interesting and interrogative perspective on what he has to say, especially his thesis that the 'encrypted' is always kept hidden as if it were dead yet it is a living dead.

The narrative core of *The Salesman* is a letter that Billy Sweeney is writing to his daughter Maeve, as she is lying comatose in a Dublin Hospital, the victim of an assault during an armed robbery at a petrol station where she worked. While *Reading in the Dark* is essentially an account of the discovery of a secret that has rendered the narrator's family and especially his mother foreign to him, *The Salesman* is the gradual confession of a number of secrets. The motifs of the need for protection and the necessity of resisting discovery are paradoxically interleaved throughout *The Salesman* with a desire to unveil and confess.

As in many modern novels, including Deane's and Morrison's work, the notion that each of us is a 'story' is used in *The Salesman*

to anchor a wider concern, with the creative and selective nature
of personal, and ultimately public, memory:

> Let me apologise to you now if I tell some things the wrong
> way around, or incompletely … It is not that I have forgotten
> those times exactly, I just remember them distantly, out of
> shape, out of their chronology, in the wrong colours.   (22)

But what links O'Connor's interest in memory with Toni
Morrison's is his interest in an individual's capacity to assume the
memories that are not actually their memories. Sweeney confesses: 'In fact sometimes, I have discovered, I clearly remember
things that never happened, or events at which I was not even
present' (22). His personal narrative, structured around recollections, some of which are the products of conscious reflection and
others of randomly triggered memories, allows the novel to range
over a long period of time and to discuss his relationship with
Maeve's mother, Grace. The narrative, like Seamus Deane's, is
linked to the etymology of the word 'recover' – meaning, for example, to reclaim as well as uncover, but also meaning re-cover. The
letter and the diary in *The Salesman* both uncover and re-cover.
The diary uncovers the events of late 1993 and previous episodes
in Billy Sweeney's life such as his courtship with Grace and their
marriage. But it also veils aspects of both. The letter and the diary
increasingly become disturbing combinations of the rational and
the irrational, evident at times in the movement into imagery: 'I
took a piece of paper from the drawer and wrote down the words
"hammer" and "knife". Then I drew a small doodle, the hanging
man' (151).

The doodle is one of the means by which what is concealed
within Billy Sweeney is revealed. The novel turns on the
dichotomy between Billy's public persona and his inner, private
self. But, again, it is useful to bring to mind here Derrida's
thoughts about the impact of the crypt upon the area in which it
is buried. The focus of O'Connor's novel is upon the impact of the
crypt upon Billy and, specifically, upon his sense of his self. His
obsession with Quinn, his vigil at the bedside of his comatose
daughter and even elements in his courtship of Grace, cast him as
foreign to himself. This is evident in the way his talking about
himself becomes increasingly dislocated and strange in the course
of his narrative – he comes to think of himself more as 'the

salesman' than Billy Sweeney. In fact, two qualities of a salesman are especially pertinent to the novel: the capacity of the salesman to spin a persuasive yarn which conceals the truth and the importance of bringing a deal to a 'close' – a word which reminds us that in *The Salesman* the narrative, and the meta narratives within it, resist closure.

At a profound level, moving between the prosperous and the seedier sides of Dublin, the text itself reflects the way Billy thinks of himself: 'Imagine if you can, two pieces of music being played at the same time one softly melodic, the other even more quiet but ugly and discordant' (151). Some of the key events in Billy's life, such as the argument between Billy and Grace at, and following, Molly's Christening and Grace's testimony at the custody hearing, suggest a side of him that is evident from aspects of the diary – cold, distant and violent. Mirroring the nature of Dublin itself, Billy vacillates between the respectable and the seedy. His surprise at Grace's account of their marriage – that they have been estranged from each other for years – also suggests how he fails to see that he has been estranged from himself. Or rather from the self that is revealed to the reader, for example, in his account of how he rushed to Grace when Maeve told him she wanted to stay in his house, and in the way he burst into her room to confront her over the condoms he has found. The 'ugly and discordant' Billy Sweeney, which acquires a more forceful presence in the narrative, is also evident in the views he projects on to others – not only Quinn whom he holds responsible for what has happened to his daughter but Grace's lover, the bank manager and even the milkman he hires as a hit man. The verbal violence in his row with Grace – a combination of passionate spontaneity and calculatingly inflicted hurt – reveals a sadistic element that also comes out when he kidnaps Quinn. This sadism is reflected in the way in which he labels and 'others' people reductively – Grace is called a 'whore' and Quinn becomes 'Q'.

The cage in which first Quinn and second Billy Sweeney himself are imprisoned is one of the key images of the crypt in the novel, and of the hidden self that is gradually unveiled in the course of Billy's narrative. Quinn's insight into Billy's 'encrypted' self, more accurate and searching than Billy's own self-knowledge, gives him his superiority over Billy. Although Billy initially locks Quinn in the outdoor aviary, he is 'caged' by Quinn's psychological intimidation. Quinn proves the stronger personality indulging in physical exercise and taunting Billy with his plans to break out. When Quinn escapes from the cage but remains within the house, he reorders the garden and carries out repairs to the house that Billy has neglected. Indeed, the house and the garden are symbolic of Billy's life, his inner self and the fundamental weakness that was one of the reasons why his wife left him.

The sparrow hawk with which Billy threatens Quinn turns out to be a metaphor for the way Quinn systematically shreds Billy's confidence until he takes to barricading himself in the attic. When Billy is released from the cage after his period of imprisonment, such is the hold that Quinn has over him that he goes out to work, concealing from others his secret that he is being held 'prisoner' by Quinn and returns to his home and to Quinn like a bird-of-prey returning to his trainer. But the fact that Quinn is holding him prisoner is not the only 'crypt' hidden within him. The hold that Quinn has over Billy is partly the product of Quinn's psychological intimidation and partly the recognition on both their parts that their secret selves have much in common with each other, including a deep-rooted loneliness – both for different reasons are separated from their families – guilt, alcoholism, and a violent personality.

Billy Sweeney's initial violence and eventual sympathy for Quinn's plight when he is holding him prisoner in his garden cage is repeated when Quinn turns the tables on Billy. In each case, the sympathy that one eventually shows to the other – symbolically realized in the image of the two green budgerigars – comes about when the one reveals the narrative of his life to the other. Each narrative illustrates the point made earlier in the novel that 'each one of us is a story, a mix of desires, experiences, fantasies'. But they also reveal how the secrets and the amount of pain which each man has kept hidden and carries around with him has affected his being. Significantly Quinn is tortured and meets his death in Billy's garden tied to an apple tree – symbolically the tree of knowledge. What the novel seems to recommend is that being human and recognizing others as human is only possible when we place the individual in his/her 'narrative' and recognize the 'crypt' – the pain and the secrets – within each of us. Lizzie demonstrates the truth of this when she tries to persuade Billy to forgive Seàn his relationship with Grace – he confesses to Billy that he is Lizzie's father. While Billy sees him reductively, Lizzie places what he did in the context of his narrative as a young and still immature priest. Billy is only able to demonstrate the same generosity after he has learned to love the man who has virtually killed his daughter by seeing him as the sum of the choices he has made, his experiences, fantasies, secrets, lies and failures.

The Salesman, like *Reading in the Dark*, is concerned with haunting, ghosts and spectres as manifestations of what in Fredric Jameson's terms, 'makes the present waver: like the vibrations of a heat wave through which the massiveness of the object world – indeed of matter itself – now shimmers like a mirage' (1999: 38). Spectrality challenges our sense of what is ever fully present, our apprehension of a world based mistakenly, as I said earlier, upon limit, finality and closure. From Billy's letters and diaries emerges a self that has never been fully present to its own life, not least because of the ways in which it has been bound up with denial and concealment. Unlike Deane's novel, *The Salesman* suggests that being fully human involves recognition of the messiness of most people's lives and being responsive to how most individual lives, albeit to varying degrees, involve the 'encryptment' and suppression of pain and trauma. The 'encryptment' of pain that is almost unbearable, and its affect upon the individual consciousness and being, is a recurring feature of Northern Ireland women's writing, discussed in the next section with particular reference to a comparison of Jennifer Johnston's *Fool's Sanctuary* (1987) and Mary Leland's *The Killeen* (1985) and a discussion of Linda Anderson's *To Stay Alive* (1984).

Foreign Bodies

A case might be made that it is the presence of northern women authors writing about late twentieth-century Northern Ireland, and about countries and histories outside the North, that most marks Northern Ireland literature in the 1980s and 1990s – Linda Anderson, Caroline Blackwood, Polly Devlin, Kathleen Ferguson, Joan Lingard, Deirdre Madden, Kitty Manning, Una Woods. The most obvious point to make about the women who have chosen to write directly or indirectly about contemporary Northern Ireland is that they are concerned with the impact of the Troubles upon people's lives especially upon the lives of women and children. On a negative note, this has led to a tendency to essentialize women's experiences as pacifist, a trend challenged by Mary

Leland's *The Killeen* which focuses on the lives of two female lovers of violent revolutionaries but also includes two women who are themselves uncompromising nationalists, ready to sacrifice the lives of others.

Criticism's tendency to see women writers in the North as concerning themselves with the impact of the Troubles on people's lives has not always meant that the profound, haunted nature of some of these texts has received due recognition. Perhaps one of the most obviously haunted novels by a woman writer about sectarianism is Jennifer Johnston's *Fool's Sanctuary*. However, it is a novel to argue with rather than from. Like many contemporary Irish novels, it is concerned with refiguring and interrogating nationalist history of the struggle for independence – in this case the events of 1919–21 – and follows a trend in Irish fiction in the 1970s and 1980s to revision the Anglo-Irish war and republicanism in the light of the impact of the post-1968 Troubles in Northern Ireland. The novel is narrated in the early 1980s by an elderly woman who lies dying in her family home, and, like many contemporary novels, it is concerned with the past and present continuum.

I say that this is a novel to argue with rather than from because its demonization of the IRA seems too easy and, unlike Mary Leland, Johnston does not present a convincing account of the personal motivations and the socio-political circumstances of the nationalists. Like Leland's novel, it concerns a woman who falls in love with a revolutionary. In this case, he refuses to obey his orders to kill her brother and her brother's friend, who are officers in the British army, and he is himself killed for betraying the republican cause.

The most obvious way of reading this novel is through the connotations of the name of the family home, 'Sanctuary', and the Shakespearian allusion in the name of the central character Miranda. At one level, the reference to *The Tempest* suggests that these texts share scepticism about retreating from life into an island of one's own. But there is more to Johnston's novel than this. The past becomes a 'foreign body' encrypted within Miranda who, hidden away in her private sanctuary, enters a kind of living death. In her relationship with a revolutionary, both Miranda and her lover are not entirely known to each other. What they keep from each other, wittingly or unwittingly, creates a deep-seated sense of estrangement within each of them. This is analogous of how the Anglo-Irish struggle often meant that revolutionaries and their lovers, the public and private, together with the tension between rhetoric and real deeds, were never fully present to, or conversant with, each other.

This is certainly the case in Leland's *The Killeen*. Whereas the principal intertext in *The Sanctuary* is Shakespeare's *The Tempest*, Leland's novel alludes to Yeats's *Cathleen Ní Houlihan* and the real Cork revolutionary Mary MacSwiney, whose brother, the Mayor of Cork, died while on hunger strike in 1920. The novel might be read as an account of the disillusionment of women initially attracted by the heroic masculinity of revolutionaries. But the text is also about concealment and its impact upon those who become implicated in it and who, however inevitably, withhold part of themselves from those with whom they become intimately involved. It is no coincidence that the IRA gunman with whom Margaret Coakley becomes emotionally entangled is hidden in the grounds of a convent where she has been sent to 'skivvy' by her widowed mother. Concealed by his brother Father Costello, the gunman, the priest and the convent itself become 'foreign bodies'. The baby which Margaret carries inside her becomes literally and figuratively a foreign body within; as the husband of Julia Mulcahy, to whom Margaret is sent to stay, becomes to his wife when he dies on hunger strike in the name of the republican cause.

The impact of knowing that these men concealed much of themselves and were never fully present to the women with whom they made love is analogous of the way in the 1920s and 1930s elements of republicanism revealed themselves as strangers to each other. *The Killeen* is set in the 1930s and Mary's lover is a foreign body not only to her but also to Eamon de Valera's republicans who in 1936 outlawed the IRA. At one level, it could be argued that the political manoeuvres and betrayals within nationalism at this time constituted what was hidden in more triumphalist versions of official republican history. Another secret within nationalism, is the extent to which nationalists in the 1930s looked toward Fascism in Europe for inspiration and were seduced by its imaginings of a nation as strong, inviolable and racially untarnished. This is exposed in the novel in the conversations between Father Costello and Julia Mulcahy's aunt. But one can also see the events of these years – the refusal of some of the republicans to accept the Treaty which brought the Irish Free State into being and Eamon de Valera's eventual acceptance of the Treaty and re-entry to the Dáil in 1927 – as products of the 'crypt' within. Those who worked together found themselves not knowing, and wondering whether they had ever really known, those who were now strangers to them. Moreover, what their former nationalist friends and colleagues had withheld from them created a void within them too.

However, the most obvious and shocking image of the crypt in Leland's novel is the Killeen itself – the place where babies who died without being baptized were buried. Indeed, it is important to understand that this is a novel about the 'crypt' to appreciate how its Part Three is better integrated with the rest of the text than some critics have allowed. This part of the novel is concerned with Margaret's illegitimate son, Thomas, whom her brother Michael agrees to adopt. In a fit of rage and shame over his illegitimacy, Thomas is killed by his grandmother and buried in the Killeen because the priest refuses to baptize him. However, the focus is upon the way that his hidden body affects the territory – literally the physical and moral landscape of Ireland. Thus, the focus is principally upon Michael who is so affected by what is concealed in the Killeen that eventually he leaves Ireland for America.

Indeed, the best of the novels about the impact of the Troubles upon those who live in Northern Ireland are profitably read within frameworks provided by Derrida's ideas about the 'crypt'. In focusing upon how the Troubles impact upon people's lives they inevitably take us into what is hidden and, in allowing what is secret to emerge from its place of concealment, have the effect of making the present 'waver'.

In Linda Anderson's fiction, as in many works about the Troubles by women writers, there are traumatic moments that are part of the wider lore of living in, and being a citizen of, contemporary Belfast. But encrypted within these moments of traumatizing violence, which are part of the broader mindscape, are harbingers of what is further encrypted within Belfast life. *To Stay Alive* is set in 1979, the beginning of the second decade of the Troubles. It is typical of many novels written about Northern Ireland in the 1980s and 1990s in that it focuses upon the resolution of the problems of a number of central characters. It opens with Dan, a Catholic medical student and one of the key protagonists, retrieving his wife's dog that has been used for target practice by a British paratrooper; it is significant that the dog is female: 'He felt the spine. Broken. The body would disintegrate if … Unless it was lifted very carefully' (7). This is the first example of the violence that surrounds Dan and his young wife in Catholic West Belfast. Their friend Aidan is the victim of a revenge killing and one of their neighbours is killed in crossfire. Crossfire itself is an important motif in this book for Dan and his wife find themselves caught between the occupying British army and the IRA. At one level, Dan and Rosaleen's experiences within this 'crossfire' anchor the novel's critique of the British army. However, the book is more complicated than this. At one point, the army are showed slides of the district to orientate themselves to the community. One of the slides, redolent of Heaney's well-known poem, 'Punishment', is of a young female victim of communal punishment. The voyeurism that is implicit in Heaney's poem is explicitly coarse in Anderson's account. The emphasis is upon violation, meanness and misogynism:

> Another slide. A young woman tethered to a lamp post, her head covered with some oily liquid, her full breasts partly bared by a rip in her shirt.
> 'This is Marta O'Hanlon.'
> 'Ohhh, I'd love to martyr her,' Shiner whispered.
> Her hair was cut off by a group of women. They poured red lead over her head until it dripped into her eyes. Men ran their hands over her body and urinated against her while women cheered them on … (24)

Several things emerge here from their, usually 'encrypted', presence within the wider communal knowledge of Belfast. First, there is the behaviour of women who go with British soldiers and the summary punishment of offenders by the paramilitary groups. Second, there is the cynical chauvinism of the British army that is not broadcast in mainland national news. But, the elision of the soldiers' reactions and the abuse heaped on the female victim by her own kind underscores a deeper crypt which has much to do with the nature of masculinity in traditional working-class communities from which both the soldiers and the men who urinate on their victim come and in which other women, too, are complicit.

At the heart of Anderson's novel is a philosophical, Derridean, concern with the fusion of the public and the private through what is 'encrypted' within each. As Anderson herself has said:

> A recurring obsession in my work is the link between public and private kinds of violence, the way 'public' violence seeps

and deforms and creates what a man says to a woman in bed, for example, and the reverse situation, too. The way all our 'privacies' create the mutilating world. (St Peter, 2000: 100)

But, having 'relocated' these privacies, the text finds itself in a kind of timelag, uncertain as to how to finally inscribe them. But Derridean notions of the 'crypt' help us to understand how its concern with the violence that is 'encrypted' within the private determines the nature of this text. For its focus is upon how what is concealed within the various private lives and histories consti-tuting the different communities affects the 'territory' in which it is embedded. By 'territory', I mean here the psychic make-up of the different characters, genders, families, communities, and institutions with which the novel is concerned. One of the princi-pal fault lines in Dan and Rosaleen's marriage is not simply their poverty but the secret of their poverty that he forces Rosaleen to keep. It becomes in turn a terrible secret, almost too painful to be borne, for in his view it is not a crime to be poor but 'the most unforgivable crime of all. Even worse than being sick' (74). His language – 'you'll tell no one our troubles' (74) – conflates the private and the public and betrays the state of inner tension with which they are forced to live.

Through this focus upon the way in which what is hidden can affect the wider sociopsychic territory in which it is concealed, *To Stay Alive* explores different layers of 'violation'. At one point in the novel, Dan's wife Rosaleen reminds her neighbours what was done to a young woman in the neighbourhood who was accused of being 'a whore to the entire British army': 'They fixed it so they would be the last guests,' said Rosaleen, picturing the wet slick of blood curling from the punctured womb (47). Another victim of communal discipline, the young woman on the slide viewed by the British army, which I mentioned earlier, is further violated by the soldiers who examine the picture. Here text and slide are elided so that the reader and the voyeuristic soldiers are almost conflated, leaving the reader positioned so as to be complicit in the young victim's ordeal. Meanwhile, Christ might be seen as violated by the associations in the account of the punishment with the crucifixion: the paint is redolent of blood from the crown of thorns; the rip in her shirt suggests the spear wound in Christ's side; and the behaviour of the men and the women echoes the

mockery that Christ endured. To complicate these different levels
of violation further, later in the novel, Rosaleen perceives Jesus as
a violator:

> She re-read the New Testament in amazement, hating the Jesus
> she found there. A righteous prig blasting fig-trees, turfing
> money-lenders out of the temple. And his cruel impossible
> demands! ... Not that he forgave his opponents. No, they were
> destined for 'everlasting torment', which he described with
> gloating malice. And, oh, how he wanted to die! He invited it,
> insisted. Elected his own betrayer.   (85)

What is presented here is not simply one character's perspective
on Christ but another example of how the 'foreign', in this case
the arrogant, self-righteous Jesus, is 'encrypted' within the familiar holy and meek man. Moreover, the echo of the crucifixion in
the slide viewed by the soldiers, reminds us, as does Leo's broken
body, that within the religious iconography of the cross, as I
mentioned earlier in discussing Seamus Deane's novel, is
'encrypted' crucifixion as a shameful and, at the time of the
passion and death of Christ, a common form of judicial
punishment:

> When Rosaleen came back with cold compresses, Leo was
> stretched on the settee. His face, usually so proud and brazen,
> was swollen with bruises and tears, his trousers hung in tatters
> over burnt legs. Rosaleen kneeled, breathing in his close pan-
> icked odour and placed a cloth on the charred skin, making
> him wince.
> 'I'm sorry, sorry,' she murmured, turning to stop her tears
> splashing on his sores. 'Moral degenerate,' she read uncom-
> prehending. There was a notice pinned to his shirt with 'Moral
> degenerate' scrawled over it! Rosaleen snatched it away.
> Their mother was patting and soothing him: 'My love, my
> love, who did it to you? Why? Was it Protestants? Where did
> you go?'
> His speech was snarled and ugly, as if his tongue was thick-
> ened: 'Tattoo. They said ... next time.'
> 'But you know nothing. You've never even been lifted.'
> 'No,' he jerked his head as if impatient. 'Keep away from bad
> women.'

He gave a sound that was half giggle, half sob. 'Said I take drugs.'
Suddenly her father loomed over them.
'Everybody!' he shouted in a raw strangled voice. 'Everybody! Everybody's rotten!'   (88)

In a complex web of allusions, *To Stay Alive* conflates different examples of how, in Derridean terms, the territory in which the 'crypt' is concealed is affected by the presence of the crypt.

The introduction of the threat of the tattoo introduces another important trope, the inscription and reinscription of the body. The passage moves from Leo's body violated by 'the new priesthood', to how he has secretly abused the body of, presumably, prostitutes, to the concealed abuse of his own body through drugs. His action is placed in a wider context – the way in which men are responsible for inscribing the female body with a particular text that legitimates the abuse of women. Rosaleen remembers her father's reaction when a man followed her home from school every day for several weeks: 'It's your own fault for tarting yourself up' (88). The father's rebuke makes him complicit in the stalking. In turning her modern appearance into a sign of moral degeneracy he violates her himself by metaphorically pinning a notice on her.

To Stay Alive conflates different examples of how those with power use the powerless. It underscores how this is legitimated and made possible by the way those with power and authority 'other' the bodies of those they exploit. Most of these incidents draw attention to what is often denied but is always 'encrypted' within these scenarios of exploitation: gender and sexual politics. At the end of the novel, Rosaleen is surrounded and sexually assaulted by four soldiers who would have raped her if she had not vomited over one of them. The assault – one of the soldiers who blocks her way clamps his hands on her breasts – is accompanied by verbal abuse in which she is labelled, because she is a Catholic who is not at church on a Sunday, as a 'heretic' and a 'bad girl'. The former label reminds us of the way the torture and execution of women by religious courts were a means of curtailing female power as well as religious subversion, and the latter reminds us that, for centuries, men had the legal right to physically punish their wives. Eventually, as the prospect of rape gets nearer, Rosaleen is reduced to an 'it' and to 'Irish' (183). In other words, how her principal assailant behave is determined by discourses about women, about the Irish, and about masculinity, and what is very often 'encrypted' within them, which in turn determines their own sense of what it means to be British, masculine and in the army.

Here, the ways in which an occupying power controls the occupied is linked to the way in which class and gender politics work through language and representation. But there is an equal emphasis in the account of this episode upon the way in which the soldier and his masculinity is seen through Rosaleen. His violence in turn crops his identity so that he becomes a collection of parts: 'His spots, his teeth, his lips, hovered near her face' (183). Within the context of Bhabha's concept of the timelag, it is significant that the text stresses that the squaddie is an adolescent, itself, of course, a state in-between boyhood and manhood. He is seen as caught between his physical–sexual relocation and the confusion of what is expected of him: 'Acne ran wild on his face. He was leering at her like a deadly adolescent who practised his menace in a mirror' (183). His attack upon Rosaleen becomes a means by which he is defined in relation to, and by, his army mates who scorn him when Rosaleen vomits over him: 'You make them come at the wrong end ...' (184). But what is intriguing is the way in which the text interleaves the public and private dimension of the encounter. The most violent words he uses are those he whispers, secretly, into her ear: 'I'm going to suck your cunt so hard your head will shrink between your shoulders ...' He conflates his private fantasy, and the violence that informs those fantasies, with the public nature of the assault:

> He was pressing his fat thing against her. His breathing became thick and wavy in her ear. 'Tough shit, tough shit,' he kept mumbling. No! Touch it! He was telling her to touch it! Vomit came into her mouth and erupted, spattering his sleeve with slimy streaks.   (183)

The crypt, then, in each of these texts by women writers focusing upon the experiences of women in Ireland and Northern Ireland, involves, as Derrida says, 'a place comprehended within another but rigorously separated from it'. What is especially interesting in Anderson's novel is the way in which it interleaves an exploration of what is secret and hidden in the various communities within Northern Ireland with what is 'encrypted' in language and discourse, so determining the status afforded women and the behaviour of men towards them. Thus, while, as Derrida said, we normally think of what is hidden as separate from what conceals it, this text, like Derrida's preface, usefully refocuses our attention upon the close relationship between what is hidden and, as far as contemporary Irish fiction is concerned, the individual or national consciousness in which it is concealed.

4

Mimicry, Authority and Subversion

Brian Moore's *The Magician's Wife* (1997),
Emma Donoghue's *Slammerkin* (2000) and
John McGahern's *Amongst Women* (1990)

The three principal texts of this chapter are connected in their preoccupation with 'mimicry' and its role, paradoxically, in both the maintenance and the secret subversion of authority. In each of these texts, these two principal preoccupations are closely interleaved because in each history is read through the interconnection of power, mimicry, authority and subversion. Homi Bhabha (1983) offers perspectives on the relationship between mimicry, power and authority in a colonial context which are applicable to Moore's *The Magician's Wife*, which is specifically concerned with France's colonization of Algeria, to Donoghue's account of women's lives in the eighteenth century and McGahern's covert critique of the Irish state in *Amongst Women*. Although Bhabha writes primarily with the colonial and postcolonial experience in mind, the relationship between power and mimicry is one that enters more generally into contexts that are dependent upon the maintenance of dominant and subordinate relations. Bhabha's essay is dependent upon another influential postcolonial theorist Edward Said, whose recognition that mimicry is an ironic, secretive interface between the dominant presence, and its panoptical vision of identity and status, and the changing perspectives of, and sense of difference among, those who are dominated.

In summary, Bhabha argues that, at one level, mimicry reflects the dominant discourse's insistence upon a recognizable 'other' in tune with its expectations as well as the accommodation to its strategies of those who are under its authority. But, at another level, mimicry is a secret sign of recalcitrance and of difference that always poses a threat to the synchronic vision of those in authority. Thus, mimicry, Bhabha maintains, reminds the dominant or colonizing power of an 'other' 'that is almost the same, but not quite' (381). For Bhabha, the ambivalence of mimicry, does not simply rupture or 'disrupt' the dominant discourse but creates an uncertainty that renders the subjected as a 'partial' or 'incomplete' presence. The subjects are incomplete because the dominant power refuses or fails to recognize or represent them fully and also because they challenge the way in which these dominant discourses seek to appear natural or normal. In other words, the success of authoritative or colonial discourse is dependent upon the creation of partial or incomplete subjects which reflect what that discourse desires of them but signify a constant rejection of it. The subjects of colonial, and indeed patriarchal discourse, occupy a space in which overtly or covertly authority and power are mocked. For mimicry 'mimes the forms of authority at the point at which it deauthorizes them' (385). The discussion of the three texts in this chapter is primarily concerned with examining how they turn on points where mimicry 'deauthorizes' authority but is also concerned with the secret nature of mimicry's subversion.

Mimicry at a number of levels is essential to Brian Moore's *The Magician's Wife*. It is set in a 'timelag', a period in 1856 when Napoleon III, fresh from victory in the Crimea, sought to buy himself and his armies some time before embarking upon his final campaign in Algeria. (The French entered Algeria in 1830, in a bid to put an end to piracy out of North Africa. Bringing 313 years of Turkish rule to an end, they eventually created a French colony that did not win its independence until 1962. The novel is set in a period when Europeans were being actively encouraged to settle in Algeria, a policy which was initiated in the 1830s and 1840s.)

The central characters in *The Magician's Wife*, the magician Henri Lambert and his wife Emmeline, undertake a significant movement in their lives by which they each also enter a timelag. In being called upon to help Napoleon buy the time he needs to recoup his forces, Henri, and his wife, enter the period of suspended time in which France, and, unknowingly, Algeria, is now situated. Henri is asked to perform tricks which will emphasize the potential power of France and which will, even if only temporarily, discredit the Bou Azziz, an Algerian marabout or spiritual leader who is considering calling a Holy War against France. This wider sense of a timelag is analogous to that which occurs in Henri and Emmeline's private and professional lives. Henri's performances are based on 'laws' and techniques that are hidden from the audience and involve a suspension of logic. His trick with an Arab boy literally involves suspending the young participant. However, the emphasis of the text is upon Emmeline who quite literally moves from her marginalized, bourgeois existence in the provisional town of Rouen to the centre of power – a week at Napoleon's court and then a period of time in the administrative centre of Algeria. The geographical shift is analogous of the cultural, emotional and psychological transformation she undergoes. The narrative is focused on this timelag in her life as a period of growth but also of self-reflection, doubt and tortured meditation:

> As her maid sluiced a last jug of water over her breasts, Emmeline stood up in the tub, wet and glistening. In the long pier mirror opposite she saw her naked body, young and slender; no one could guess that twice I have carried a dead child in my womb. I look like a virgin. It's Henri who is old, not I. And in these clothes, in this world – Compiègne has changed me.   (63)

At the opening of the novel, we encounter Emmeline's husband who has moved from the centre, where he enjoyed the reputation of being Europe's greatest living magician, to a more marginalized position as an inventor of mechanical gadgetry. Napoleon, or more precisely the Head of Arab Affairs in Algeria Colonel Deniau, offers Henri the opportunity to place himself once again at the centre. In other words, he has to place his normal life in suspension. The timelag which Emmeline enters is one in which she begins to think of herself and France differently but is uncertain as to how she will finally re-inscribe herself and her country. However, the period of time spent in the employment of Napolean's court causes no such problems for Henri who perceives it as a marvellous opportunity to fulfil what he always felt himself capable of.

Bhabha's ideas about mimicry are especially pertinent to this text because to a large extent Emmeline's doubts and anxieties arise from the requirement upon her to mime the forms of authority that are controlling herself and her husband. However, not only does she find herself being compelled to mime the forms of French colonial authority but the forms of her husband's authority. In each case, she is required to do so at the point at which they are, in Bhabha's term, 'deauthorized':

> Emmeline felt her face grow hot. Just as she had feared, the others in the carriage were aristocrats whose every glance in her direction seemed to warn that despite Madame Cournet's coaching and Monsieur West's elaborate toilette she would remain for them beyond the pale, a doctor's daughter, half educated in a Rouennais convent, provincial beyond redemption and, despite his fame and pretensions, the wife of a person who performed on stage. (14–15)

Emmeline's husband is less critical of the whole process of mimicry than his more reflective wife. Indeed, he conflates mimicry and mimesis. In his stage shows, he dresses soberly and mimics the voice of a scientist in order to give himself professional authority without pondering how his act deauthorizes the authority which he tries to copy, and leaves himself a partial 'object' in that he is neither fully a professional nor a performer. This is enhanced, of course, by the fact that his whole career is based on professional tricks and secrets; the expertise affords him some kind of 'professional' status but the trickery and the secrets make of him something of a charlatan. What Emmeline recognizes, and he doesn't, is that at Napoleon's court her husband is a 'partial' object because the court does not fully recognize or acknowledge him, as we also discover it does not fully accept the bankers and financiers upon whom Napoleon is dependent:

> Emmeline noticed that the rooms to which these more privileged guests were led seemed to be suites, many of them overlooking the park. The remaining guests must climb yet another staircase to reach the upper floors of the château. At last, with just one other couple, Emmeline and Lambert ascended a final staircase to reach a floor just under the roof. (16)

The emphasis of the text, however, is not upon the way in which Henri is treated but Emmeline's recognition of it. As such, she represents the fluidity and shifting sense of difference in the lived experiences of those who are dominated which threatens the synoptic vision of those in authority:

> She did not answer for at that moment a chamberlain approached and asked if they would like to dance. 'If we can get the dancing properly started,' the chamberlain said, 'then the Empress may join in.'
> At once, as though he were a servant not a guest, her husband took her arm and led her on to the dance floor.
> 'Why are we dancing?' she said. 'You don't like dancing. Why do something we don't want to do?'   (24)

Like the colonized people who make a face to meet the colonizing authority, Henri is not only unacceptable to his superiors but less than himself, as the 'false laugh' he acquires suggests (32).

Staging the Present

The real magician in Moore's novel is not Henri but Colonel Deniau who is able to appear, like Satan, in a variety of guises:

> [Emmeline] looked at Deniau now as he lay back on the cushions eating the Arab food delicately with his fingers, she looked at the fine white robe that covered his body, at the curved dagger in his ornate belt, at his bare feet in the red sandals, at his sun-darkened face, this man who made allusions which could lead to an affair …   (104)

But, once again, the focus is not upon the magician but the subversive potential in Emmeline's perception of how, in deauthorizing the authority he mimics – in this case of an Arab leader – he himself is never fully present:

> Today's true devotion was reserved for the flag, symbol of recent victory, displayed not as an act of Christian piety but in a gesture of triumph in the temple of a conquered race. She searched the faces of the official party until she found Deniau who stood among the most senior officers, left hand on his

ceremonial sword, his eyes on the newly raised colours, his voice chanting the patriotic verse. Was this the man who, two days ago, lay on silken cushions wearing an Arab robe and telling her that Africa had changed him?   (109)

The contrast to which these passages draw attention exemplifies how the narration moves along, and through, openings between authority, mimicry and subversion, and in doing so is often anchored in the extent to which subjects and objects share a material space. But what is most important to this text is the persistent positioning of Emmeline's critique of the French colonial project and of her husband at points where objects are divested of any one set of connotations.

When Emmeline first arrives in Algeria, she is impressed by the complexly codified nature of Algerian society where the nineteenth-century European and non-European binarism she had expected has given way to internal conflict and division:

Looking up at the ship were Arabs, a race she had known only from drawings and paintings, now suddenly real, men with short beards and moustaches, their heads shaven except for a long lock of hair on top. They wore ankle-length robes, the garment fastened to their heads by a rope of camel hair which served as a turban. Over this robe many wore long flowing cloaks. They were shod in primitive ox-hide sandals, but Emmeline noticed that a few who seemed of higher rank wore high yellow leather boots. There was also a score of Arab women, most of them young, dressed in wide woollen shirts, tied at the waist with a rope and fastened at the breast with large iron pins. Their hair was plaited in long tresses and on their arms and legs they wore bracelets of silver and iron. Their faces shocked her. Many were tattooed. In their ears were large rings and their nails were dyed red-brown with henna.   (82–3)

Here the various objects and modes of dress elide the imperialist fantasies which they have helped determine, as Emmeline becomes aware not only of the divisions within Algeria but the codified nature of objects generally. Her appreciation of the elusive nature of the way in which objects and clothes are used to extend and control one's cultural identity, especially as far as gendered and racialized associations are concerned, is particularly pronounced in her readings of the different European ceremonies which she is required to witness or participate in. Here the text may be profitably read alongside Virginia Woolf's *Three Guineas* (1938) in which Woolf draws attention to the codified nature of masculine uniforms:

> Every button, rosette and stripe seems to have symbolic meaning. Some have the right to wear plain buttons only; others rosettes; some may wear a single stripe; others three, four, five or six. And each curl or stripe is sewn on at precisely the right distance apart; it may be one inch for one man, one inch and a quarter for another. Rules again regulate the gold wire on the shoulders, the braid on the trousers, the cockades on the hats – but no single pair of eyes can observe all these distinctions, let alone account for them accurately.   (178)

But an important distinction between Moore and Woolf's approach to the subject is his greater concern with the way in which objects are associated with fluid rather than fixed meanings and the impact that this has on cultural identification generally. The so-called 'miracles' performed by Henri are themselves dependent upon objects which do not perform their expected functions. This highlights one of the central messages of this text that, in terms of their cultural significance, objects are continually coded and recodified. This in turn becomes in the novel the essence of corporeal identity. For example, the Arab objects with which Deniau is associated on one of the occasions when he is trying to seduce Emmeline – the cushions, white robe, curved dagger and sandals – are slipped from their primary Algerian categorization and recodified in a mimicry of Arab culture determined by, and determining, the European imperialist fantasies of the East as an exotic and sexualized 'other'. Deniau's persistent, and somewhat secretive, pursuit of Emmeline, in order to ensure her co-operation, as much as the spies that follow her, is indicative of the threat which her awareness of the ambivalence of mimicry poses to the colonialist project. Throughout the text, the focalization of which the reader is most aware is Emmeline's, located, as in the account of the ceremony in the passage earlier, at the point of reversal: 'the flag, symbol of recent victory, displayed not as an act of Christian piety but in a gesture of triumph in the temple of a conquered race'. Reversal is a key feature in the novel's depiction of ceremony – evident, for example, in the contrast between the *curée* and the Sunday mass:

> Above her, the Empress knelt in a tableau of devotion, hands joined in prayer, her eyes on the upraised chalice, the same Empress who last night had smiled in pleasure as she presided over the satanic celebration of the kill. (69)

Emmeline's personal narrative culminates in the most significant of the text's reversals when she confides her husband's professional secrets and the purpose behind their presence in Algeria to Bou Azziz.

Apart from Bou Azziz, the character with the strongest presence in the text, which is also one of the most talked about, is Napoleon himself. Like Henri's tricks themselves, he is designed to be talked about, demonstrating how words can themselves function as objects, extending the cultural and corporeal identity of the nation's subjects. This is evident, for example, in the way Deniau speaks of Napoleon: 'And he himself is an extraordinary figure. Think of it. He has come from exile, seized power and crowned himself as Emperor of France. An amazing achievement!' (21). In this respect, the representation of Napoleon is analogous to the tricks which are expected of Henri, as Napoleon himself inadvertently acknowledges: 'What we need to convince the Arabs is something even more spectacular, something which will both frighten and amaze them' (58). In order to extend the cultural identity of the French people, and secure their loyalty, this vision of Napoleon has to present itself, and be presented, in synchronic terms. In other words, to invest the nation with transcendent significance. But, it is dependent upon a diachronic narrative of Napoleon's life which has changed and evolved over time and like the lifescripts in some of the novels discussed in the preceding chapter, it involves secrets and silences. The latter poses a threat to the sense of omnipotence that the figure of Napoleon III is intended to convey.

Ironically, in the context of the earlier quotation, Deniau is speaking to Emmeline whose presence at Napoleon's court opens up a gap between Napoleon as a transcendent symbol of the conquering and unconquerable modern French nation and Napoleon as the potentially vulnerable, flesh and blood subject, evident all too clearly in his secret, and sometimes not so secret, pursuit of women.

The material space, which Emmeline shares with Napoleon, is one in which she is subjected to 'a long lascivious caress' (59), and one in which the Emperor touches her buttocks and thighs while alluding to a possible affair between them. It is also one in which the Empress is clearly suspicious of, and unhappy with, her presence. But, again, the emphasis is upon Emmeline's recognition of ambivalence rather than the frailty of Napoleon himself: 'It was then that Emmeline saw that the Emperor seemed ill: he grimaced with pain as he bent forward to pick up a folder on his desk; his eyes were circled by dark shadows, his face was puffy and she realized, with shock, that his cheeks were rouged' (57).

Women out of Clothes

The three novels discussed in this chapter see writing 'historically based texts' as a kind of 'mapping' rather than a 'tracing' of history. Indeed, history itself emerges from these novels as 'mapping'. This distinction between 'mapping' and 'tracing', so central to this chapter and, I believe, to these novels, is one that I have derived not from historians but from geographers. Contemporary geographers Steve Pile and Nigel Thrift (1995) define 'mapping' as being a form of 'way finding' and different from 'tracing' in that the latter is more closely associated with definition and fixity:

> What distinguishes the map from the tracing is that it is entirely oriented towards experimentation in contact with the real. The map does not reproduce an unconscious closed in upon itself; it constructs the unconscious ... The map is open and connectable in all of its dimensions; it is detachable, reversible, susceptible to constant modification. It can be torn, reversed, adapted to any kind of mounting, reworked by an individual group or social formation ... A map has multiple entryways, as opposed to the tracing which always comes back 'to the same'. The map has to do with performance ... (1)

The usefulness of transferring Pile and Thrift's distinction between 'mapping' and 'tracing' from geography to history is especially evident in Emma Donoghue's novel. As she herself explains in an appendix to *Slammerkin*, it is based on fragments about the life of a sixteen-year-old girl, Mary Saunders, hanged for murder in Monmouth in 1764. The text introduces several characters based on individuals at the time that had no contact with the 'real' Mary Saunders and a number of characters that never actually existed. Nevertheless, the novel can be seen as an exercise in 'mapping', as defined earlier, rather than simply 'fiction' because it offers the reader 'multiple entryways' into Mary Saunders's life and into modern women's history. In writing Mary's history from a feminist perspective, the novel is an exploration of how what we might see as a fixed and defined history is, like any map, 'detachable, reversible, susceptible to constant modification'. As we take 'multiple entryways' into various histories through the principal novels of this chapter, we see that history conceived of as 'mapping' rather than 'tracing' does not always bring us back 'to the same'. In seizing on a point made in the probably fictitious account of Mary's life in the broadsheet written for distribution at her execution – that Mary killed her employer 'because she longed for "fine clothes"' (422) – *Slammerkin*, to adapt Pile and Thrift's words, 'does not reproduce an unconscious closed in upon itself; it constructs the unconscious'. In doing so, it is 'open' and 'connectable' in many directions including the way in which power relations in society are dependent upon the mimicry of those who have authority by those who are subservient, especially women, at the same time that authority itself is revealed as precarious by the subversive potential of this mimicry.

Thus, *Slammerkin*, like each of the novels in this chapter, conceives of history as 'mapping' as a feminist project. Not in any crude sense, Donoghue explores the implications for women of history as 'his story'. At one point, having fled London and ended up in a seamstress's household in Monmouth, it dawns on Mary that 'she'd wandered out of her own story into another, and was lost' (185). Although most of the characters in the novel are unwittingly the subjects of other people's narratives, a point to which I shall return later, this is truer for the women than the men. And it may be said to be more true for some of the women than for others. When Mary's employer in Monmouth, Mrs Jones, tries to curry favour with her maid after she has beaten her by suggesting 'Aren't we all servants, one way or another', Mary quickly retorts: 'Maybe so, madam. But some get whipped and some do the whipping' (364).

Even a cursory reflection on this episode in Mary's life is enough to demonstrate the text's interest in history as a narrative with different 'entryways'. Who is responsible for Mary's beating – Mrs Jones, Mr Jones with whom Mary has had sex for which he feels guilty, or Mrs Morgan, the valued, genteel client whom Mary has inadvertently insulted? Moreover, the fact that Mary is bent over the back of a runaway black slave, who has herself received whippings in her past life, is itself a detail which, at one level, blurs the boundary between the two while, at another level, underlines the distinction between them.

Although, at one level, *Slammerkin* is a very different historical novel from *The Magician's Wife*, each is based within timelags; emphasizes the importance of mimicry in maintaining and secretly subverting authority; and is concerned not so much with events as the central protagonist's responses to these events. At the centre of *Slammerkin*, there are two timelags: the period when Mary is a prostitute in London and the period she spends as a maid/trainee seamstress in Monmouth. As in *The Magician's Wife*, the emphasis falls upon the central character's analysis of the psychological and cultural implications of these geographical shifts. In each, she conspicuously occupies a space, to employ Bhabha's terms once again, between 'relocation' and 'reinscription'.

Mary adapts to the life of the prostitute – so convincingly that we forget that she is a child in our terms – but then in Monmouth eventually tries to secretly undo how that life has reconstructed her. Donoghue's focus on the prostitute is a reminder of how prostitutes acquired a more obvious presence in the metropolis in the eighteenth century. In this respect, they remind us of Bhabha's arguments which I invoked in Chapter 1, particularly his point that when the socially marginalized emerge from the margins, a spatial shift occurs. Of course, prostitutes still occupied a marginalized position in eighteenth-century towns and cities, but there is no denying that they acquired a more conspicuous presence. In effect, Donoghue picks up on the same idea as Bhabha; the spatial movement that occurred when prostitutes became a more visible part of the metropolis can be envisaged in geographical, social and metaphorical terms. Like all who constitute the socially marginalized, prostitutes, Donoghue recognizes, are not only labelled as 'different' by the kind of spaces they occupy and their perceived status in the dominant society but are 'othered' by the dominant discourse through which they are represented. Donoghue, like Bhabha, suggests that when socially marginalized groups begin to achieve recognition, they become a more significant 'other' within the dominant discourse. Thus, Mary finds herself situated both within and outside the dominant discourses that define gender identities and social behaviours. Mary herself, like the figure of the prostitute which in the eighteenth century was becoming a more subversive presence, occupies the 'in-between' position, between relocation and reinscription, to which Bhabha attaches importance.

Ironically, Mary's journey from London to Monmouth is the reverse of the journey taken by her mother. Monmouth itself, like the prostitute's lodgings in London, is an in-between place. Culturally and geographically, it is neither fully English nor fully Welsh. But more importantly for the novel, it occupies a border position in Mary's personal narrative; at one level, it is a real part of her history but at another it is a lie which, at times, becomes a secret fantasy where Mary tries for a while to step aside from her past and reinvent herself. On her way to court, Mary has 'the impression she was going into the wilderness, crossing into a country beyond time' (388). From the outset, Mary stepped, or tried to step, 'beyond time' in coming, albeit reluctantly, to this small claustrophobic town. Other characters in the Monmouth section also appear to try move beyond time, especially Daffy Cadwaladyr, or, Mrs Ash, who having found herself 'no longer mother, no longer wife' (182), is forced to become a wet nurse. But Mary is the most radical case, occupying a fictive space and secretly presenting herself as something she is not to Mr and Mrs Jones. While Monmouth is the place her mother came from, she journeys to a house of a family she does not know with stories of her mother that are inventions designed to persuade them to take her in. Indeed, she comes to recognize that 'she'd wandered out of her own story into another, and was lost' (185). When Mrs Jones beats Mary for endangering Mrs Morgan's patronage, she thinks of her as Mary Saunders rather than simply Mary, reminding the reader that in entering a story that is not quite her own, Mary has always been a partial object to others, as they have been to her.

The word 'lost' in the preceding quotation anticipates the description of Monmouth as a 'wilderness' which, too, has biblical connotations. But the novel redefines in feminist terms, largely through its stress upon the importance of women taking control of their own individuality and body, what 'lost' and 'wilderness' mean. The importance of being fully present to oneself, of being the subject in one's own narrative rather than a pawn or even less in someone else's, is a salient trope in this novel. The dangers in stepping out of one's own story is one of the lessons hammered home by Doll, the prostitute who befriends Mary in London. When she finds Mary beaten, raped and abandoned by soldiers in a ditch, she turns the idea of Mary being lost around – now she has discovered her identity as a woman in violent, eighteenth-century English society: 'Been made a woman of, ain't you?' (37). Doll's voice, directly or as remembered by Mary, dominates the first part of the novel, set in London and haunts the second part set in Monmouth where, remembered or imagined by Mary, it frequently interrupts the text. It is a voice which stresses the importance of being oneself and of being subversive, even secretly, rather than submissive. While scrubbing Mrs Jones's stairs, Mary imagines or remembers Doll's mocking voice: '*like any old skivvy*' (176). Eventually, Doll's voice becomes a projection of her own repressed stoicism: '*Monmouth's a hidey-hole, that's all*, said Doll in her head. *Like that stinking ditch we crouched in when the bread riot ran amok, remember? Anything can be borne for a while*' (185). But it also serves as a projection of the dominated's capacity to trick those who think they have complete authority: 'Deceiving the Joneses was all too simple. *Easy as pissing the bed*, as Doll used to say' (242).

Here, it is important to remember Bhabha's thesis, which I introduced in Chapter 1, that marginalized voices question the frames of reference that inform a society's narratives about itself. Doll does not simply provide a view of society from the perspective of an underclass, but questions the very way in which the concept of society is conceived. Thus, Doll is an important presence in *Slammerkin*, a focal point for the way Donoghue's novel occupies an in-between space from where it questions not only the discourses but also the frames of reference that they employ.

Doll teaches Mary what being a woman, albeit one who ostensibly sells her body, means in a society where the definitions of prostitution are quite fluid: 'It was the way the world was. It was the bargain most women made, whether wife or whore, one side of the sheet or another' (59). That the respectable can be seen as prostitutes is an argument of fellow whore Nan Pullen: 'Masters and mistresses were only cullies by another name... You pretended to be satisfied, or grateful, even' (185). As a prostitute, Mary quickly discovers: 'The trick was to pretend to be excited herself. An intake of breath, a catch in the voice: it fooled the cullies every time, and speeded them up like nothing else' (69). In making the point that servants and employees, like prostitutes, only 'pretended to be satisfied', Nan Pullen is anticipating Bhabha's thesis, with which I opened this chapter, that those who are subject to the authority of others are a 'partial' or 'incomplete' presence which challenges the way in which dominant discourses appear natural or normal.

Throughout the first part of the novel, the prostitutes mimic and mock the respectable classes in the cut and flamboyance of their clothes. The mockery lies to a great extent in the way prostitutes make a figure and a face:

> [Mary] dressed in the brightest colours she could find on the stalls of Monmouth Street – pinks and purples and oranges – and never cared if they clashed, so long as the cullies kept looking. She knew herself to be wanted. She wore her rouged face like a carnival mask.   (60)

That Mary buys her clothes from Monmouth Street proves ironic given her role later in her life as a seamstress in Monmouth. But here she has control, sometimes secretly, over the 'mask' she wishes to assume, whereas in Monmouth, her new master is a staymaker who in effect fashions women's bodies according to his secret fantasy or society's ideal image of what they should look like.

Mary observes when she sees Mrs Morgan's slammerkin: 'The harlots all wanted to dress like ladies and the ladies returned the compliment, it seemed' (178). The point is made forcefully by the different roles occupied by the slammerkin in the London and the Monmouth sections. In the latter, it is a sought after morning gown, while in the former it is a dress favoured by prostitutes because it opens at the front. Indeed, Mary's friend, Doll, sees the whore and the slammerkin as synonymous: 'Slovenly, slatternly sluts and slipshod, sleazy slammerkins that we are' (51). The prostitutes' mimicry of the respectable is an example of how, in Bhabha's thesis, 'the look of surveillance [by those in authority] returns as the displacing gaze of the disciplined' (383–4). In the second part of the novel, the point is well made in Mrs Jones's punishment of Mary. We might remember that when Mary first sees Mrs Morgan's slammerkin, she 'hid a grin' (178). The slippage in Mrs Jones's explanation as to why she is going to beat Mary reinforces the notion that Mary's 'crime', in her half-hidden grin, is to return 'the look of surveillance': 'You laughed at Mrs Morgan'; 'It was the way you looked at her, when you were laughing'; 'what lady could bear to be looked at in that way' (361).

However, the prostitutes in London also mimic the way in which female identity is being increasingly constructed in terms of appearance and the way in which women are themselves becoming commodities. As Doll observes, *'clothes make the woman'*. The prostitute is an extreme example of this:

> It seemed to Mary that these days there was nothing else you could place your trust in. Clothes were as lasting as money, and sweeter to the hand and eye; they made you beautiful and others sick with envy. On Sundays she went off to Hyde Park to see what the quality were wearing these days as they rode about showing themselves off; her eyes sought out the tiny details of pleats or buttons, the altered curve of a set of new hoops.   (89)

The attention she gives to detail as a spectator has an ironic reversal in the second part of the novel when, in making dresses for the rich and famous, she has to be attentive to detail. The privileging of clothes is evident when she is punished; her back is bared partly to increase the pain of the birching and partly to spare her dress the same injury as her flesh.

Both *Slammerkin* and *The Magician's Wife* are concerned with the cultural significance of clothes. But more importantly Donoghue's novel shares Moore's concern with how objects are associated with fluid rather than fixed meanings, are continually coded and recodified, and the impact that this has on cultural identity generally. In *Slammerkin*, as in *The Magician's Wife*, the codification of different modes of dress is the essence of corporeal as well as cultural identity. Both novels emphasize the central protagonist's confusion in the midst of this newfound appreciation of the fluidity of the corporeal. In Emmeline's case, she is made generally more socially aware and critical by the behaviour of Napoleon and Deniau's easy assumption of the dress codes and objects of the Orient. Mary's eyes are opened by Doll: 'In these uncertain times, Mary was learning, a duchess was sometimes just a stroller who'd picked the right honourable cully' (78). The prostitute who says *'clothes make a woman'* also says *'clothes are the greatest lie ever told'* (77). What the novel does, though, is to deconstruct the word 'lie' here. Clothes mark the boundary between corporeal identity, culturally constructed norms and expectations, and personal, as well as socially propagated, fantasies:

> Anyway, Susan Digot wouldn't likely recognise her child-as-was, all gussied up in a flowered jacket-bodice and a worn silk skirt buoyed out by a pair of improvers. Mary looked like a woman of the town, these days. She smelt different, even, with the mouth-watering lemony reek of Hungary water.   (77)

Mary's work as a seamstress provides a commentary upon the relationship she perceived between herself, dressed from a stall in the Seven Dials, and the so-called noble women whose clothes she saw herself mirroring but mocking at the same time. Learning to see through Mrs Jones's eyes, but retaining Doll's scepticism, Mary recognizes that, whereas the lower orders may mimic those in authority, they can never bridge the advantage of economic superiority. Mary's hidden horde of money, derived from renewing her prostitute activities in Monmouth, becomes the means by which she hopes to regain control over her body and identity, but also, eventually, becomes a kind of secret fetish. In the second part of the novel, it mirrors her personal wardrobe in the first part. There, her clothes, like the money, have a practical but also a fetishistic role in her life. In them she invests her secret fantasies. Under Mrs Jones's influence, Mary's earlier fantasies begin to unravel:

> Mary had always had a feel for clothes and what they meant. But these days she was learning to read a costume like a book, decipher all the little signs of rank or poverty. She was developing a nose for vulgarity; much of the stuff she'd paid out her earnings for, at the stalls of the Seven Dials, now struck her as shoddy tat.   (207)

But what also occurs is a shift in Mary's understanding of where the boundary between the clothed and the unclothed is located. Mr Jones creates stays to shape and transform the female body.

They are, in Doll's words, a lie; producing a shape that is an illusion. Mary, on the other hand, is discovering that

> what mattered just as much as what someone wore was how they carried it off. The best silk sack gown could be ruined on a stooping, countryish customer. It was all in the gaze, the stance, the set of the shoulders. Mary set herself to learning how to move as if the body – in all its damp indignity – was as sleek and upright as the dress.   (207–8)

The details here – 'the gaze, the stance, the set of the shoulders' – are significant because they are the means by which the slave and the servant can express their subversion secretly, without appearing overly disrespectful. They are also the means by which the dominated can appear erotically attractive to their superiors. Mr Jones, who finds himself secretly attracted to Mary, noticing 'under her blue bodice her chest was as taut as a sapling', also finds seductive her 'dreadfully teasing manner' (275). 'For fifteen, she was a full-figured woman' in her master's eyes, and 'full-figured' refers to both her physical and mental maturity, evident in the way she mocks and makes fun of him.

The Spectacle of Tyranny

Brian Moore's linking of the spectacle of authority with the permeable limits of the cultural and corporeal identity of those in power, evident in the behaviour of Deniau and Napoleon, is one that can be found in a number of contemporary Irish novels. It is much in evidence in *Amongst Women*, a novel that interleaves domestic relations, religious discourses and public politics. Although it is concerned with the way fathers become, or rather are allowed to become, tyrants, it is also a critique of the damaging effects of Catholic discourse on families and on the lives of women in particular. Bhabha's essay about mimicry in a colonial context is appropriate to this novel because in it 'the look of surveillance returns as the displacing gaze of the disciplined, where the observer becomes observed and "partial" representation rearticulates the whole notion of *identity* ...' (383–4).

The novel is focused on the disintegrating family of a former republican army commander who failed to win the position and

authority he hoped for in the army of the new state. His tyranni-
cal hold over his family is one of the factors that drive his children
away, one by one, to London and Dublin. One of the intertexts in
this book, especially in its emphasis upon 'the displacing gaze of
the disciplined', is D. H. Lawrence's semi-autobiographical novel
Sons and Lovers, which helps to account for the speculative nature
of McGahern's brand of realism, for, like Lawrence's fiction, his
writing is driven by cultural as well as social critique. Both novels are set in rural or semi-rural areas; in Lawrence's case it is
rural Nottinghamshire that has become industrialized with the
coming of the mines. What McGahern in effect does is to trans-
pose Lawrence's analysis of the working-class family as a space
of conflict, a site of shifting power allegiances and irreconcilable
differences, into rural, working-class Ireland. But, in doing so, he
retains the emphasis upon how the tyrant is perceived and undermined by those who are dominated, recognizing the secret
subversion within what is never fully obedience.

In these respects, Moran echoes Lawrence's father figure
Walter Morel. Although Morel is a miner, both are patriarchal,
holding on to traditional working-class notions of masculinity
that are challenged by their wives and by the apparent emas-
culization, in their terms, of one of their sons. Moran's wife, Rose,
in the story is his second wife whom he brings into a family of
grown-up, or near mature, children. Like Lawrence's Morel, he is
charming in courtship only to prove boorish, violent and bullying
in marriage. At his best, Morel displays a spontaneity and
warmth that is not embraced by his middle-class wife, Gertrude,
who feels trapped in the marriage and lives out her social aspira-
tions through the lives of her children, especially Paul, whom she
is adamant will not follow his father to the mines. Morel provided
McGahern with a model for a Father who could be proud of his
family at one moment and a canker within it at another; whose
silent, often secretive, brooding presence could be as oppressive
as his explosive outbursts. The shift in the name from Morel to
Moran – M (or) an – emphasizes Moran's 'manliness' and the
oppressive male domination of Irish society.

Both texts suggest that the law of the Father is not as complete
and all embracing as one might think. The moral authority of the
mother is further developed in McGahern's novel through the
women's appreciation of the beauty and vitality of nature, which
for Moran is largely a place of work. The fact that Moran is a

former guerrilla leader is an important development of Lawrence's depiction of a working-class family. McGahern's family is analogous of the Irish Free State and Republic. This is a strategy that enables him to use the very notion of the family, on which Eamon de Valera based his vision of the new country, to expose it as a site of oppression, and of division and conflict along gender, regional and class lines. It also allows him to explore, at the micro level, the resistant and complicitous, sometimes secretly complicitous, psychologies which the Republic and its ideals brought into being.

Even a cursory summary of *Amongst Women* suggests that this is a novel about ghosts. The domineering Moran tries in old age to come to terms with his life as a father, the ways in which his family has turned out, and his past as a guerrilla leader in the War of Independence. There are several significant family meals in the first part of the novel, especially the recreation of Monaghan Day and the Christmas meal when Moran is courting Rose Brady. At both there are absent presences: the ghost of Moran's fellow columnist from the war, McQuaid, who used always to join Moran for the Monaghan Day family feast; and, more significantly, his eldest son Luke. The way Moran's daughters recreate Monaghan Day as it used to be encapsulates the way nationalist historical discourse has transformed the War of Independence:

> Forgotten was the fearful nail-biting exercise Monaghan Day had always been for the whole house; with distance it had become large, heroic, blood-mystical, something from which the impossible could be snatched.   (2)

The daughters create a feast which mimics the original and, in effect, becomes a 'partial' event that mocks Moran's authority and vision. Haunted by the ghost of how it had been, the Monaghan Day feast is analogous of how Moran is haunted by memories of what the war itself was really like: 'It was a bad business. We didn't shoot at women and children like the Tans but we were a bunch of killers' (5). McQuaid himself is a memory haunted by other memories of him as 'a drunken black-guard' (4). The secret, 'encrypted' aspect of the war exists alongside the nationalist, public view of it. But what is withheld affects those who live with real or inherited memories of how the Republic was brought into being. It leaves them, as it leaves Moran – forced to brood in secret whether, with so many families disrupted and so many in exile, it was all worth it.

Moran's daughters invoke McQuaid's presence at the feast to usher in memories of when the Day meant much to Moran. But what they succeed in doing is invoking the ghost of the Day when McQuaid severed his friendship with Moran. That previous meal was itself haunted by tales of what had been kept secret, such as Moran's involvement with one of the Maquire girls. In fact, this episode provides a vital clue to Moran's psychological make-up, and to one of the salient tropes in the text: Moran becomes 'angry as ever at any baring of the inviolate secrecy he instinctively kept around himself' (19). Even at his most charming, Moran is haunted by his temper, and by an aspect of his personality that is dominant and domineering and which makes involvement with others difficult.

The title of the novel encapsulates Moran's position in the family and in the community – he is indeed a man amongst women – and invokes 'The Hail Mary' prayer of the Rosary:

> Hail Mary, full of grace! The Lord is with you; blessed are you among women, and blessed is the fruit of your womb, Jesus. Holy Mary, Mother of God, pray for us sinners now and at the hour of our death.

The Hail Mary prayer singles out Mary as 'blessed … among women'. To some extent it is possible to see Moran, too, as 'blessed … among women'. After all he occupies a privileged position. But because Catholicism, the Constitution and the Rosary place women at the centre of affection in the home, he is haunted rather than blessed. The extent to which he is haunted is a secret, which he tries to withhold even from himself. The repression of this secret self is analogous to the way in which the family keeps secret his violence and domination over them, as is evident when his future mother-in-law quizzes Maggie:

> 'People say he used beat ye.'
> 'People said that because Daddy never let us mix with them.'
> 'Did he not beat ye?'
> 'No … now and again when we were bold, but like any house.'
> Shame as much as love prompted the denial. (34)

Even allowing for public scrutiny of Moran and Rose together and the children's apprehension at meeting their prospective stepmother, what is withheld makes the family seem 'foreign', an uncomfortable presence when they attend the Saturday night concert:

> They knew all the people entering the hall, and those that occupied seats close to them smiled and spoke to them. They felt nervous and compromised ... The small group became more the centre of attention than the stage itself.   (32)

Throughout the text Moran is associated with the Rosary. As Siobhán Holland (2000) points out, he relies upon it 'to promote his authority over his family and, in his use of prayer to support his claims to power' (70). Drawing on Antoinette Quinn's work, Holland reminds us that 'the order of prayers in the Rosary ... stresses Moran's dominance over his children and his wife' (71). The Family Rosary begins with those present holding the Crucifix of their Rosary in the right hand and making the Sign of the Cross. The cycle starts with the leader; in the novel this would always be Moran, saying the Apostles' Creed. But Moran's dominance is challenged if not undermined on several accounts. First, as Holland says, 'the narrator's focus on the use of the Rosary in the Moran household draws attention to those moments of inconsistency and contradiction when Moran's claims to power are made vulnerable to attack' (69). Second, and ironically, as Holland goes on to say, 'the Rosary and the Constitution can be unclear about the kind of family they are validating because Marian and Catholic nationalist mythologies both place great stress on the mother as the natural focus of attention and affection in the home' (69–71). Thus, Moran relies on 'a prayer cycle which ... makes his authority vulnerable to parody and erosion' (71).

However, it is not only the prayer cycle which 'makes [Moran's] authority vulnerable to parody and erosion'. It is the way in which he is forced to recognize, but is unable to explore, that his family is at best a 'partial object'. Luke's absent presence throughout the text is a reminder of this. His accusing gaze is visible through the remaining children's surveillance, through their fear and, sometimes their secret contempt, of Moran's behaviour and moods. Like the colonizer, he is stripped of his authority through their rituals of observed rather than real obedience. At one point, after he has driven his second son Michael away, he tries to make reparation to Sheila: 'Anything I ever did was done for what I thought was in the best interests of those concerned. Sometimes what I did might have been misguided but it was always meant for the best' (126). It is a hollow admission that evades rather than confronts the real problem. Moran, like Morel, has been more interested in imposing his will on his family than recognizing how his children stand separate from him yet with him at the same time. Thus, not only have his children been partial subjects in relation to himself but he has never been fully present to them. Those episodes in the text in which his daughters embrace him, or try to embrace him, fully provide us with scenes of great generosity. The death of Morel is a case in point:

> [His daughters] were so bound together by the illness that they felt close to being powerful together. Such was the strength of the instinct that they felt they could force their beloved to remain in life if only they could, together, turn his will around. Since they had the power of birth there was no reason why they couldn't will this life free of death ... It ran counter to the way he had managed his own life. He had never in all his life bowed in anything to a mere Other.   (178)

Moran has managed his life with only rare shows of humility; as the First Joyful Mystery of the Rosary makes clear, humility is a feminine quality associated with the Virgin Mary when told of her role. Moran's daughters display a charity, of which his son Luke is not capable, in spending so much time with him when he is ill; it is a charity analogous to that remembered in the second Joyful Mystery of the Rosary when Mary visits Elizabeth, the mother of John the Baptist, and remains with her for three months before John's birth.

The secret Moran keeps from himself constructs an 'encrypted', foreign being within him which is evident in the contradictions in his behaviour. When he is responsive to the warm being within, to the 'feminine' within his family, Moran, like Morel, is a different man from the tyrant who turns his sons against him:

> The sight of his daughters in sleeveless dresses was relief from the lonely tedium of the work.

'I'm planning to knock this meadow before the evening is out,'
he told them before they left and joked, 'You'll have to harden
your hands before you leave.'
'They are not that soft, Daddy.'
As they walked away from him through the greenness, the
pale blue above them, Maggie said, her voice thick with emotion, 'Daddy is just lovely when he's like that.'   (81)

Here Maggie applies an especially feminine epithet to her father,
and one more inappropriate to his behaviour at other times it is
difficult to imagine. The way Moran's family becomes fragmented is an ironic reflection on the Catholic assertion that 'The
family that prays together ... stays together'. But it also suggests
that if the Rosary is to keep the family together it is through a
redefinition of what constitutes masculinity and authority and
through a re-examination of the family with the father figure at its
head. The family has to be seen more as a collection of beads held
together on a string. Each family member has its own presence,
centre of gravity, as each has his/her own part in the recitation of
the Rosary. In this respect, the novel seems to be making the same
point as Roddy Doyle in *The Snapper*, discussed in Chapter 7, that
the future of the family as a transcendent signifier in Ireland
depends upon a redefinition of the family.

   Thus, the title of the novel may be read as directing our
attention, as Doyle does in his novel, away from male or father-
centred perspectives to values and behaviours more traditionally
associated with women. The women in the novel are a diverse
group, and it would be wrong to interpret this novel as a text
anchored in essentialist concepts of femininity. But, certainly in
the first part of the novel, women are associated with a heightened sensitivity to the beauty in nature; a fact to which the repetition of the phrase 'dear presence' seems designed to draw our
attention. We learn that, although the Moran's girls have worked
hard in the fields as children, 'each field and tree had become
a dear presence' (80). The phrase is repeated in the account of
Rose walking back to her family which Moran has visited for the
first time:

She walked slowly back down the lane, savouring the rich
peace, the strength she felt. This narrow lane was dear to her.
Sleepless in Scotland she walked it many times in her mind.

The wild strawberries, the wiry grasses, the black fruit of the
vetches on the banks were all dear presences.   (30)

The application of this phrase in describing the Moran girls and
Rose's sensibilities anticipates the way in which the women from
both families fuse together, and come to see each other as 'dear
presences':

To leave the ever-present tension of Great Meadow was like
shedding stiff, formal clothes or kicking off pinching shoes.
Old Mrs Brady never took to Moran but she grew fond of the
children ... In a few months Roses's home place and Moran's
house were almost interwoven.   (33)

The question as to whether the title of the novel points the
reader toward a female or male centre parallels the unclear and
contradictory nature of the Rosary as far as the female is concerned which Holland stresses. Women in the novel are presented
as potential saviours of men. This is first suggested in the account
of the last Monaghan Day supper attended by Moran and
McQuaid in the story of Mary Duignan, whose association with
the Virgin Mother in her name is taken further in her marriage to
a carpenter and her role as a mediatrix in saving the columnists
from the Tans. Rose, of course, is identified specifically with the
Rosary through her name but she also recognizes that Moran 'had
lived in the stone house with too much responsibility for too long'
(36). Michael, under Rose's influence, acquires a feminine sensi-
bility which is associated with Rose's flower garden, rather than
his father's vegetables, where

he could often be found, at first helping Rose, then taking over
and extending the garden ... This both amused and irritated
Moran.
'I suppose one of these days you'll be getting yourself a
skirt.'   (64–5)

At the end of the novel, after Moran's funeral, Sheila remarks of
the men who talk pleasantly together with their children around
them: 'Will you look at the men. They're more like a crowd of
women' (184).
However, Lawrence's influence is especially evident in the
way the novel examines the 'masculine' and the 'feminine', which

Holland sees as one of the principal concerns of the text, in terms of oppression without recourse to a simple 'oppressor' and 'oppressed' binarism. The emphasis is upon the dialectic between the two. At one point, the preparations for Christmas seem to stress the analogy between the family and the Catholic Church. In the house, the daughters, despite everything that has occurred, derive a sense of superiority from belonging to the family: 'only Moran, their beloved father: within his shadow and the walls of his house they felt that they would never die' (93–4).

It is worth noting that the 'feminisation' of Michael, too, occurs in quite subtle ways. On her return from London, Maggie brings him 'a saffron tie to go with his hair' (79); this kind of careful matching of clothes with one's hair is not normally a signifier of masculinity. She also brings him 'seeds with pictures of flowers on the packets'. In effect, Maggie reverses the traditional practice of a man giving flowers to a woman. But we also have here a woman giving a man seed. Although she is living primarily in England, joining the ranks of Irish exiles, Maggie still thinks of her role in the family. If anything, her exile makes her 'feminisa-tion' of the family – reflected in the 'big box of soft-centred choco-lates' they eat – more overt.

It becomes clear in this account of Maggie's return that Moran's authority is dependent upon not admitting to what he has done to the family. Given the privilege accorded the father and eldest son relationship in the patriarchal family, Luke's per-sistent absence is a telling indictment of Moran. Sheila's question to Maggie – 'What's Luke like now?' – is highly significant for she might have asked what Luke was doing or how often Maggie saw him. Her question reinforces the way in which children must inevitably grow away from their parents, and, at one level, are never more than partial subjects within their parents' gaze. There are moments in the novel when Moran suggests that he might embrace Michael's 'difference', but they are short-lived. When all the girls have left home, he touches the boy's hair in an unusual display of affection. But, at the same time, he challenges the 'feminisation' of Michael: 'They've mollied you for too long. You'll have to grow up and fight your corner' (91). This does not simply mean that the boy must learn to be more independent; he has to grow out of care and love into separateness and violence which is an important dimension of Moran's definition of mas-culinity. However, it picks up recurring motifs in *Sons and Lovers*

which cross a simple 'male' and 'female' binarism – the importance of not allowing oneself to be smothered and the significance
of being with, yet separate from, others, especially those with
whom we are most intimate.

Throughout *Amongst Women*, one is conscious, as in *Sons and
Lovers*, that this is a novel that runs deeper than an exploration of
the 'masculine' in relation to the 'feminine', even though, at times,
McGahern does seem to be appropriating a familiar binarism in
modern Irish fiction whereby men are associated with violence
and women, linked to stoical suffering, are generally pacifist. For
example, the same night that Maggie brings Michael his present of
a saffron tie, and Sheila, perhaps carelessly but possibly deliberately, asks about Luke, Moran recites the Rosary 'as if the very
dwelling on suffering, death and human supplication would scat-
ter all flimsy vanities of a greater world' (79). This has a distinctive
Lawrentian echo; D. H. Lawrence frequently suggested that at the
centre of Christianity is death and suffering rather than life,
although many Christians would no doubt disagree. Here 'flimsy
vanities' refers to what the daughters bring into the house. But joy
and pleasure are set against thoughts of death and suffering. In
traditional medieval Christian iconography, proceeding 'blindly'
is associated with foolishly following the ways of the world and
the flesh, eventually leading to damnation. But when Maggie
comes home and women 'embraced blindly and kissed one
another' (78), 'blindly' is associated with joy and happiness.

However, an important similarity between McGahern's work
and Lawrence's is that the joy and happiness – in *Amongst
Women*, associated more with the women, and less often than in
Lawrence's novel with the family as a whole or with men – is
indicative of something that is prelinguistic; with what, in French
feminist terms, might be thought of as the 'chora'. Julia Kristeva
(1984b) originally proposed the concept of chora where she
appropriated the term from Plato to mean something akin to
vocal or kinetic rhythm. In *Amongst Women*, it is evident in the
jokingness of the female voice and the pleasure and joy in calling
out each other's names: 'Sheila, Maggie, Michael, Mona, Rose,
Rose, Rose, Rose' (96). What emerges in the novel – in, for example, those rare moments when Moran and his daughters come
together – is the connection that Kristeva stressed between the
chora and the instinctual and the pre-symbolic. Kristeva associated the pre-symbolic with the 'feminine' and the symbolic with

the 'masculine'. The way a mother sings and makes sounds to her child would be seen in Kristevan terms as a manifestation of the chora, of the pre-verbal. In summary, such pre-symbolic and instinctual rhythms may be seen, Kristeva argues, as disrupted by the emphasis in our culture upon symbolic language and upon the type of understanding associated in European culture with male rationality. For eventually, the initial song and rhythmic sounds made by the mother are replaced by language in which the emphasis is upon the communication of a different kind of meaning. In other words, the symbolic interrupts the chora and marginalizes it, although it may be seen as being preserved in poetic language. Kristeva's stress upon the female body, espe-cially the mother's body, as the site of the chora would enable us to read the novel as one in which the chora is an important trope in this novel. Significantly, Moran's name is not called but the women do shout Michael's, the more feminine male. Holland draws attention to the significance of Rose's name and the fact that her influence in the family increases as Moran's decreases. Here, Rose's name, Queen of the family and analogous to the Queen of the Rosary, is the most repeated. But there is, as in Kristeva's theoretical work, a distinction between the 'masculine' and the 'feminine' that does not entirely accord with culturally constructed notions of male and female.

Moran's attempt to assert himself, as Holland argues, through his recitation of the Rosary is undermined, at one level, in what perhaps we might call, with the chora in mind, a 'feminine' way, by 'muted responses', coughing, rustling newspapers and rasp of coat buttons on furniture. But there is more going on here than that. To adapt Bhabha's words, the voice of surveillance is secretly returned by the displacing responses of the disciplined. That is to say, at one level, the symbolic, the word and the Law of the Father, are undermined by the feminine, and the pre-verbal. But, at another level, this passage is about the way in which the authority of the colonizer is undermined by the subtle subver-sive behaviours – a secretly mocking kind of mimicry – of the colonized or dominated.

Although, as is said in the account of the day when Maggie brings home her presents, that the children may behave like a shoal of fish without the net, what is inside the net, whether visible or invisible, is not necessarily absolute obedience. The rituals of obe-dience in the Moran household are based upon what we might

conceive of as behaviours that accord to the will of the tyrant or colonizer; they think, like the colonizer, in terms of objectives, accom-
plishments and goals: 'to clear the table, to brush away crumbs, to
wash, to dry, to return each thing to its place' (79). But they are disrupted by mockery within this apparent obedience: the 'muted
energy; whispers, jokes, little scolding asides'. Obedience can be
merely a mimic of expectations: 'Ingratiating smiles and words
were threaded in and out of the whole whirl of busyness' (79).

Amongst Women encourages us to think, as Michel Foucault does
in 'The Use of Pleasure', in terms of a morality as a set of imposed
rules (associated in the novel with Moran and the large beads of the
Rosary) and 'ethics' concerned with the behaviour of individuals in
relation to the values that are advocated to them. While the former,
and especially Moran, place the emphasis upon what Foucault
calls 'techniques of domination', the latter stresses what he calls
'techniques of self'. In effect, the novel might be read as playing off
these two concepts of the self in relation to power against each
other: the one, associated with Moran, in which the self is conceived in terms of status, functions and activities, and the other,
associated with what Moran could become and with his daughters
and his second wife, in which power is achieved through how
one's sovereignty over oneself is denoted. As we see clearly at the
end of the novel, the 'old guard' signified by the now deceased
Moran is set against Michael as a different kind of man:

> At the gate they paused firmly to wait for the men who lagged
> well behind on the path and were chatting and laughing pleas-
> antly together, their children around them.
> 'Will you look at the men. They're more like a crowd of
> women,' Sheila said, remarking on the slow frivolity of their
> pace. 'The way Michel, the skit, is getting Sean and Mark to
> laugh you'd think they were coming from a dance.'   (184)

Clearly the comparison of the men to 'a crowd of women' suggests the positive feminization of men. But the passage also
implies that it will be this newfound masculinity that will be significant in shaping the new generation. It is in some respects, an
over romanticized conclusion. For example, it eschews the generations that it will take for the violence with which families in
certain areas of Ireland have grown up, and taken an active part
in, can be exorcised. That said, there is also a hint of ambiguity

here. The phrase 'a crowd of women' is not entirely complimentary, and may imply a criticism of the men. These concluding remarks have to be taken in context with the speaker whose sister, without correction from the others, commented of their father: 'He may be gone home but he'll always be with us,' Maggie spoke for them all 'He'll never leave us now' (183). There is a dark, ominous side to this that undermines what comes after as well as the revision of masculinity that appears to be championed throughout the text. It is ominous if seen as applying only to a particular generation – to the daughters rather than their children – but if more than this, it becomes a depressing thought indeed.

Each of the texts discussed in this chapter are very different from each other. But they each read history through the interconnection, which is sometimes concealed in authoritative discourse, of power, obedience and subversion. But what particularly links them is their preoccupation with 'mimicry' and its role, paradoxically, in both the maintenance and the secret subversion of authority. The next chapter examines how some significant texts by women writers further interrogate the role of discourse in determining power and gender relations.

5

Unspoken Desires

Jennifer Johnston's Later Novels, Emma
Donoghue's *Stir-fry* (1994) and Kathleen
Ferguson's *The Maid's Tale* (1994)

The previous chapters have argued for the significance of
Bhabha's ideas about what happens when the previously silenced
or marginalized emerge from the margins for contemporary Irish
fiction. Particularly relevant to the work by women writers, which
is the subject of this chapter, is Bhabha's thesis that previously
marginalized voices, emerging from and in turn determining the
spatio-cultural shift in a nation's ideas of itself, confront and contradict the dominant discourses that have been directly or indirectly responsible for their silence and marginalization.

In developing his thesis, Bhabha argues that the voices of the
previously silenced also question the frames of reference that
inform the nation's narrative about itself. In this chapter, I want to
explore how far this is borne out by some key texts by women
authors. It hardly needs stating that the contemporary Irish novel
confronts and contradicts the discourses defining, for example,
Irishness, nation, home, belonging, exile, sexuality, desire, religion
and spirituality. But Bhabha's essay prompts us to ponder further
the consequences for the novel of it occupying an in-between
space from where it questions not only the discourses but also the
frames of reference that they employ. But we have to ask, how successful is contemporary Irish fiction, particularly women's writing, in occupying, to build on Bhabha's notion of an 'interrogative
space', a space of 'radical openness', while at the same time straddling traditional representation and 'unrepresentability'.

There is a case for saying that the contemporary Irish novel is
never fully present to its own present. Again, Bhabha's concept of

97

a timelag helps us to understand the relation between the past and the present that is being worked through in novels from Ireland and Northern Ireland. The space between 'relocation' and 'reinscription' for which he argues involves an encounter with 'newness'. But this encounter with 'newness', he maintains, is not part of the continuum of past and present. What makes this idea relevant to an Irish context is that he is not suggesting that the encounter is outside 'history'. Rather Bhabha's argument is that the encounter with newness is not part of the past–present continuum because the past is refigured. And it is refigured in ways that interrupt the present.

Bhabha maintains that the in-between space is really a space 'beyond' which becomes a space of intervention in the here and now. As Elleke Boehmer, drawing on Julia Kristeva observes: 'Writing is "transformative", operating through the displacement of what is already signified, bringing forth the not-yet-imagined and the transgressive' (1991: 10). Boehmer argues that women's writing can interrupt 'the language of official nationalist discourse and literature with a woman's vocality'. But also because 'national identity rests on received images of national history and topography', women can remap the nationalist geographies and histories through narrating their own experiences (10).

Thus, envisaging a 'space beyond' as a means of interrupting the past–present continuum has proved important for women writers from Ireland and Northern Ireland, and especially those who move imaginatively as well as literally between the two. This is evident in the work of Jennifer Johnston whose novel *Fool's Sanctuary* I briefly compared with Mary Leland's *The Killeen* in Chapter 3. Johnston's *The Christmas Tree* (1981), too, is written around an interruption of the past and present continuum that anticipates many novels written by Irish and Northern Ireland women that were to follow. Like Kathleen Ferguson's *The Maid's Tale* (1994), discussed later in this chapter, it is a first-person narrative of a woman who is trying to make sense of her life. In this case, it is Constance Keating who is dying of leukaemia. Thus, Bhabha's concept of a timelag provides an appropriate framework in which to examine this text. One can think of Constance as having moved from a previously silenced or marginalized position because her life has been distorted by the influence of men, and held in check in many respects by the influence of her father and by the publisher who rejects her manuscript.

But it is also significant to think of this novel in terms of the way in which Bhabha's thesis, as I argued in Chapter 3, is best applied to many Irish novels in tandem with Freud's concept of Nachträglichkeit. Although Constance tries to recreate her past life chronologically, the linearity is disrupted by the present, 19–26 December, in which she is working and the, frequently unwelcome, eruption into her consciousness of past events.

However, *The Christmas Tree*, exemplifying the way in which Johnston tends to concentrate her narratives in short periods of time, demonstrates how for many Irish writers the timelag which Bhabha sees in largely positive terms is a space marked by anxiety and confusion. This is certainly the case for the central protagonist of *The Christmas Tree*, positioned between life and death. She occupies a timelag – waiting for the end – in which she has been relocated but is uncertain of how she will finally reinscribe her life history, if, indeed, she will have sufficient time to do so. She occupies an in-between state in other ways, too. Through the influence of alcohol and painkilling drugs, she is trapped between reality and fantasy. She has also returned to her father's house, to his bedroom in fact and works in his study. The latter is a reminder that her father had wanted to write a book but had never succeeded in doing so. The house becomes an in-between space in itself. For no longer the house of her father, it is not hers either. Indeed, in writing her own book, Constance might be seen as fulfilling, as a surrogate, her father's ambitions, and in having a child, the birth of which coincided with her father's death, she might be seen as fulfilling her mother's ambitions for her. Her mother had died two years before and it was at her deathbed that Constance had decided to have a child. The in-between space in which she is located is one of reorientation, but it is also one of disorientation, that might turn out to be, at best, an unfulfilled and unfulfilling space, not least because Constance cannot finish the narrative of her life without some one to help her and she clearly will not live to see her child grow up.

Because of the contexts that gave rise to them, the book that Constance is writing and the child that she brings to her father's house for Christmas are not simply part of the past and present continuum from her parent to herself. They represent the space that, finally, Constance is trying to carve out for herself. This is emphasized by the fact that Constance decides to lose her virginity and have a child, thus ostensibly entering history, when her mother dies. But the mother's death puts the child outside of the mother–daughter continuum, and, since the child is born when the father dies, the child is also outside the father–daughter continuum.

Since Constance herself is located on the eve of death and in an alcoholic and drug induced state, the condition of being outside of time is an important trope in this text. In one sense, both her father and her mother's ambitions for her are outside of time, as both die before they are realized. Bridie May, the hired help, who has the responsibility for completing Constance's narrative after her death, is also outside of time in that she is born illegitimate, and was abandoned by her mother. Thus, like Constance's child, she is outside the mother–daughter continuum herself. Moreover, not only is Constance's own daughter conceived after the death of her mother, but she is also illegitimate. The significance of the in-between space in this context is reinforced by the fact that Constance's lover, and the child's father, is a displaced Polish Jew.

Despite its seeming 'spectrality', the in-between and illegitimate space is the beyond which Johnston clearly believes women writers should occupy, not least because it is a transformative as well as transgressive space in which the known signifiers are displaced. Significantly, the male publisher who rejects Constance's book explains that he must think in terms of a second and third novel, where there is a discernible sense of development. He cannot entertain a manuscript that might be a one-off, occupying, in other words, its own space outside of a sequential process. But the potentially negative side of displacing the known signifiers is that the past, the present and identity itself acquire a kind of spectrality which is one of the ways in which the Christmas Tree with its blue lights, occupying the temporary space of the Christmas season, might be perceived. When Jacob returns to collect the daughter he had not known existed, he takes from the house a child that to him is more spectre than flesh-and-blood daughter – he aligns her with his Jewish past and takes her to England. Indeed, he reconfigures her as one of his dead female ancestors who will now re-enter his life as a ghost through the child, and enable him to work out the past that he has been unable to confront. As such, there is an analogy between this future ghostly visitation and the spectral appearances of Constance's mother in her last weeks of writing and recreating. Thus, in severing the mother–daughter, motherland-writer, bond, there are further dangers that lie in the spectrality with which the signified, including the past, is then rendered.

Placing Johnston's work within a framework provided by Bhabha's timelag helps us to understand the enigmatic quality which has sometimes bemused critics and led to her work being misunderstood and underrated. Her place within modern Irish writing in English is confirmed at the level of her popularity – her work has large readerships in Ireland, United Kingdom, United States and Western Europe. But this popularity, despite three major awards, has not been matched by critical acclaim. Moreover, for a writer who enjoys such popularity and who has consistently produced serious, publishable novels, there is a dearth of critical studies. Adverse criticism of Johnston has included criticism of her tendency to sentimentality, her repetitiveness and the improbability of some of her plots. Generally speaking, it is difficult to deny the criticism at one level. But most of it comes from naturalistic or historical approaches to her fiction that do not offer the best frameworks within which to discuss it.

Apart from exposing ostensible weaknesses in the plot and structure of Johnston's fiction, a naturalistic approach makes for fairly depressing reading. She appears to be preoccupied with decay – for example, of the Big House in her earlier novels. Characters, like Constance Keating in *The Christmas Tree* and Miranda in *Fool's Sanctuary* (1987) are dying. Relationships in so many of the novels are doomed and projects such as Hawthorne's renovation of the station in *The Railway Station Man* (1984) head for unavoidable disaster. However, Johnston is always going to fall foul of this kind of critical approach because, as I have tried to illustrate in reading *The Christmas Tree*, she is not, and does not appear to have set out to be, a naturalistic novelist. Her characters are not meant to seduce us into believing that they are unproblematically real. They are sites of ideological conflict or embodiments of ideological positions that are challenged, like Miranda's optimism, for example, not just by what happens to that character at the level of the story but also by the larger interplay of ideas within the narrative as a whole. This is where the interest of the reader who wishes to take Johnston on her own terms must lie and critical discussion must concentrate on following the ideological conflicts through the pattern of recurring motifs, of thesis and counter thesis, of the fusion of the natural with the mythical.

The way in which Helen in *The Railway Station Man* conceives her own art provides insight into the nature of Johnston's work. She sees herself as primarily seeking to express a truth of which she is not fully aware, and gathering thoughts that cannot necessarily be expressed in a coherent way. If we substitute a writer's language, symbolism and motifs for Helen's brush strokes, we are left with the impression that Johnston is letting us know that she is working with ideas that she finds difficult to tackle in coherent, logical, linear prose – hence, the cyclical, complex and often contradictory nature of her narratives.

Locations in Johnston's novels are not physical places, but sites of various and usually competing discourses. From her early, albeit not especially original, interest in the Big House and the waning of the Anglo-Irish ascendancy, Johnston has been interested in premises as locations of ideological premises. For example, the school that Helen attends in *The Railway Station Man* is remembered for the conceptual parameters she encountered there. In her account of the premises in which she first lived as a married woman, the focus is upon the view from the window. What she stresses is that from her window everything seemed to be constantly changing – analogous of the kind of in-between space that Constance occupies at the end of her life while working on her narrative. Typical of a painter, the emphasis falls upon the changing colours, the light and the dark. So that in looking from the window one seems to occupy a space in which the known is displaced from stabilizing referents. Helen obviously welcomes certain features of this view: its constant changing; the fact that there are no strongly defined lines; and the general sense that everything coheres within this larger sense of change. This engagement with change and disentanglement from rigid definition is contrasted with the determinism expressed by people who look out on days when the view is so clear that the walls appear to lose their definitions and conclude with certainty that it will rain!

Thus, *The Railway Station Man* illustrates a point that holds true for all Johnston's work. The emphasis upon change at the beginning of the novel anticipates the way in which the novel focuses upon the subject not as coherent and unified but as complex, contradictory and ever changing. Indeed, most of Johnston's novels, and certainly her later works, seem to suggest that it is only in recognizing oneself as such that freedom from known, linguistic determinants is possible. Johnston's novels embody, if

I may allude to the French linguistic theorist Roland Barthes for a moment, a 'writerly' concept of identity in which a character, such as Helen, is marked by, but not necessarily constructed by, sociohistorical determinants because she has the capacity to recreate and reimagine.

Johnston's concern with place as the embodiment of competing discourses, with a performative concept of identity and with the situated subject as changing and non-unified is rooted in her identity as an Irish writer and as a woman in environments which, as in her novels, are oppressively gendered. This helps to explain the reconfiguration of identity and identity politics in her work from the collective – the family, the community and the nation – to the individual. Indeed, it is only recently that we have seen materialist–feminist theory being applied to Johnston's work. But what has been done so far in this area has still failed to appreciate the extent to which Johnston reads the environment in terms of a gendered and ideological geography. In *The Railway Station Man*, Johnston explores how far subjectivity may become a space for the subversion of established 'reality' that is of male-ordered space. We can follow this argument through the novel by noticing the parallels between the constrictive view of art in school and college and the advice she is given by her father whose thinking is as neat and well-ordered as his appearance. He lives by the maxim that one must keep within structures. In contradistinction to her father, and recalling the open and radical in-between space which Constance comes to occupy in *The Christmas Tree*, Helen's own paintings are symbolically unframed. They are elemental – scenes of sky, sea and bare hills – and are full of unfettered energy and light. In the course of the novel, the activity of painting for Helen becomes increasingly physical, exploratory and revelatory. The descriptions of her at work stress her bodily engagement with it and the physical effort involved – crouching, leaning and stretching. When Father Quinlan buys one of her pictures, he immediately wants to frame it – to contain it and define its subject matter in terms of a recognizable genre. The irony is reinforced by the fact that he, like Helen, spends much time on his knees, in his garden. But he does so in order to tidy the garden, to provide it with a frame as it were. Roger, with whom Helen is having a liaison, also, mounts her pictures in wooden frames that are described as 'prim'.

One of the dangers in Johnston's writings is that they do, as is the case in *The Railway Station Man*, tend toward a rather essentialist male–female binarism. Throughout the novel, Helen is framed and defined by the general spatial arrangements surrounding her, and these restrictive environments are associated with men, while the liberating spaces are associated with the female and the feminine. In addition to the examples referred to earlier, she is defined by Dan as a 'boring woman', seen by her grown-up sons only as a mother to be at their beck and call and treated by her father as if she were a child. The narrative drive of the novel is provided by Helen's desire, literally and metaphorically, to discover her own space. In *The Railway Station Man*, as in *Fool's Sanctuary*, the movement from the urban, a world of masculine violence, to the country becomes an important metaphor. Eventually, Helen moves into a shed where she works. But the male characters do not understand the importance of the possession of space. After spending a night with Roger, Helen has to hurry home – to reclaim her own definition of herself (one of her first actions is to see herself undressed in the mirror) that can only happen in a space that is not constructed by others. The dialogue between Roger who follows her home and Helen is riddled with references to space. Roger's response, that his head is full of her, denies her her own space. In shouting after her that she is 'a funny woman', Roger epitomizes how, through the female address in their male-determined language, men diminish women. Within this context, the skinny-dipping episode in which she undresses for herself and not for the male gaze, assumes increased significance. Here, drifting in her own space, as it were, Helen enters a secret kind of timelag. Typically, it is one where danger as well as freedom looms:

> You could feel the current pulling you as you lay upon the water. It wanted you to go towards the rocks at the southern end of the beach and then if you weren't careful away out into the ocean … She lay on her back and allowed herself to drift. She knew for how long she could indulge herself in that pleasure before turning over and swimming strongly back into the safety of the breaking waves. (45)

Johnston's novels are not exclusively hinged, as some critics have suggested, on an art-for-art's-sake versus political commitment debate, though it is a topic with which they are concerned. Rather, they are primarily concerned with the search for ways of achieving a sense of identity, disentangled from the determinism of the socially constructed and gendered linguistic and cultural environment. There are no ready solutions. In the reconfiguration of identity from the collective to the individual, there is a risk of apolitical dislocation and a diffusion of identity, as Helen eventually confesses to Roger. What really bothers her though is the way in which her sense of her own identity is predicated on freeing the known from their stabilizing referents. In this situation, without the certainty on which it depends, political commitment is difficult. Thus, Helen ends up envying Roger his conviction.

In rediscovering herself, Helen moves beyond the symbolic, the masculine and the land:

> She stood up and pulled off her jersey and shirt and then her jeans and her pants and ran across the sand into the sea. She waded out over the breaking line of waves and then, falling forward onto the water, she swam straight out to sea, something that she normally wouldn't dream of doing, fear always keeping her within scrabbling distance of the land. She swam for a good six or seven minutes, thinking of nothing but the movement of her body through the water, the soft cleaving of arm after arm, the rhythm of her outstretched legs beating, then suddenly frightened by her own courage she turned and swam back towards the shore. The rhythm was lost and her limbs began to feel the strain. She faltered, splashed, gulped mouthfuls of water. (104)

Thus, her 'true sense' of self is linked to what is traditionally associated with women – rhythm and water. Surrounded by water, suggestive of amniotic fluids, and thinking only of her body, she is in a somewhat secretive state of being which returns her to what is beyond language. When she loses that state of being, she finds herself faltering and gulping. The suggestion is that there is a natural, essentially female sense of being that can be undermined by the masculine. Her enjoyment of it – 'What a life mermaids must lead, she thought' – is interrupted by the tall, looming figure of Damian Sweeney. He behaves very differently in the water from Helen – almost trying to struggle with it and overcome it:

> Suddenly in a great explosion of energy he rolled into the foam and leapt up into the air again. He twirled round, his arms

high above his head and then down he went again, rolling
again. Up he came and ran through the shallow water kicking
great sparkling fountains up ahead of him as he ran.   (105)

What a lot of critics have identified as sentimentality in
Johnston's work may be more accurately seen as pathos arising
from the way in which, for Johnston, creating a writerly identity
inevitably involves, as it does for Helen, patching over absence.
The personal sense of loss felt by characters such as Constance,
Helen and Miranda is, in microcosm, a much larger social and
political absence. Their small existentialist crises mirror, sometimes quite literally, the larger historical ones for women. The
notion of the trans-historical or mythical subject is not easily
available to women in Johnston's novels because of the way
she perceives the problematized nature of the situated subject,
threatened by the spectrality of the 'beyond' which they enter in
rewriting their life scripts.

Emotional Stir-fry

Written in 1994, Emma Donoghue's *Stir-fry* and Kathleen
Ferguson's *The Maid's Tale*, set in the middle of the twentieth century, give a voice to previously silenced experiences of women.
Stir-fry is concerned with same-sex relationships among women
and *The Maid's Tale* with women who have been exiled within the
Catholic Church but also trapped by it and its ideologies.
Ostensibly they might appear to be very different novels. *Stir-fry*
is the third-person narrative of a 17-year-old, Maria Murphy, who
has arrived in Dublin from her small, country town to study at
university. The fact that Maria is attending university at all is testimony to the liberalizing effect of the modernizing economic
reforms of the Lemass era. In the period 1959–66, they created a
climate in which liberal ideas might be developed and topics
around which there had been an unhealthy silence, such as sexual behaviour, could be discussed, even if not entirely openly.
Donoghue's novel is a version of the innocent abroad narrative,
as Maria unwittingly ends up sharing a flat with a lesbian couple.
The Maid's Tale is a first-person narrative of Brigid Keen, a woman
in her fifties who has spent her adult life as a Catholic priest's
housekeeper. Her father, now incarcerated in a mental hospital,

killed her mother in a fit of passion. As a result, Brigid and her brother and sister were brought up in an orphanage in Derry run by the Sisters of Mercy. Although *The Maid's Tale* has a slightly longer time span than *Stir-fry*, both texts provide a perspective on the discourses surrounding women's sexuality in Ireland in the 1950s and 1960s. But in writing of the 1950s and 1960s, these authors provide a critique of the slowness with which reform moved in Ireland in the second half of the twentieth century. For example, same-sex experience even in the 1990s existed within a fluid socio-political situation which itself might be described as something of a stir-fry. The 1885 British acts which criminalized homosexuality, and which were retained in the Irish Free State and the Republic, were only repealed in 1993.

Each of these two novels, like Jennifer Johnston's work, is concerned with the way in which desire is determined, complicated and distorted by the discourses in which it is articulated. This makes the title of Donoghue's book especially pertinent. At a literal level, stir-fry refers to the meal that the lesbian couple, Ruth and Jael, serve Maria when she first visits their flat. It is also the metaphor that Ruth uses in her letter to Maria, near the end of the novel, explaining how the relationships among the three of them proved more complicated than she had expected:

> It's sort of like a stir-fry, that's the only way I can think of to describe it, don't laugh. I thought you could chop up lots of different vegetables and mix them in and raise the heat, and they'd all make each other taste better. It never occurred to me that ginger and fennel might clash. (199)

Ruth is referring to the way Maria has fallen in love with her but is attracted to Jael. At another level, the entire novel might be thought of as a stir-fry. Like many contemporary Irish novels, it is a generic stir-fry: an innocent-abroad novel, as I suggested above; a coming-out novel; a sexual bildungsroman; and, at times, a campus novel. In each case, Donoghue's text disrupts the conventional generic conventions and the traditional expectations of these familiar forms. A number of feminist texts revise the bildungsroman – initially concerned, like Dickens's *Great Expectations*, for example, with the rise of a young man in society – in order to explore female subjectivity. But Donoghue goes further and adapts the narrative to a young woman's growing consciousness of her same-sex desire. The title also refers to the melting pot of Irish metropolitan experience, to the nature of memory and the complexity of individual, especially female, desire.

The emphasis of the text falls upon Maria's own emotional stir-fry, anticipated at the beginning of the novel when she makes her way up the stairs to Ruth and Jael's flat: 'Between two steps Maria found herself in darkness' (9). Maria enters darkness metaphorically and literally. The steps image encapsulates how she is caught between the two terms of the socially determined binarism of heterosexuality and homosexuality. At this point, the novel also suggests that Maria is emerging from conventional depictions of femininity, especially as configured by the ostensibly radical glossy magazines targeting women. On her way to the flat, she discards her copy of *Her* magazine, containing articles on breast cancer, standing up to the boss and desirability in men, together with others on subjects that reinforce the status quo for women, such as slimming. Literally relocating herself, she finds it difficult to redefine herself. Indeed, at this point in the text, she considers collecting the magazine on her way back down the stairs.

Maria's process of 'coming out' mirrors the emergence of modern Ireland itself, and the way that in the second half of the twentieth century, Ireland moved into a space that was not yet fully defined. But even then there was resistance. This movement as far as the status of women and sexual relations, especially same-sex relations, in the 1950s and 1960s was concerned was only partial and uneven, especially when Dublin was compared with more remote rural areas. In Eamon de Valera's ideologically constructed nation state, it was often difficult in the rural areas for women to break from prevailing discourses about gender that the Constitution enshrined. And even within Dublin itself developments affecting women were not always wholly supported. Liberalism was invariably a middle-class affair. Urban, middle-class women had for long enjoyed the advantages of being able to participate in organizations such as the Gaelic league, the suffrage associations and the Irish Women Workers' Union. Maria, by no means typical of young women from rural areas, brings to the city an emerging scepticism about the way female identity is conventionally figured. But, it has to be said that the knowledge that Maria, as a country girl, brings to the city is one that Irish women have had to pass among themselves in their own, secretive ways. Maria's own movement, physical and psychological, begins, as it did for those women in rural Ireland who were, or indeed were able, to be more outward looking and were willing to take risks, with the discovery of a feminist text. In this case, her sense of being was 'interrupted' by finding in her local library a 'tattered copy' of Germaine Greer's radical feminist book, or so it was perceived at the time, *The Female Eunuch*. The unease with which she reads this book is indicative of the way liberal, feminist attitudes in the country areas were inscribed with more secrecy than in the urban areas. Thus, there is no simple binarism in this novel between innocent country and sophisticated metropolis. However, the opportunities provided by the city are not gainsaid. The city offered women more experiences than the rural areas and made a wider variety of perspectives available to them. But women in the city could be as complicit in their own oppression as women in the country.

The extent to which even the educated in the city might be implicated in the oppression of women, and women themselves not recognize how their equality has to be fought for and negotiated on a daily basis, is evident from the incident which Maria witnesses involving the engineering students. The men in the Department throw a fellow, female student in the pond. It is, as one of the male characters says, an act of 'adolescent macho thuggery' (25). But it is more than that because of what is 'encrypted' within the incident. First, the event is dependent upon traditions – each year the engineers try to beat the previous record for the number of young women thrown in the pond – and upon discourses that permit men to abuse women. Donoghue focuses upon how what is 'encrypted' within this act is concealed – by, for example, a so-called sense of fun and by time-honoured ritual. Looking at this incident through the Derridean lens which we discussed in previous chapters, what is 'encrypted' in this act is separate from the wider context yet has a dialectic relation with it. Donoghue, in Derridean terms, is interested in the effect of concealment upon the wider 'territory' in which the crypt is buried. The effect is evident in the purported chivalry that accompanies the deed – the men guiltily retrieve the soaked victim's sandals and wrap her in a laboratory coat – and in the embarrassed laughter of the on-lookers. Also 'encrypted' within this event, is the way in which women have been defined as subject to men for centuries. The incident has resonance of the ducking stool and similar punishments meted out to women in earlier times suspected of witchcraft, which were a means of controlling female power. It cannot be overlooked here that women, through higher education, are entering a world dominated by men. The point is made by Maria – 'She's no witch, she's a bimbo' (24) – who thereby reveals how she has herself been relocated but is not certain of the direction and the limits of her reinscription. Her in-between state is underscored by the presence of the student from Galway who claims that what they have witnessed is 'sick' but can still argue: 'If she's going to be in their class for four years she won't want a reputation for not being able to take a joke' (25).

Stir-fry is the principal trope whereby the physical and the emotional confusion of the in-between are expressed in this text. It refers the reader literally to the physical entanglement of sex, suggested cryptically by the address of Ruth and Jael's flat, number 69, and more specifically when Maria catches sight of the two women on the table: 'Her eyes tried to untangle its elements' (68). The passage itself suggests entanglement – 'Ruth, cross-legged on the table, her back curved like a comma, and Jael, leaning into it, kissing her' (68) – and untangling as Maria tries to visually untangle what she is witnessing and also make sense of what is happening. Here 'untangling' for Maria means trying to understand what she sees within the conventional structures within which desire is constructed. She has yet to reach the stage when the larger linguistic and ideological frameworks within which desire is articulated is questioned: 'The kiss, their joint body, the table, all seemed to belong to a parallel world' (68).

Even more overtly, entanglement is stressed when Maria sees Ruth and her lover actually having sex: 'She could see firelight edging over a tangle of limbs. It wavered on Jael's long brown back arched over Ruth, their arms like the dark interlacing bars of a hedge' (98). The entanglement is not simply in the bodies of the lovers but in Maria's complex reaction, for she is beginning to recognize that she loves Ruth but desires Jael – hence the way her eyes focus on Jael's back is stressed in a sensual way. (Eventually, in rejecting Jael's seduction, Maria comes to recognize her true feelings for Ruth.) What is also emphasized this time is the way in which she is emotionally caught up with the scene – she has to wrench herself away. Not surprisingly, Maria's attempt to untangle what she sees is juxtaposed with the entanglement of the bodies: 'Maria had to strain to hear the rough breathing, the indistinguishable words' (98). But it is not only the words that are 'indistinguishable' – it is impossible for her to tell who is making which sounds. Eventually, Maria returns to her bed and assumes the 'foetal position'. The phrase 'the foetal position' makes it sound like a sexual position, which takes us back to the cryptic house number, and undermines the innocence suggested by Maria's assumption of this shape. Her response to this scene and to the kiss is couched in formulaic terms. Here she sees herself as a voyeur whereas previously she had tripped out clichés that she couldn't seem to get beyond: 'consenting adults', 'nobody's business but their own', 'different strokes' (73).

Set in the mid-twentieth century but written in the 1990s, *Stir-fry* is a novel as much about the way prejudices and preconceptions are preserved in established and popular discourse as about same-sex relations. It opens with Maria struggling to decipher Ruth and Jael's card advertising for a flatmate. While she is able to work out that they are two feminists, the reference to 'NO BIGOTS' passes her by. On her way up to their flat she is not as disarmed as she should be by her own assimilation of her brother's stereotypes of feminists:

> Not a whiff of lentils, she thought, as she was guided round a bend and up another flight of stairs. How many feminists does it take to screw in a light-bulb? One to screw in the light-bulb, one to stir the lentil casserole, and one to object to the use of the word 'screw'. (9)

What Maria learns by experience – from her initial reading of *The Female Eunuch* in her hometown library, to her experiences at the university, to her relationships with Ruth and Jael – is that discourses can open up or close down possibilities. The door, which can exclude or allow entry, is one of the key tropes in the novel:

> Maria slashed through the bead curtain. Ruth's door was shut. She stood outside, her fingers against the wood, waiting for the right words to come. Not a sound from behind the door. What was she expecting – a sob, breaking glass, the snapping strings of a guitar?
> Her thoughts were interrupted by a flush, and suddenly Ruth was behind her, toothbrush in hand.
> 'Hi,' said Maria, her back to the door.
> 'Did you want something?' Ruth's voice was barely audible.
> Light caught the wet bristles of the toothbrush. Maria stared at it stupidly. 'Just to say goodnight.'
> 'Sweet dreams, Maria.' Ruth shut the door behind her. (210–11)

This passage may be read on many different levels. The passage begins with Maria determiningly breaking through the bead curtain through which she had previously witnessed Ruth and Jael making love and come to the knowledge not only of their relationship but of her sexual feelings and desires also. The bead curtain suggests, then, that she saw as through dark glass. Even, now, she is still not fully aware of her feelings for Ruth over Jael. The closed door represents how she, consciously or unconsciously, perceives Ruth's stance toward her. It is also the emotional door that she must open within herself. More important, it is a linguistic door that is closed to her. Without the language to articulate her same-sex desires to herself, she is unable to explore them, let alone express how she feels to Ruth. Hence, she stands outside the door, in a kind of timelag, unable to find the right words. The passage suggests that may be Maria is locked within conventional discourses and the way forward for her is to step outside. Significantly, while she believes that Ruth is on the other side of the door, her friend appears from behind. There are suggestions that Maria needs to acquire a more female oriented language than she has been used to. From behind the door, she does not imagine verbal sounds but simply sounds. The reference to a toothbrush is interesting within the context of this passage. Ruth, in effect, is refreshing her mouth – the part of the body concerned with articulation. Her question opens a door for Maria, and for a while both stand together in the timelag created. It is a question which relocates Maria from a position whereby she is the timid girl standing outside Ruth's door to one where she and Ruth become involved with each other. The temporal space is filled with Ruth staring not simply at the toothbrush but at its bristles that have obvious vulvac connotations. Although it is Ruth who eventually closes the door, in effect, it is Maria who closes it. 'Sweet dreams' picks up on the fact that she has obviously seen Maria staring at the bristles.

This passage is juxtaposed with the one in which Ruth enters her room. Again the emphasis is upon the significance of opening and closing doors:

> Maria lay inert, flexing her stiff neck. When her door creaked open slowly, she blinked, then squeezed her eyes shut. It was Ruth; she had made out her silhouette in the dark. Nothing happened for a full minute. Maria knew she was being looked

at, and her mouth hanging [sic] slightly open. Finally Ruth's voice came out of the black. 'Are you awake?'
Go away. Maria was dead. She was limp like a tracker who didn't want to be eaten by the bear. Go away.
After a few seconds she heard the rustle of paper, then a murmur of words that she could not distinguish; it could have been 'Good luck'. (211)

This time Ruth not only enters Maria's darkened room but also emerges from the depths of her subconscious. This is not simply Ruth standing in front of her but a figure on whom is projected Maria's affections and what Maria imagines to be Ruth's desires for her. This time Ruth is more spectre than person. The repression of her own desires means that what Maria perceives is exaggerated and threatening. What is being concealed by each of them is turning them into ghosts in relation to each other and is being expressed in rather grotesque spectrality – Maria envisaging herself as a tracker in danger of being eaten by a bear. This is symbolic of how she perceives the dangers not only of Ruth's but her own, hitherto repressed, sexuality. Her eyes squeezed shut are analogous of the tightly closed door that excludes the new possibilities open to her. Again, the central image is of a timelag. Not only is there another silence in which no one moves or speaks but also Maria is in an in-between state, between sleeping and waking, analogous of the in-between state she occupies as regards her feelings for the other woman. Again, too, there is a suggestion of the inadequacy of language. In the previous passage, Ruth was barely audible, and now Maria has difficulty in deciphering her final words. Both these passages, of course, are about the inaudible – what is not being expressed but is clearly present between them. Again Ruth's question can be read in different ways – asking Maria whether she is not sleeping in the literal sense or whether she is awake to her own feelings.

The conclusions that Maria comes to at the end of the novel are only partially thought out because there are still so many issues to be resolved in her life as there are for gay and lesbian people in Ireland generally in the 1990s. Not the least of these is that in committing to same-sex relationships, one may be excluding oneself from one's family or traditional community and excluding oneself from the spiritual support of the Catholic faith. Thus, same-sex partners invariably find themselves in a community that has to offer alternative channels of support. At times, we might feel that Ruth and Jael's spiritedness is excessive, but it is an index of the personal energy and spiritual reserves necessary to commit to a same-sex relationship in a nation state itself in a condition of limbo. As in *The Maid's Tale*, the conclusion leaves the text in a state of limbo. Maria makes a spur of the moment decision, but it is based on finally opening her eyes:

> Jael began speaking, then stopped herself, and realization crept across her face. 'I see. God, I hadn't even thought of that.'
> 'Of what?' And then Maria stopped, because she knew.
> 'That makes sense of a lot of things.'
> They looked at each other in bewilderment. 'It does, doesn't it?' said Maria, mostly to herself.
> Jael cleared her throat. 'How come I never saw?'
> 'I didn't either, till now.'
> 'She'll be at her mother's,' said Jael automatically, breaking the silence.
> 'Oh. I'll be off, so,' said Maria slowly.   (230)

This passage may be read simply in relation to Maria, Jael and Ruth. Or it may be seen as analogous of the situation within which Ireland wakes up to the part that same-sex desire has had in people's lives within the Republic. Maria's love for Ruth emerges from the inner crypt within which it has been concealed – analogous of the emergence of lesbianism in Ireland from its marginalized position. On both levels, the passage points to the 'beyond' – where much will begin to make sense. The key images here are of silence being broken and of relocation and reinscription. There is also a sense of being caught in a timelag. The final image is of Ruth opening the door to Maria. The reader does not know, any more than Maria, how she will be received. We cannot be certain as to what decisions each of them will now make.

The conclusion of *Stir-fry* locates Maria in an 'in-between' space, literally between 'reinscription' and 'relocation'. Like many of the women characters in Johnston's novels, she has emerged from a previously silenced position that has also been, and to some extent still is, marked by secrecy. In doing so, like Helen in *The Railway Station Man*, she is a vehicle by which the text, as much as the protagonist herself, confronts the dominant discourses that have been directly or indirectly responsible for her silence and marginalization.

Ghosting Desire

The 'in-between' spaces in which Constance and Maria in the novels discussed earlier find themselves are not only places from which the dominant discourses determining gendered identity and sexual relations are interrogated but also spaces of confusion and uncertainty in which what has been hidden is not easily confronted. Such spaces give first-person narratives in women's fiction dealing with suppressed desire a shadowy and cryptic quality comparable to that in Joseph O'Connor's *The Salesman*, discussed in Chapter 3. In many of these narratives, it is not only suppressed desire that acquires a spectral quality but, because the narrator is not fully present to her own presence (in both senses of the word), the voice of the protagonist herself has a haunted quality.

Not surprisingly, then, in its concern with suppressed desire and a narrator who is thereby removed from her own sense of being, *The Maid's Tale* conflates various meanings of the word 'ghost'. Brigid Keen's life in a Catholic orphanage, following her mother's murder by her father, and in service to Father Mann is like a false spectral image caused by imperfect diffraction: 'The Catholic Church was father, mother and family to me for over fifty years' (1). Indeed, the voice we listen to is the product of imperfect diffraction, for Brigid has been adversely influenced by her Catholic upbringing. At one point she bemoans: 'But I'll tell you this much, my mind took fifty years to get free. Many as grew up with me wasn't near as lucky' (2). Despite her efforts to get free, she remains a haunted personality. In order to stress the extent to which, because of the Catholic context of her life, the seeming spectrality of her own being is intertwined with Catholicism, many of the different meanings of the word 'ghost' invoked in the text have religious origins. The echo of the Holy Trinity in the first of the preceding quotations, underscores the way the novel interleaves secular and religious notions of the word 'ghost'. The effect of this in the text is to accentuate the archaic meaning of the word as 'animus' or soul, and the suggestion, through Holy Ghost and the structure of the word itself, (g)host,

of the Eucharist. The linking here of animus and one of the sacra-
ments by which Christians are intended to attain 'grace' is appropriate because the emphasis in the text falls upon the search for a
spiritual freedom which does not deny the body.

Like *Stir-fry*, *The Maid's Tale* can be read as a feminist rewriting
of the bildungsroman. The crucial figure in the book in this
respect is Aunt Grace. It is Aunt Grace who really makes Brigid
see herself as a prisoner:

> 'Look at the colour of you!' says she. 'You look like you've
> never seen the sun in years. And those clothes you were wear-
> ing when I came in! They're like something your grandmother
> would've worn. You might as well be in mourning. How can
> you stand it, locked up here, year in, year out?'   (101)

When Brigid sees the clothes that Grace has brought her – 'all figure hugging and sexy' (98) – she is appalled and excited at the
same time. But their 'foreignness' to her – '[they are] only fit for a
movie star' (98) – is an indication of the extent to which her own
sexual body has become something alien to her. Thus, like *Stir-fry*,
this is a novel that has a central female character estranged from
her own sexual desires. Additionally, what Brigid seems to feel
most is the invasion of her private emotional and physical space
at Bethel House to which she is sent as a child. Nicknamed
Shamey, after a simpleton in a radio drama, and haunted by a line
from the play, she becomes a scapegoat for the frustrations,
shame and anger of the other children. Her body becomes the
object of their verbal abuse.

As a child, Brigid occupies a paradoxical subject position;
being alone yet constantly feeling her private space is threatened.
Her life revolves around secrecy and a lack of trust. As she herself
complains, she grew up like the other girls 'with not a soul [she]
could trust to talk to' (4). Not surprisingly, she finds the domain
of intimate relations problematic. But more than that, the reader,
especially in the first half of the book, finds it hard to take anything on its own terms. Saying one thing, Brigid frequently means
or suggests another. Half articulated meanings create a ghost
presence within what purports to be fully expressed.

This ghost presence is comparable to what the postcolonial
critic Gayatri Spivak, in an introduction to one of Jacques
Derrida's works, identifies as a 'trace'. Here she is taking issue

with an aspect of linguistic theory developed by the Swiss linguist Ferdinand de Saussere. In summary, Saussere was generally responsible for a sea change in the study of language. Rejecting previous approaches that examined how language changed over time, he took language out of its historical context and focused upon the rules governing, and the elements within, language at any given time. Despite this, Spivak maintains that language is never fully present to its present but contains 'traces' of the past. She argues:

> In spite of itself, Sausserean linguistics recognizes the structure of the sign to be a trace-structure. And Freud's psychoanalysis, to some extent in spite of itself, recognizes the structure of experience itself to be a trace, not a presence-structure. (Derrida, 1976: xvii)

Indeed, for much of the text, Brigid's narrative is a 'trace-structure' and her experiences, as she relates them, are not a 'presence-structure'. This is evident, for example, in her views of Mary Bosco, of whose relationship with Father Mann Brigid is jealous:

> Of course I did what Father ordered me to do in the beginning and told her he wasn't there. And, I'll tell you this, I didn't have no pangs of guilt neither. What business had she putting in on Father every night of the week? It was too much to expect, even of a priest. Not another soul in the parish ever dared put in on Father the same way. (85)

Eventually, she admits the truth to herself and the reader about her feelings for Father Mann and realizes what a mistake she has made. But the problems then revealed are not only self-deception but, as in O'Connor's *The Salesman*, the way in which the secret that Brigid has kept within herself has created, to adapt a concept from Nicolas Abraham in the text for which Derrida wrote his preface on the crypt, an alien or foreign being within her:

> Looking back, I seem to have spent most of my life jealous of one person or another when it comes to the Father. I resented the people that come to him with their problems, when me that lived under the same roof didn't dare open my mouth to him unless it was something to do with the housekeeping I had to say. (89)

The alien being within her is accentuated by the way in which she proves to be a rather poor reflection of the Virgin Mary as a mediatrix. She does not assist those who want help from the priest with the same sympathy as one would hope Mary would petition Christ on behalf of sinners. The secrets that we eventually learn her father has withheld, or been forced to withhold, from her turn her into a stranger to herself. Father Mann's sister-in-law, Miriam, perceives her as 'a stranger in the house', and her alienation from those with whom she should have a more comfortable relation means that others see her as kind of grotesque. As Miriam observes: 'There's something the matter with her. She trembles. She acts like a frightened rabbit' (117).

Secrets and Lies

While Brigid's narrative is driven by her perception of her life from within, it incorporates, despite Brigid's filtering of them, a sufficient number of other points of view for the reader to see her relationship with Father Mann from the outside. Indeed, the nativity crypt that is described at one point in the text serves as a metaphor for the 'encrypted' nature of the relationship between himself and Brigid. 'A queer jumble of pieces', it includes Mary with a 'soppy look', and Joseph 'weighed down under an oversized halo' (96). Evident here, too, is Brigid's tendency to deny someone has any negative attributes. The way she sees Mary regarding Joseph with a 'soppy look' is analogous of how she sees the other women in the parish looking at Father Mann. But Brigid places Father Mann on a pedestal. She denies to herself that Father Mann actually encourages the attentions of his parishioners. Instead, she only sees him, in essentially asexual terms, as burdened by his duties and responsibilities. In fact, this is a convenient way for her to see him because both are then in a similar position, and one that legitimates the exclusion of sexual desire between them.

Brigid is also oblivious of any connections that might be made between her own situation and the fact that her mother has been murdered in a crime of passion. If she were honest with herself, she might realize that living with a man who has taken a vow of celibacy as his house keeper, in other words in a relationship where no sex is demanded or given, is subconsciously what she desires. She possibly chooses to live with a man this way because it avoids her having to enter a sexual relationship. Like many women who have been scarred by trauma early in life, there is a masochistic side to Brigid. In entering a post with Father Mann, she confines herself to living in a working relationship with a man with whom she would like to have a sexual relationship. Subconsciously, again, she appears to have chosen a relationship in which betrayal and hurt are highly likely. But it is not just what happens eventually; she lives with a perpetual sense of pain and betrayal as she watches the other women with the Father: 'God forgive me but I envied them getting his affection like that, for nothing. While I attended him hand and foot all day. And for what?' (89). Brigid holds on to an emotional fidelity even though it means denying to herself aspects of Father Mann's life which are probably apparent to every one else. Indeed, in many respects, Brigid exhibits what in psychology is sometimes called 'inverse co-dependency'. This term is normally taken to refer to how a partner in a relationship with someone suffering from emotional trauma devotes themselves so totally to the person dependent on them that they submerge their own needs and become addicted to the needs of the other. In her dependence on Father Mann, Brigid's caretaking role becomes obsessive or 'hyperactive'. This obsessiveness becomes a means by which she thinks she is avoiding domination, betrayal and exploitation by a male while this is not the case.

Father Mann, whose whole career as a priest is a denial of the secrets about his own needs and desires which he confides to Brigid, is also haunted by what he conceals:

> Now Mary had made a habit of calling on Father before this and I put no pass on it on account of who she was. Father aye gave her the same time he give anybody else – no more nor no less – till this night when the two of them didn't come out of the study till well after twelve o'clock. When I asked him if he wanted anything else he bit the head off me. I swear I never seen him in a temper like that before. He had his fists clenched tight like he was ready for murder. I blamed that Mary Bosco for taking it out of him.   (32–3)

In Brigid's description of him, Father Mann not only appears to be estranged from himself but also coiled in repression. His 'fists clenched tight' signify his deep, emotional closure and denial. Thus, the wider subject of this narrative is the impenetrable entanglement of the 'other' within the self. In Father Mann's case, it is the man within the priest, and in Brigid's case, the sexual woman within the asexual figure of the priest's housekeeper – the fact that what she really wants is the man and not Mann. The relationship between Brigid and the Father is not based on intimacy but the extent to which, in the midst of his familiarity to her, he remains unfamiliar:

> He liked me to keep the house a particular way and he liked the place to be quiet all the time. This was so people who come to see him would feel at their ease, he says to me. He liked his dinner set down on time as well, in case he was called away. At night he had his wee fixed ways with him that I come to know by heart. He'd go round every room in the house before he went to bed and pull the plugs out of the walls. He had this terrible dread of being burned in his bed, he says to me one time when I forgot to put the fireguard up. Every night he took a bath just the same. I'd hear the water running, just so long. And he'd spend exactly fifteen minutes in there. He filled the water to the self same level – just below the middle – every time.   (36–7)

Ferguson embarks upon a configuration of identity here based upon concealments that render a subject a stranger to him or herself. In Father Mann's case, obsessive repetition and pathological precision serve to guard the self against the eruption, often in violence, of what is 'encrypted' within.

In Jacques Derrida's terms, what we have here is the 'crypt', 'enclosed within the self, but as a foreign place, prohibited, excluded' (1986: xxxv). Ferguson, though, is interested in the relation between Brigid's own recognition of her exclusion and her refusal to admit that she shares an understanding of Father Mann as a result. The Father's obsessive behaviour is comparable to the way Brigid secretly relies upon rhyming Hail Mary's and Glory-be-to-the Fathers back to front. His outburst following Mary Bosco's long vigil is comparable to the bouts of temper that Brigid had to control at Bethel House: 'The bouts of temper got rarer as I got older. After a while I couldn't say what I thought or felt any more, or if I thought or felt anything' (19). Brigid, in her denial of intellectual curiosity and her refusal to have opinions and feelings, and Father Mann, in his pedantic obsessiveness, become less than themselves. In a Derridean sense, they become traces in their own narratives. Derrida (1976) relates 'trace' to 'the alterity of a past that never was and can never be lived in the originary or modified form of presence' (70). In its entirety, the novel is a narrative of a past that never was because of the amount of repression and denial upon which it was based. It is one to which neither Brigid nor the Father were fully present.

Repressed Hosts

Father Mann and his maid become like the hosts that Brigid makes for the Communion. The cross on the host is a signifier of a complex liminal space: between life and death; mortality and immortality; sin and grace; the body and the spirit; glorious cross and humiliating public torture. It reminds us of the liminal space which Mann and Brigid occupy. For example, Brigid is located between body and spirit because she is not quite either; and between the humiliation of being Mann's maid and the status which such a post carries in the Catholic community. The 'other' as phantom erases the boundary between self and other. Thus, the Father represses the man within him, but it returns as a phantom to erase the boundary between man and priest – literally the boundary between Mann and man. It returns, as in Father Mann's case, as the repressed.

The hosts, pressed from the wafer biscuits and stored in card boxes, are analogous of the convent girls, the nuns and the priests pressed within the Catholic Church; the 'other' pressed on them like the crosses on the host. It is the ghostly trace of the 'other' that seems to fascinate Ferguson. The Algerian psychoanalytic critic Hélène Cixous argues:

> What is intolerable is that the Ghost erases the limit which exists between two states, neither alive nor dead; passing through, the dead man returns to the manner of the Repressed. It is his coming back that makes the ghost what he is, just as it is the return of the Repressed that inscribes repression. (Cit Buse and Stott 1999: 13)

What makes Mann and Brigid appear to be ghostly figures in themselves is that what they have repressed returns, as Freud suggested in his concept of Nachträglichkeit introduced in Chapter 3, to their consciousness as spectres. It is the process of returning which is the highly charged signifier – making the repressed known as the repressed – just as, for Derrida, it is the process of concealing that marks out what is concealed as the concealed. Hence, the focus upon the text falls upon the processes of returning, revealing and concealing. These processes are embodied in the very nature of Brigid's prose as her comments on Mary Bosco and her relationship with the Father to which I referred earlier all too clearly suggest.

The cross on the host is a complex signifier because at one level it suggests all that cannot be easily assimilated into the Christian theology, including its pagan origins. The ghost, and the other as ghost, represents that which resists assimilation, as do the contents of Brigid's nightmares:

> The only problem was the dreams had a bad tendency to get out of hand. I mind a real bleak period when every time my head hit the pillow, I'd see my father – or who I took to be my father – for I hadn't seen the man at the time. He never had the same face twice but I knew him to be my father never the same. Pictures, like snap-shots, of my mother's grave plagued me about this time too. I had no peace with them.   (19)

Since her father here has many faces, he would seem to be symbolic of the threatening presence of masculinity. They may also be suggestive of how her father's ghostly presence in her psyche determines her attitude toward men, and people in general. He is what Brigid and her sister Dympna have repressed for years and which Aunt Grace makes them confront when she takes them to the mental hospital in which he is incarcerated. The episode draws analogies between the way that the Keen sister's father becomes the dominant secret in their psyche and the way that mental patients generally are society's secret. We encounter the patients' transformation into grotesques before we see Brigid's father:

> I'll never forget them haggard, crazy faces as long as I live. They were that twisted up with seething rage and frustration, and their eyes was black and brooding with dread and despair. Most of them was anaemic and blotchy from living indoors so long and their bodies was withered from lack of exercise.   (105)

The patients are turned into grotesques – become 'twisted up' – by what they are forced to repress. Their craziness might be seen as a product of the repression that has created within them a foreignness with which it has been difficult for them to live. As in the case of Patrick McCabe's *The Butcher Boy*, discussed in Chapter 8, the madness here is not meant to be a faithful representation of mental illness. It is intended to function figuratively, for the reader to pick up on, what Brigid begins to see, the similarities between the condition of these patients and Brigid herself. The 'seething rage and frustration', akin to Brigid's own inner torment, has made ghostly presences of them. They are more spectral than flesh and blood. Moreover, as occasionally in Father Mann's case, the secrets within them find expression in violence. Indeed, this is the aspect that dominates Brigid's initial impression of them:

> The man in the first bed was bloated with medicine and glared at us over his fat cheeks. Next to him was a man who talked to himself and made signs of the cross in the air. He cursed and blasphemed and give us the fingers. Another one came right across to us and eyed us up and down like he'd never seen a woman before.   (105)

Thus, the patients are grotesques because of what they repress and because of what society projects on to them. The part that the nurses play in keeping these people hidden from society contributes to turning them into 'grotesques'. Staff respond with violence to any trace of dissent, as in the case of the two male nurses and in the Sister's threats to Brigid's father. But they, too, are indications of how society develops an 'alien being' by marginalizing or denying the mentally ill. When we come to the encounter between the Keen sisters and their father, we see the father as the grotesque they have created – they stare at the back of his head for a long time, fearful to walk around and see his face.

The twist in the narrative is that Brigid's father has an unexpectedly disturbing impact upon her. The ghost in her life turns out to be within her own self. He reinforces the truth about herself to which Aunt Grace first introduced her: that she has allowed herself to become Father Mann's prisoner. 'But you're as bad. You let them do it to you. You choose a civilised kind of battering. But that's all it is' (110). The ghosts, like Aunt Grace, who mysteriously drops into her life and then just as suddenly disappears, assist Brigid by telling her what she already knew but did not want to face. The Sister, who unlocks barred gates, is analogous of the gatekeeper within Brigid's own psyche; protecting her encrypted, alien self. But at this point in the narrative 'projection' and 'introjection' are blurred. Brigid has not simply projected her secret anxieties on to her father, she has internalized them so that he comes from within: 'When I looked in the mirror, I seen his face staring back at me. My face was just like his and this scared the living daylights out of me' (110). Without the rigorous enforcements of her psychic gatekeeper, the boundary between self and other becomes as permeable as that between past, present and future.

Following the visit to her father, Brigid sees Mrs Boyle, 'the oddest old woman', when she lights her candle in the church. The one key detail about her is that she 'wore clothes you'd never see nobody else wearing' (112). It suggests, if we recall what Aunt Grace said about her niece, that Brigid sees herself as an old woman. A ghost from the future, Old Mrs Boyle makes Brigid aware of time: 'The wax old Mrs Boyle had dropped on my hand was hardening' (112). Brigid reaches the period in her life when the future in which she is an old woman or dead haunts the present.

By the time she enters Knockmaroon, Brigid has come to think of ghosts as something menacing and frightening:

> The place was that empty and eerie late at night it would scare the devil out of you between strange creaks and noises and shadows coming out of nowhere at me. I kept expecting a murderer to land in any minute. And I was feared stiff of ghosts into the bargain. Inside was full of dark corners and crannies for them to hide in, not to mention the dark barns and storehouses was outside. Every room I went into and every corner I turned round, I expected to run into some of the people lived and died in the house before father and me come.   (175)

Her confession that she was 'feared stiff of ghosts' is odd, given her earlier admission:

> I fell in love with the house – Knockmaroon, it was called – for it reeked of the past. I used to imagine the people that lived there before me and I'd see them coming and going around the

place, in old clothes, like they still lived there. I sucked the excitement out of the walls of that place the way you'd suck the flavour out of honeysuckle. (143)

Throughout the novel, we are encouraged to think of houses and their pasts in terms of families and their secrets, and of rooms as metaphors for minds: Brigid has to realize the significance of her admission: 'I kept my room, like I kept my life, bare and spare for I never could stand clutter' (142). The first Knockmaroon passage above transforms the meaning of ghosts as it metaphorizes the physical being of the place. The 'strange creaks and noises and shadows coming out of nowhere' refer not so much to the house as to the workings of Brigid's own psyche. The passage suggests that perhaps the ghosts that haunt us are not the dead. But that the 'strange creaks and noises and shadows' have instead to do with our physical or mental impairment. Old Mrs Boyle becomes a physical grotesque in Brigid's eyes: 'Her face was covered in black wrinkles and she had long hairs growing out of her chin' (112). In other words, she is a product of the projection of Brigid's fears and anxieties.

In each of these novels, the in-between space is really a space 'beyond' that becomes, as I suggested earlier, a space of intervention in the here and now. Elleke Boehmer's argument that women's writing can interrupt 'the language of official nationalist discourse and literature with a woman's vocality' begs a number of questions about that vocality – not least the extent to which it is part of an in-between space and emerges from margins that have been shrouded in secrecy – with which Johnston, Donoghue and Ferguson are concerned. However, it is not only that these writers create protagonists who 'remap the nationalist geographies and histories' but also that they operate, as Boehmer says of postcolonial women writers more generally, through 'the displacement of what is already signified'.

6

Fetishizing Absence

Dermot Bolger's *Father's Music* (1997) and
Emily's Shoes (1992)

Father's Music and *Emily's Shoes* deal with themes that have not
been the subject of serious fiction in Ireland and Northern Ireland
previously: self-harm and shoe fetishism. They are concerned
with activities which are linked in different ways to maintaining
a kind of emotional control and which are shrouded with secrecy.
Each of these novels also explores the subject of absence, and,
what might be called, the fetishization of absence.

Language as a system of signs is the basis of European
Sausserean linguistics to which I referred in the previous
chapter. Gayatri Spivak, in the introduction to Derrida's text
(1976) which I mentioned in that context, draws attention to 'the
strange "being" of the sign: half of it always "not there" and the
other half always "not that". The structure of the sign is determined by the trace or track of that other which is forever absent'
(xvii). Her thesis that language is determined by 'the trace or
track of that which is forever absent' is an especially pertinent
framework within which to discuss Bolger's fiction. Towards the
end of *Emily's Shoes*, Michael, besieged by pilgrims who want to
see the Virgin Mary in his doorjamb, thinks of himself as a
'haunted man' (225). Bolger's novels are invariably based on men
and women haunted by absence, and they encapsulate Bolger's
larger concern with the in-between position of being 'not there'
and 'not that' – with the trace itself.

Bolger's novels are invariably concerned with timelags or periods of 'suspended time'. In *The Valparaiso Voyage* (2002), Brendan
Brogan takes the opportunity of his involvement in an accident to
place himself outside of time by faking his own death in order to

126

disappear. However, he remains haunted by his childhood. In *Temptation* (2000), every year, a middle-aged woman, Alison Gill, goes for a five-day break with her family to a hotel in Wexford. Ostensibly, that short holiday provides her with an opportunity to place herself outside of the preoccupations with aging and the changes in her body that otherwise haunt her. But what really enables her to do so is an affair that she has when her husband is suddenly recalled to Dublin. It provides her with 'a second life'.

The concept of a second life is explicitly explored, of course, in the earlier novel with that title. Following a near death experience, photographer Sean Blake comes to think of himself as a spectre – in the words of the nurses who care for him, one of 'The Walking Dead'. This makes him realize the extent to which he has always been a ghost in his own life: 'In the spare room I was both part of the house and yet outside it. Often during the day I might have been a ghost at the window, listening to the sounds of life below me' (33). He is a ghost at the window in several senses quite apart from him thinking of himself as having died once. First, the near death experience gives Sean a different sense of time, in which the present is 'just one random fragment of a progression stretching backwards and forwards' (35). In this 'progression' what appears to be solid, including houses and one's sense of self, becomes ghost-like:

> If I could only see it, the hallway would be one continuous blur of movement. Children in black boots stomping across patterned lino; a toddler proudly shuffling out in his father's shoes; a woman cooking a pig's head, passing right through me to open the back door at the sound of a bicycle in the lane; a girl allowing herself to be pressed back against the door and kissed, her skirted legs opening and closing around a boy's spread hand.   (35–6)

Second, he is haunted by a double absence in his life: his mother who gave birth to him in a rural convent and his father who deserted her.

Like Tracey in *Father's Music*, the novel to which I shall turn in a moment, Sean is structured by the absences in his life. The text focuses on how he has 'changed, no longer able to focus on the world we had built up, cursed and haunted by gaps in [his] life' (54). But, in fact, he has always been haunted by these absences.

As in Tracey's case, his mother erupts into his consciousness. Here, Sean's biological mother is linked with a childhood fear that she might appear and take him from his adoptive parents and with an adult fear that, if he found her, she would reject him again. These fears create a secret, encrypted self within him that is projected on to a phantasm of his mother as 'a callous invisible woman in my subconscious' (55) and turn the Botanic Gardens he is not allowed to visit into an imago. Photographing these Gardens and ensuring his parents see the developed film becomes a 'declaration of [his] difference' from them (58).

The novel interleaves the revelation of Sean's sense of difference with disclosures about his mother in a third-person narrative. For her part, she is haunted by memories of her first child:

> And, though she tried to stop the thought coming, where was her own? Padraig, Paudi. A boy with the bluest eyes, a boy who had cried while she struggled to teach him to suck at her breast. (23)

Like Sean, but for different reasons, she is a ghost in her own life. Like her son, she has no past – when she married no relatives of her side of the family were present – and she has been given another name, Elizabeth. Elizabeth is haunted by the ghost name 'Lizzy'; as Sean, too, has a ghost name Padraig. In fact, she is a ghost in her husband Jack's life for he loves not so much her as 'what he thought of as her' (22). She loves him because he did not desert her, which makes him a phantasm conjured by her experience of Sean's father. A further analogy between mother and son is that Sean's placement of his own life among the ghosts who have inhabited their house corresponds to the ghosts at the convent amongst whom Elizabeth places herself:

> Where were those girls now? she asked herself. The girls who had worked with her in the convent kitchens in Sligo, the girls who scrubbed the floors in the laundry, the bloated girls who had stopped work only when the labour pains came? Where were the other girls who were sent by the nuns to work for their board in rich homes in Dublin and Cork? (23)

Elizabeth's secrets make her a stranger to her husband and to her children, especially Sharon. While Aunt Ellen provides Sharon with a family background, Elizabeth's disappearances remind her that part of her mother will always be absent from her. Moreover, her father, too, has secrets which make him a stranger not only to Elizabeth but his children, as Sharon, his eldest daughter, discovers when, on clearing out his tool shed, she finds a secret horde of adult magazines devoted to spanking:

> Something told her that she should stop, should put his ashes in that shed and the padlock back on and then set it alight, like Aunt Ellen had told her Irish tinkers did when someone died. She opened a plastic refuse sack and began to clear the old tins of congealed paint from the higher shelves, lifting down the newspapers, biting her lip but not crying as she handled the mildewed copies of *Janus, Blushes* and *Spanking Letters*.   (25)

But, as in *Emily's Shoes*, the narrative turns on moments when a sense that there is something else becomes something which cannot be imagined. It occurs quite early in the chronology of Sean's narrative when his wife, Geraldine, becomes concerned at his fits and later in Lizzy's narrative when her daughter discovers her 'palms pressed against the [kitchen] window' seeming 'like a moth trapped there on the glass'. Then she realizes that 'inside meant nothing to her mother. The garden had been her real home, as the shed had been her father's' (145). The neglected garden, like her husband's shed, becomes an emblem of the secret life that will return to haunt their children as what they withheld haunted them. The most obvious example of a person haunted by an 'encrypted' being within is Lizzy's brother, Tom, who chooses the Church rather than marriage to disguise his homosexuality. It is a secret he cannot confide even to his sister when she confesses to him that she is pregnant. But the secret that creates a bizarre being within him is his betrayal of his sister; that he let her be taken from the house while he hid in his room.

Many of these tropes – the trace itself, the reconfiguring of the past and the present, the void created within by repressed secret selves, the projection of phantasms on to others and the mother's haunting presence – are important to *Father's Music* and *Emily's Shoes*. The name of the central character in *Father's Music*, Tracey Evans, is clearly significant. She acts as a conduit for the various meanings of the word 'ghost': a trace or semblance of something; a displaced image or a false spectral line caused by imperfect diffraction; and a returning or haunting memory or image.

The Unadjusted Subject

Father's Music is one of the most haunted texts of the 1990s. In her promiscuity and self-centredness, the wayward protagonist Tracey Evans reflects the way independent, sexually assertive females were perceived in America and Britain between the wars as 'unadjusted'. The term 'unadjusted girl' was coined by the Chicago criminologist W. I. Thomas in 1923 and gave rise to a configuration of the independent, sexually assertive woman that dominated the media for a generation and which some believe has never been fully challenged. From a Marxist–Foucauldian perspective, the unadjusted female challenges the subjection or submissive state of mind required for an individual to contribute to the larger interest of capitalism. This is evident in the way Tracey delights in turning the tables on those, especially middle-class men, who try to make use of her:

> I'd enjoy their predicament in trying to manoeuvre me from their beds in time to make a dash for work. Sometimes, with the more nervous types, I'd sleepily turn over, letting them stew with visions of a ransacked flat on their return and mes-sages scrawled in lipstick for neighbours to read.   (13)

But Tracey is more than a radical female. Her promiscuity rep-resents one extreme of what psychoanalysts might think of as 'boundary problems'. Her transitory affairs with men suggest not only loose but unpredictable boundaries. This type of behaviour has been identified as a characteristic of what has been called Traumatic Re-enactment Syndrome (TRS) where people re-enact some form of physical, mental and/or emotional abuse from childhood. According to psychoanalytic theory, as Dusty Miller argues, individuals who cut and/or abuse themselves 'may have a strong wish to feel sexually ruthless and dominant' (1994: 136). Certainly Tracey's sexual relationships, especially the sex she has with Luke that opens the novel, appear to be a form of 'acting out'. As Miller says of TRS women, 'she may feel a sense of mastery or even revenge in choosing to be sexual with partners she does not really know or like, or in flaunting a provocative, flamboyant sexual lifestyle' (136). Although Miller's study of self-harm focuses upon women, and the sufferer in Bolger's novel is female, it is important to recognize that self-harm is a phenomenon that involves many men, especially young men, as well as women in Ireland.

In plot terms, Tracey is haunted by memories of her dead mother, and her mother's brief relationship with an Irish fiddler much older than herself, Frank Sweeney, who was to become her father. One of the consequences of this is that her sense of self becomes a false spectral image, and her family history an imperfect diffraction resulting, we are initially led to believe, from her sense of how her father abused her mother emotionally and physically in their brief relationship. As a child, her body becomes the object of self-loathing and, simultaneously, a site where self-inflicted abuse becomes a means of resisting what has happened to her:

> Then, just as suddenly, it hurts less, as if an amphetamine was unleashed into my blood stream. The sensation is of giddy exhilaration. If my body is theirs to move about, then these scars are my graffiti, scrawled on it. It is no longer myself I'm hurting, but their possession. Without warning, the elixir fades and the brief, startling high is gone. Only a throbbing pain is left, another bewildering layer of guilt, and a fear of discovery which makes me dress next morning with the door locked. (65)

Tracey's case appears similar to women 'whose rage, pain, and shame lead them to hurt themselves, re-enact the trauma inflicted on them in childhood through a pattern of behaviours, a set of personality styles, and a number of predictable and distressing problems in living' (Miller, 26). For Tracey the pattern of behaviours include her promiscuity, her affairs with older men and her excessively independent and assertive personality. But it also includes the way in which pain and the infliction of pain and humiliation enter her sexual relations. Her relationships accord with the key characteristics that Miller identifies with TRS: '(1) the sense of being at war with one's own body; (2) excessive secrecy as a central organizing principle of life; (3) inability to self-protect, often evident in a specific kind of fragmentation of the self; and (4) relationships in which the struggle for control overshadows all else' (26–7). The novel turns on one of the central paradoxes associated with TRS: while Tracey like the stereotypical TRS sufferer appears to be out of control, in fact, she is living the illusion that she is in control. Whether she is cutting herself or purging her body in excessive, promiscuous sex, Tracey reflects the reasons why women suffering from TRS cut themselves:

> Self-destructive behaviour often provides a sense of relief. It can provide escape from feelings of rage or grief. It can relieve the self-injuror from the sensation of numbness. It can reduce feelings of anxiety.   (Miller, 27)

Father's Music is one of the few serious works of fiction to engage with TRS. In including this dimension in the novel, Bolger makes an important contribution to exploring in fiction subjectivity where the sense of self has been shaped by abuse and/or neglect. In aesthetic terms, it is Tracey's experiences that determine the rhythm of the novel. It follows the TRS sufferer's pattern of 'eliciting help and then rejecting it, asking for closeness and then destroying the longed-for relationship' (Miller, 126).

The novel is a quest narrative – Tracey's search for her father – that draws on the flight story and the thriller while the physical quest is analogous of a deeper, psychological journey undertaken by the central protagonist. In other words, the quest novel is reinvented through the lens of a TRS sufferer. Miller (1994) argues: 'The TRS woman faces a complex and difficult set of relationships with her family of origin. Each relationship has some unfinished business, some shadow of an internalised dynamic' (142). The 'shadows' in Tracey's case include her mother, her grandmother, her father and her grandfather.

A Mother's Pain

Although the novel is called *Father's Music*, it is, as Tracey herself says, as much about her 'mother's pain' (17). The ostensible confusion as to whether Tracey's quest is for her father or mother again anchors the novel in Tracey's TRS experience, for such sufferers, even if they are able to understand that they carry representations of their parents within themselves, may have difficulty in separating the two parents (Miller, 144). The way Tracey comes to view her family – 'Our problems just festered and broke out as hidden wounds' (240) – becomes an analogy of how her mother's pain breaks into her consciousness. Her love making with the older Luke Duggan, from a notorious Dublin criminal family, is haunted by the thoughts of her mother having sex with her father:

> Luke pulls my legs higher, positions a pillow under my tensed
> back. I don't want to ever open my eyes. The music is so loud
> and quick it seems sweet torture. It courses through me. I can
> see his old face playing, that capped man with nicotined teeth
> and tufts of greying hairs in his nostrils.   (3)

There are numerous points in the narrative when her mother's
presence erupts into her consciousness. The model of the unconscious in this text is closer to that of psychoanalysts like Melanie
Klein rather than the Freudian concept of repressed trauma that
needs to be unearthed and come to terms with. The Kleinian
model sees traumatic memories are ever present in proximity to
stored non-traumatic recollections. A memory or sensation situated in close proximity to the traumatic memory can often stimu-
late or trigger it. Hence, Tracey is haunted by the trace of her
mother. Other European feminist psychoanalysts such as Julia
Kristeva have argued that we all mourn our mothers from the
time when we are separated at birth by the breaking of the umbil-
ical cord. In that sense, we are all estranged, initially from our
mothers and ultimately from ourselves, because we all carry an
unfulfilled sense of having lost our mothers. But in Tracey's case,
this sense of estrangement is exaggerated: 'I should be over her
death by now, but too much guilt seemed involved to properly
mourn her' (17). The grieving family at Christy's funeral stimu-
lates Tracey's repressed desire and the need to mourn her mother.

However, what the text is primarily concerned with is the extent
to which Tracey chooses to be haunted by thoughts of her mother,
and particularly her mother's sexual relationship with her father.
Admittedly surfacing memories of her mother take her by surprise:

> The image kept recurring, even in school, a stumpy unwashed
> penis jutting in and out as the rubber snaps and gathers at the
> base among ancient curls. Still they rut on, oblivious to my fate
> passing between them, a fugitive seed meant to be flung into a
> ditch, a tadpole struggling up stream to blight that white-
> bellied Englishwoman's life.   (62)

This pattern again is not untypical of the TRS sufferer. The way
'memories' of her mother and father having sex intrude into her

sex with Luke is redolent of how for TRS sufferers' 'sexual pleasure is interrupted either by memories of the abuse or by flashbacks' (Miller, 1994: 134). But what Bolger does is to explore the boundaries between 'inherited' and 'direct' memory and between 'recollection' and 'recreation'. Her 'memories' and imagined ideas about her Father having sex with her mother would appear to make Tracey think that she should hate sex. Her sex with Luke borders on self-inflicted pain. It is dangerous sex and she knows it: 'How crazy was he and what danger had I placed myself in?' (32). Is she, one might legitimately ask, trying to master the trauma of her relationship with her father by reliving pain over and over again? On leaving Luke after having had sex with him at the outset of the novel, Tracey, thinking of her father and probably her abduction as a child, admits: 'Luke wasn't the first Irishman to touch me. I had fooled myself into thinking I could banish such memories' (32). Another emotion apart from enjoyment, fear and vulnerability that she experiences at these times is shame.

On many occasions, Tracey's recollections of her mother seem to have been deliberately invoked and embroidered. Even the image of her mother's face in the passage quoted earlier is as much a construction as a recollection, highlighting one source of Tracey's low self-esteem and self-loathing. Her sense of herself as 'a fugitive seed' determines the course that her sex life takes; she becomes both the 'other woman' and the partner of a criminal, ending up literally on the run at one point. Having thought of herself as a fugitive child, she uses the concept to punish herself just as in her love making with Luke he becomes the agency of her punishment. She allows him to use and abuse her body in ways that his wife would not permit. It is no coincidence that she enters into an affair with a man who, like her own father in relation to her mother, is old enough to be her father. Her feelings towards her father are a confusion of love and hate, desire and attraction. Deserted by him, Tracey configures her father through Luke as the abusive father of fairy tale. The absent good father, the ghost that haunts his brilliance as a fiddle player, is projected on to her granddad Pete.

In the account of her mother and her grandparents there are hints of secrets that have been kept across a generation. While psychoanalytic theorists such as Kristeva have suggested that our estrangement from our mothers come back to haunt us, Bolger suggests that it is not so much this as haunts us, or even in

Freudian terms primal scenes of trauma from our infancy, but secrets that those we love have withheld from us. The psychoanalytic theorist Nicholas Abraham argues that all human subjects are haunted by 'the gaps left within us by the secrets of others' (1994: 171). Tracey admits: 'I was afraid to ask about secrets they kept from me, and ashamed, in turn, to tell them the secrets which I had buried inside me' (63). Secrets withheld from her grandparents, unknown to Tracey, eventually drive a wedge between herself and her grandfather:

> The very time a family needs comfort. You stole her ashes. You knew how much that would hurt and you were hurting people who loved you. But that's all you've done for years, wrapped up in your private world. There's no pain like Tracey's pain. (254)

That Tracey has been wrapped up in her own secret world is more a cause of the rift between them than the stealing of the ashes. Of course, in keeping her secrets Tracey is able, like most TRS sufferers, to keep an 'impenetrable boundary between herself and everyone else' (Miller, 29). The relationship between Luke and Tracey is typical of that involving a woman suffering from TRS. For Tracey's self-harmful behaviours haunt them: 'No matter how many ways she asks others for contact, she is always ambivalent and is simultaneously finding ways to distance herself from the very people she cries out to' (Miller, 1994: 45). At the end of the sex scene that opens the novel, Tracey is angry with herself: 'I had broken every rule I ever taught myself for protection against this self-destructive urge. I simply wanted to get safely out of that door' (33).

By linking secrecy with TRS, Bolger breathes new life into what is a familiar trope in Irish fiction. In creating a TRS character who suffers from self-abuse, Bolger enters into a type of TRS personality where secrecy is perhaps most prevalent, not least because self-mutilation as a form of self-abusive behaviour is unacceptable to everyone else in that person's life, as is evident from Tracey's mother and grandmother's reaction to her. But the most significant void inside Tracey is that created by the family's denial of her father: 'I told friends ... that all my mother remembered was that he was strong, white and French' (63). According to Abraham, such a void creates 'a bizarre foreign body' within us which can lead to violence (1994: 175). This alien within is projected, in Tracy's case, into the phantasm of the bad father, who is introjected to become part of her body: 'Callous, ignorant and selfish, he had been a man who would sooner play music then wash himself. A man who walked away at the first hint of responsibility, leaving his tainted blood coursing through my veins' (63). The violence she inflicts on herself is a projection of her hatred of him. How she feels becomes one of many secrets that she keeps from her mother and her grandmother, turning her in her grandmother's eyes into a foreign body within herself: 'Outside of home there was no public rebellion I couldn't shame her with, but once inside the front door I was shrunk into being a child again as Gran railed against me wanting to rip my jeans or have my hair cropped' (63).

While her grandmother implicitly interprets the situation in terms of the dual conflict between a 'good' and 'bad' self, Tracey, like most TRS sufferers, thinks in terms of a Triadic Self. The three aspects of the Triadic Self, according to Miller, are the victim, the abuser and the non-protecting bystander. At one level, the victim, the wounded child within, in Tracey's case is the child who feels her father has abused her and whom her mother seemed to desert in dying. In Tracey's case the internalized abuser is her father who deserted her and father who abused her grandmother. But her mother, again a trace of her great grandmother, is also the non-protecting bystander.

In the first part of the novel, Tracey thinks of herself as 'a pawn' between her mother and her grandmother. Not only Tracey's father but also her mother becomes a grotesque to her. In Dublin with Luke, she finds herself haunted by, or deliberately choosing to haunt herself by, the walks she and her deserted mother took together when she was a child. While the reader comes to see Tracey's mother from her point of view as 'pathetic and deranged', there are hints of further secrets in her parents and grandparent's lives which find expression in, for example, the cigarette butts 'crumpled like spent cartridges in her [mother's] bedside ashtray' (63). The novel is really about Tracey's discovery of their secrets. The major secret that has passed from one generation to another has turned Tracey's grandmother, in her eyes, into an alien being, which doesn't seem ever to have been young.

In Dublin, another ghost, a spectral projection of her mother's, displaces Frank Sweeney, as a grotesque phantasm: 'Yet even at his age he had strong arms that could swing her through the air, my mother told me. He could spin a story for a full hour and never lose one person's attention' (108). The difference between this and Tracey's images of Frank Sweeney make both suspect. In particular, the text encourages the reader to ask, what is Tracey's mother's phantasm of her husband a reaction against? The big family secret, of course, is that Tracey's mother was the offspring of child abuse between her great grandfather and her grandmother. It is this secret which Tracey comes to believe turned her grandmother into a stranger to the family. At the same time, it turns her daughter into a phantasm: 'But I think that every time your Gran looked at her ... well, you'd see him come out in little things, the shape of your mother's nose and the way she smiled sometimes' (293).

Obsession

In *The Maid's Tale*, Mary Healy sticks 'like glue to people for fear they'd go away and leave her' (3). This secret insecurity turns Mary into an emotional grotesque. Her physical appearance – 'thin skin the colour of rice-paper, and freckles just like a wee fella, and pooky hair' (3) – is analogous of the foreign body created within by the death of her father. In *Emily's Shoes* (1992), Bolger writes a narrative, structured around deaths, sexual experiences and pairs of shoes, of a man from childhood to early middle age who suffers from a similar kind of insecurity as Ferguson's Mary. The extent to which the secret fear of being abandoned haunts him is evident when he finally confesses to the young woman who, stereotypically, rescues him from himself: 'I'm scared that you'll vanish' (260) and 'I need you so much I'm frightened my need will scare you away' (264). The death of his father at sea, and of his mother later in his childhood, leaves him with an inner void and fears that he keeps as secrets within.

Fetishism is a, usually, secret fixation on an object that is not in itself sexual in nature but which is compulsively needed in order for the individual to obtain gratification. Thus, Tracey's fixation on the absent father when she is making love turns this absence into a secret, compulsive need without which she cannot obtain the sexual gratification she desires from Luke. Quite evidently, the significance of her father, and his absence, goes back to her childhood. It is generally assumed that fetishism has its origins in a person's childhood and this is certainly the case with Bolger's

shoe fetishist. Aunt Emily fills the gap in a surrogate Oedipal relationship. But his confused and desperate needs are projected on
to her lipstick red, high-heeled shoes. At one level, they reassure
him: 'The months of waking in the mornings [after his mother's
death] afraid that I would be taken away, of waking at night to
remember the red sheen of Emily's shoes on the stairs like an icon
to cling on to' (66). But they become entangled with his confused,
adolescent sexuality, leading to a secret shoe fetish that dominates
the rest of his life. Within, for the most part, an outwardly conventional librarian, the fetishist is a foreign being that he tries, frequently and unsuccessfully, to expel.

This inner, obsessed self acts as a gatekeeper, directing and
determining his emotional and sexual being. This is evident from
his adolescent fantasies, such as the one involving the cyclist
fallen from her bike:

> She tries to shy away as I kneel beside her in the grass but I
> catch a hold of her bare leg. She is at my mercy as I slowly prise
> her shoe off. Nothing else occurs between us but I can still
> almost feel her hot swollen shin, the smoothness of her ankle,
> her slight gasp of pain or release as the shoe is slipped
> off.   (61)

There are traces here of generic male fantasy; Michael is in control, and the female is helpless, submissive and dependent upon
him. Such a scene as an occasion for physical intimacy is the very
stuff of male sexual fantasy as the phrase 'nothing else occurs
between us' suggests. But whereas the stereotypical male fantasy
might entertain the prospect of intercourse or surreptitiously eye-
ing parts of the body more usually associated with sex, Michael's
focus is on the cyclist's shoes. The pattern here is the familiar one
in his life; he desires both shoes as objects, new or second hand,
and shoes in relation to the feet and ankles of the wearer.

Even though Emily marries quickly, thereafter only communi-
cating on Michael's birthdays, she becomes more his real aunt
than Aunt Maire, haunting the rest of his life. Michael eventually
admits to the reader that 'part of me has always been alone in
Emily's house and has dreamt of nothing except her shoes' (181).
This is both a general observation and a reference to a specific
behaviour that haunts him – walking around the house in his
aunt's footwear. Told that it is for the better if he no longer visits

the hospitalized Maggie, Michael lies in his room: 'But it was safe there, sweating beneath the eiderdown, feeling the clasp of those shoes on my feet. Nothing could change in that room as long as I lay there. I could remain the age I always was, alone in Emily's house wearing nothing except Emily's shoes' (166). Here the language not only conjures up specific behaviours from his past but is haunted, in the reference to the sweating and the 'clasp' of the shoes, by details from earlier in the text to which I will return later.

Even as an adolescent, having introjected the image of Emily's shoes, Michael projects the phantasm on to women he sees on the street – 'I couldn't look up, I just followed the crisp clip of her polished shoes until they were lost among the grey worn feet of the shoppers' (72) – and on to women he hears about in other people's conversations: 'I could see the girl in my mind, blonde hair and white skin, blushing as she did undid the final button on her blouse, her bare legs stretching down to my aunt's black high heels' (72). The distinction between real and imagined becomes blurred; like Emily, each becomes a phantasm, or ghost, within his psyche. But it is not so much they, as their shoes. Their being, and their sexuality, is defined only in relation to the shoes they wear. When he makes love to Maggie, having met her again in Clonsilla, he asks her to keep on her shoes. They assume a spectral presence that diverts Michael's attention from her body:

> Below Maggie's raised buttocks I could see the scuffed soles of her shoes. They faced towards me, nakedly exposed … They seemed to offer me her life story, saying this is who I really am, neither ashamed nor proud. I felt such tenderness as I entered her flesh, felt that we would never be more naked to each other than with her shoes between us, that we could never surrender such perfect trust. (130)

A phrase, 'nakedly exposed', that we might have expected to be applied to Maggie's body is transferred to the soles of her shoes. This underscores how although Michael is physically entering her flesh, imaginatively he is entering her shoes. What this does is to depersonalize and objectify the whole process of his lovemaking. But, of course, it is further complicated because the ghost that haunts him as he dwells on Maggie's shoes is the sensual experience of wearing his aunt's shoes years before:

> I put the shoes on the floor and closed my eyes. I was naked, I
> was Cinderella. Each slender shoe fitted my white feet. I stood
> tall in them, I tried to walk and found my body twisting into
> new shapes as I learnt how to balance. The crisp click of a heel
> on the stairs, each step amplified through the empty rooms.
> And the way I forgot everything except the feel of leather, the
> way it gripped my instep, supported me, made me strong and
> secure.   (60–1)

In this boyhood experience, the shoe is a vulvac image and his
foot a substitute for the penis. But the emphasis is upon safety
and security. There is also a strong sense of the fluidity of his corporeal identity as he tries on different pairs of shoes. His sexual
maturity results not in a rejection of this fetishism but a more conscious and in-depth understanding of it:

> [Maggie] kicked her black shoes off on to the floor. I bent down
> and picked one up. It felt warm inside and slightly moist. I had
> read somewhere that when the foot sweats it releases secretions
> like those from the sexual organs. Her scent excited me. She
> watched me curiously as I ran my fingers over the shoe.   (128)

The feminine other that defines his masculinity is something
he wants to experience for himself. But what comes to dominate
his experience is not only the confusion of masculine self and
female other but the fear that he might be revealed, expressed for
example in his dream about appearing in the library wearing
women's shoes. The 'encrypted', secret self within Michael
reveals itself in his cryptic behaviour such as asking Maggie to
keep her shoes on while they make love. It is this behaviour that
appears weird or uncanny to his partners. Watching him finger
her shoes, Maggie is forced to ask whether he is holding something back, prompting him to confide in someone for the first
time about his shoe fetish. It is the reactions of intimate others to
him that defines him as uncanny. Through Michael's relationship
with Maggie, Bolger begins to explore the theme that acquires
pride of place in *Father's Music*: the extent to which withheld
secrets create a foreign body, turning somebody one thinks one
knows into a stranger. When Maggie eventually confesses to
Michael that she had a breakdown in Canada, what is not yet

revealed begins to define her: 'Canada was mentioned more and more like a jigsaw that I had to make sense of. Although I understood that she had had a nervous breakdown, there was something else, something that I could only guess at' (137).

A significant distinction between Michael's initial meeting with Clare and his reunion with Maggie is that Clare is more overtly the object of Michel's fetishism. While she looks to one trace on his doorjamb, he manipulates her into removing her shoes, fixated by a different set of traces:

> The leather was cool but inside I could sense the warmth of her skin. The figure 7 was barely distinguishable in gold ink. The priest tried to lean forward, peering towards the knot of wood as the girl approached. She gave a sharp intake of breath and knelt down, leaning forward on her knees so I could see the outline of her panties through the white cloth. Her bare feet were twisted sensually and almost painfully by the way in which she knelt. I held her shoes tight against my chest, suddenly feeling almost as faint and breathless as herself. (215)

When Clare eventually enquires 'Are you planning to keep me here as your bare-foot prisoner?' (217), it is clear that she realizes that there is 'something else'. What she can only guess at is revealed much later. When he eventually confesses his secret to her, her response is less incredulous than Maggie's and less humiliating for him than the child's in his dream set in the library. In this respect, the novel, like *A Second Life*, involves the cliché of a man's soul being saved by an understanding woman. The conclusion of the novel replays to some extent the cyclist fantasy but goes beyond it. Removing Clare's shoes he throws them down the cliff face before doing the same with his own. Their soles/souls are free at last.

The commodification of the body is conflated in modern fiction, as in advertising from the nineteenth century onwards, with the cut or 'cropped' fragmented figure. Late twentieth-century fiction, such as Dermot Bolger's *Emily's Shoes*, has more explicitly explored the fetishization of the cropped figure. Shoe fetishism that is the subject of Bolger's novel is especially associated with the cropping of the body in so far as it encourages the voyeur to see, usually the female, body fragmentarily. As Valerie Steele (1996) points out, high-heeled shoes, one of the most commonly fetishized forms of female footwear, affects the wearer's gait and posture: 'By putting the lower part of the body in a state of tension, the movement of the hips and buttocks is emphasised and the back is arched, thrusting the bosom forward' (111). The subject thus becomes hips, buttocks, back and bosoms. The novel, divided into three parts, is structured around deaths, shoes and sexual experiences as the narrator moves from childhood to the oncoming of middle age. But the exploration of the sexual satisfaction from part-images anchors a larger concern with the cut, fetishized and transitory nature of modern pleasure and of the wider experience of the postmodern.

Bolger's novel can be seen in the wider context of postmodern art, especially the work of artists such as Louise Bourgeois and Cindy Sherman, where the body, rendered as 'the body-in-pieces', undermines notions of a unified and unambiguously gendered subject. Bolger's novel stresses corporeal and psychological fragmentation. As Michael observes, recollecting his childhood and adolescence: 'When I see myself in those years I see myself alone, a succession of solitary images of different rooms and streets ... The boy in the rain outside the hospital, the naked boy in high heels in Emily's front room, the boy alone on the rail of the boat after leaving her house' (81). But he seeks always to overcome disintegrative effects of destabilizing childhood experiences – in this case the death of Michael's fisherman father at sea who is literally a lost soul – and reclaim his own true soul. In this respect, his fetishism, like self-harm, is a form of control.

Bolger's *Emily's Shoes* is written around a phantom. The lives of the narrator and Clare, who eventually saves him, are united at the lighthouse from which Clare's father watched his father drown; the two lives to be connected in the lives of their children in a way which is outside, beyond, their own lives:

> And Clare's father climbing down the ladder from the tower where the huge lamp swung, watching the ship until it was lost beyond the horizon. Two men face to face across the dark water, unable to see one another, not aware of each other's names. The lights of a passing ship, the flash of a revolving beacon. And here their offspring were, decades later, lost on the edge of the world. (262)

Through this coincidence, the narrative achieves a coherence and connectedness that it seems to struggle towards in its obsession with the fragmentary. One way of looking at fetishism is to see the fetish object as a kind of talisman that makes what is terrifying to the fetishist palatable. In this novel, the shoe fetishism enables Michael to survive fragmentation, to cope with a life haunted by the loss of his father.

Bolger's fiction may usefully be read through specific psycho-analytic studies such as Miller's exploration of self-harm. But, like many of the texts discussed in the previous chapters, they provide the basis for developing Jacques Derrida's ideas about what is secret and 'encrypted'. These texts argue a Derridean focus not so much upon what is hidden but the process of con-cealing. This provides Bolger with a useful perspective on self-harm and fetishism, envisaging both as a secret removed from the public face which the protagonists present but also, at a deep and concealed level of which the individual involved is not fully aware, affecting the wider sense of that person's being – as Derrida argues the 'topoi' (the grounds) is influenced by the crypt which is buried in them.

7

'Mater Dolorosa'

Abject Mothers in Roddy Doyle's *The Snapper* (1990) and Mary Morrissy's *Mother of Pearl* (1995)

Roddy Doyle's *The Snapper* (1990) is the second of three novels devoted to the fictitious Rabbitte family in Barrytown, Dublin. The others are *The Commitments* (1987) and *The Van* (1991). Characterized by their emphasis upon the present and the different voices of the working-class community of North Dublin, they shifted the agenda according to which Irishness was generally explored and discussed in the late 1980s and early 1990s. This was in itself an important development as the urban working class had often been marginalized in Ireland by de Valera's vision of a rural and agricultural nation state. Voices predominate in this trilogy; at one level, the texts appear to be more like play scripts than novels, eschewing the kind of authorial description and the kind of narrative exposition we normally associate with a novel. In particular, Ireland is presented as a country open to its own traditional influences but also absorbing influences from Great Britain and the United States, and, perhaps in its emphasis upon the latter, underestimating the impact of European influence on the Dublin economy. The traditional signifiers of identity in Ireland, including religion, are displaced by others with which young people in most parts of the developed western world can identify: music, sport, television, radio, film, and, to a lesser extent, literature. There is optimism in these novels, especially *The Commitments*, which is analogous of that of the buzzing metropolis itself. Although largely unemployed or obtaining money from the black economy, the youths in

The Commitments find a promise in music and in the idea of belonging to a band. The reality of their lives and the unlikelihood of 'making it' in the music business are not gainsaid. We never lose sight of the discrepancy between the dream and the reality exemplified in the incongruence between the sleek image the backing singers try to convey and the day-to-day crudeness of their lives; or in the possibility that their star musician Joey earned his nickname 'lips' not from his trumpet playing but the number of women he seduced. The dream image of Joey who is able to seduce Jimmy Jr with the list of famous names he has played with is undermined by the reality of an elderly man in carpet slippers who has to care for a sick mother. Nevertheless, at another level, it does not matter whether his stories are true or not. Like the barefaced cheek of the locals who come to the audition, it is the ability to take the risk and dream of something beyond one's disaffected present that is important. However, the Barrytown trilogy offers more of a critique of modernity than its ostensible celebration of the presentness of contemporary Ireland in *The Commitments* might suggest.

The Snapper is more tightly focused than the first novel, with fewer characters, and is a more overtly feminist text. Indeed, one of the best ways of approaching the novel is through the European psychoanalyst and cultural critic Julia Kristeva's observation about the way women have been traditionally marginalized in social and historical discourse:

> Women seem to feel that they are the causalities, that they have been left out of the sociosymbolic contract of language as the fundamental social bond ... [They] attempt to break the code, in the wake of contemporary art, to shatter language, to find a specific discourse closer to the body and emotions, to the unnameable repressed by the social contract. (Belsey and Moore, 1997: 206)

Doyle's book explores women's attempt to 'break the code' from the point of view of a young, urban, Irish, working-class woman whereas Kristeva appears to assume that female identity is only a matter of gender. At the heart of Doyle's novel is the relationship that develops, or at times fails to develop, between Sharon and her father.

Strangers at Modernity's Door

Early in *The Snapper*, Sharon's father, after she has disclosed her secret that she is pregnant, invites her to the pub for a drink only to discover that they have nothing really to talk about and are uncomfortable with each other in this context. Jimmy seems unable to cope with being so close to his daughter as an individual like himself, without the protective screens at home – her mother's presence, the rest of the family and his role as 'father'. It is significant that he enquires of Sharon about Jimmy Jr's sexuality. Uncomfortable with having to behave as a man in a different context than usual with his daughter, he displaces what is to be the beginning of his own revised masculinity by airing suspicions about his son's masculinity. This in itself raises a number of issues that are not fully explored in this novel, in particular how men relate to their heterosexuality, and the extent to which heterosexuality is often a mapping of the self which serves to normalize a particular pattern of power and sexual relationships. They are issues which Doyle takes further, though again without coming to any persuasive resolution, in *The Van* in the relationship between Jimmy and his best mate and the way he finds himself responding to stories of extramarital affairs, his own son's girlfriends and local young women:

> The sewing factory girls got a half day on Fridays. The first time Jimmy Sr'd looked at them on a Friday, from his bedroom window, he'd felt the blood rushing through his head, walloping off the sides, like he was watching a blue video and he was afraid that Veronica would come in and catch him. There was a gang of them – all of them seemed to be in denim mini-skirts – outside Sullivans... He'd looked at them for ages. He even dived back onto the bed when one of them was looking his way. He'd been afraid to go back and look out the window. But he did, and then they went, their heels making a great sound; he'd always loved that sound – he always woke up when he heard it. He'd felt like a right cunt then, gawking out the window; like a fuckin' pervert. (111)

Here Doyle tries to engage with the modernist distinction between 'culture' and 'nature', the way in which sexuality and gender have come to be seen by liberal intellectuals as primarily a product of the former. But in Jimmy's attempts to have extramarital sex himself, the novel also explores the extent to which male heterosexuality has traditionally been constructed around notions of conquest and performance as a way of proving itself to other men.

The scene in the pub between father and daughter encapsulates how *The Snapper* as a whole is positioned, in Bhabha's terms, between 'relocation' and 'reinscription'. Trying to engage in a dialogue with Sharon, Jimmy is forced to recognize how little he knows about their bodies and sexualities. He has always taken the body, like his masculinity, for granted. Father and daughter have emerged from the marginalized positions they occupy in each other's lives but neither is able to define exactly the new spaces which they occupy, although each is intent upon doing so. The novel is characterized by protagonists assuming a more centred position within their own lives and their immediate environment whether it be the family or the local community. The most intimate moment between Jimmy and his daughter occurs in her bedroom as she is on the point of leaving home. He recognizes that she is not just his daughter but also someone who, despite the levels of intimacy between them, will always be, in part, a stranger to him, as any child must be to their parents. Moreover, he recognizes, how this has created, and will create a void, within himself unless he acknowledges that we are all strangers to each other, and ultimately a stranger to ourselves:

> Sharon heard the stairs creaking. She threw a bundle of knickers onto the bed.
> Jimmy Sr knocked, and came in.
> ... Don't go, Sharon.
> – I have to.
> She stopped messing with the clothes.
> – Yeh don't have to. –
> Jimmy Sr looked across, out the window. His eyes were shiny. He kept blinking.
> He gulped, but the lump kept rising.
> – I'm cryin', Sharon, sorry. I didn't mean to.
> He pulled the sleeve of his jumper over his fist and wiped his eyes with it.
> – Sorry, Sharon.
> He looked at her. She looked as if she didn't know how she should look, what expression she should have on.   (161)

Here, there is an interesting inversion of Catholic theology where the Virgin Mary kneels before her son and asks forgiveness of the Father. The father, metaphorically, kneels before his daughter and asks her forgiveness.

Estrangement from oneself and from one's own family is a recurring theme in the contemporary Irish novel. George O'Brien maintains that there are several clearly discernible types of exile narrative in Irish literature including exile resulting from banishment because of conscience; geographical transition as 'the final phase in a series of much more challenging psychological disruptions', exile as analogous of the life of the artist; exile as a condition to be overcome. (2000: 35–55) What unites them is that exile brings about a new awareness, in other words 'exile discovers the protagonists' (2000: 51), and often modernizes their outlook.

Doyle's Barry town trilogy is one of a number of Irish texts that challenge whether the contemporary, geographical exile novel is really an exploration of marginalization, of which exile is only one manifestation. They also challenge the extent to which 'geographical exile' is viable as a category of experience distinct from other forms of exile; whether it is possible to be 'psychologically', even spatially exiled, in one's home territory or in one's family. The subject position it explores is one where there is no absolute sense of belonging in a culture or locality which has traditionally posited an absolute sense of belonging. While Irish literary criticism has stressed the importance to the Irish novel of exile, I want to suggest the importance of the elision of exile and estrangement in fiction where the discovery of the privacy of the self and personal morality is almost inevitability at odds with institutionalized (church, family, state) outlooks; political, class and regional affiliations; and normative sexual practices.

The most imaginative theorist to have linked exile and estrangement is Julia Kristeva. As I said in the previous chapter, Kristeva, following Lacan, maintains that to become a subject we have to separate from our first object, the mother. This is the primary separation that is necessary for us to achieve maturity and perceive of ourselves as separate from the world outside of us. But, according to Kristeva, it also continually haunts us and makes us forever estranged. For Kristeva, the infinite creative possibilities of language that we find in literature offer a kind of consolation for the loss, and absent presence, of the enfolding womb. Language provides us with an opportunity to incorporate the outside world from which we feel estranged into our language and psyche, extending, as it were, our psychic being.

New Men and New Women

The movement embraced by characters within *The Snapper*, which makes them strangers to themselves, each other and their former sense of self, is analogous of the socio-spatial movement represented by the novel as a whole, for the text gives a voice to the socially marginalized working class of North Dublin. The voice which it gives the young Dublin working class has led to it being associated with what came to be called for a while 'Northside dirty realism'. Apart from unhelpfully eliding the work of very different authors, the concept of a school of writing devoted to the dirty realism of Dublin, developed by Ferdia MacAnna and traceable to the 1960s, can underemphasize Doyle's preoccupation in the Barrytown trilogy with that liminal space of which Bhabha writes. Within this context, the geographical location of the book is highly significant, for the Dublin suburbs are themselves zones of contested meanings where 'relocation' and 'reinscription', the utopian and dystopian, come up against each other, sometimes violently. In writing about working-class suburbs, Doyle locates his text in a place that literally has no stability and sense of certainty. More importantly, from the point of view of Bhabha's thesis, it is not simply conventional authorities that are challenged but the frames of reference that define them. In this respect, there are two dominant consciousnesses within the book, neither of which are entirely identifiable with the author: the consciousness of the emergent, new male which is critical of the traditional masculinity which it displaces and is primarily but not exclusively identified with Jimmy; and the consciousness of the aggressively independent, young working-class woman who challenges traditional modes of abuse and humiliation to which she has been subject and is mainly focused upon Sharon.

Ostensibly, *The Snapper* appears to push the boundaries of Catholic respectability as far as one might imagine. Sharon, as a representative northern Dublin girl, is made pregnant, in a moment of drunken sex, by a married man who is old enough to be her father and is the father of one of her closest friends. This story line not only gives a voice to a young Irish, urban working-class woman but brings from the margins truths about the behaviour of so-called respectably married men and the issue of what today might be called 'date rape' which have been too often concealed. But more than this, it begins to engage with the way in which sexually aroused men are represented in a Cartesian duality between mind and body. George Burgess, once aroused by Sharon, is unable to do anything but surrender to his animal urges, accepting in a sense that his body is not fully involved in his definition of himself. This separates Burgess from Jimmy Sr who does, at least, seriously ponder the way in which men's relations to their own body and to women's bodies can be incorporated in a rational way of thinking about themselves. In other words, Jimmy can be thought of as giving a voice to his physicality as well as his masculinity.

The Snapper is an unusual novel, also, in presenting an intimate portrayal of the relationship between a father and his daughter. Independently minded and assertive, Sharon chooses to keep the child. The time scale of the novel is her pregnancy but the new life in the text is not in her womb but in her father who becomes, as a result of the interest he shows in his daughter's pregnancy, a new man, and apparently a better lover to his wife. By 'better' the text suggests better able to understand the other person's needs and not separating sexuality from care and intimacy. Initially, Jimmy is unable to cope with intimacy, using gifts and offerings – he hands out money or says nice things – as substitutes for the true expression of his feelings. The fact that Bertie hands out calculators to his friends in the pub, as if to express the fondness for them which he is unable to articulate in any other way, confirms the sense of a working-class culture in which men especially are not simply unable to express their feelings other than through their actions but are strangers to their own intimacy, emotionally and sexually. After shouting at his wife, Jimmy tries to make it up to her by sending one of the children to buy her a chocolate ice cream. The choice of a chocolate ice is an interesting one on a number of levels: it is a luxury treat, but in terms of its shape, the way it has to be eaten, the intermingling of light and dark, and the creamy milkiness of the eating experience it provides, it is also an obvious and provocative image of displaced sexuality. Food – from the way a 'fry up' lifts Jimmy's spirits to the appeasement and compensation signified by the portion of chips Jimmy frequently brings Veronica when he returns home late from the pub – functions as the key emotional currency in the family. What Sharon does is to prompt him into thinking about how men's relationships with the body have been developed, or have failed to develop, over time. In particular, he comes to realize how the ways in which we relate to our bodies impact upon our wider relations and our sense of our own sexualities, including, as in Jimmy's case, the fears he carries related to homophobia.

There are numerous ways in which the changing nature of Jimmy may be read. The most obvious way of doing so is to place Jimmy's revisioning of himself in context with what was happening to masculinity in the 1980s in response to feminist criticism of what constituted appropriate masculine attitudes and behaviour. This revealed itself in various guises such as remasculinization in the Reagan years in response to the post Vietnam War deconstruction of traditional 'maleness', the 'New Man' and the 'Men's Movement'. The feminine side of men emerged from the margins to which it had been relegated by post-Second World War culture. But masculinity was plunged, as a consequence, into a state of uncertainty – some might even say crisis.

The portrayal of Jimmy Sr may be read as a sympathetic critique of the new man. Thus, the 'in-between' nature of *The Snapper*, the narrative is located between Sharon becoming pregnant and giving birth, is a thematic as well as a structural device. Jimmy Sr is in the in-between state that Bhabha describes. Emerging from his traditional identity, marred it would appear from the opening pages of the novel by sexism, racism and homophobia, he is uncertain about his new identity. But the refocusing of masculinity in the 1980s and 1990s also underscored masculinity not as given but as a linguistic and cultural construction. In other words, masculinity and concomitant concepts such as 'father', 'provider' and 'law giver' were stressed simply as that: constructions.

Thus, it is difficult, not to read *The Snapper* in relation, for example, to Joyce's depiction of fathers who fail to assert their authority in *The Dubliners*. But Jimmy finally establishes his position in the family by discovering the instinctual within himself and entering into a new, and potentially problematic relationship, with his daughter. Wittingly or unwittingly, the novel follows psychoanalytic theory in its acceptance of an autonomous, inner, emotional, psychic life. But it is concerned with the relation between a person's inner life and their relations with those around them and more with the way in which this is brought into being through one person's feelings for another. The novel, consciously or unconsciously, rewrites Lacan's thesis that it is the masculine-oriented symbolic world that provides the perspectives in which the mother–child dyad is conceived. Once the normalizing of certain attitudes and behaviours through dominant heterosexual discourses of masculinity is accepted, these 'traditional' perspectives, the novel suggests, are open to becoming more fluid. Jimmy steps outside his conventionally masculinized language and preconceptions to see pregnancy and, ultimately the mother–child relationship, from the point of view of the mother. The novel inverts Lacan's idea, based on Freudian psychoanalysis, that the mother–child dyad is defined not only by the symbolic but by the threat which the father poses to that dyad in interrupting it and in introducing the child to the symbolic. The text leaves us with the impression that the father will not come between mother and child in the same way that Lacan has argued. Jimmy discovers, in other words, the 'instinctual drive and continuous relation to the mother' which Julia Kristeva, drawing on Lacan, argues that the symbolic represses (1982: 9).

But if the novel reclaims the father–daughter dyad which has been displaced by the father–son dyad in many Irish texts, it leaves the father–mother dyad somewhat traditionally limited, even though Jimmy acquires sufficient knowledge to better satisfy his wife sexually. In his changing relationship with his daughter, Jimmy acquires a knowledge of the maternal that bolsters his, albeit somewhat limited, masculinity and resists the infantilization that occurs when his wife subverts him.

Sharon, too, may be interpreted against a tradition of representing the maternal and the mother–child dyad in Irish literature and culture. The absence of the father enables her, it is anticipated, to bring the child up in a symbolic structure of her choosing. Her decision to name the child after its father is then surprising unless we read it as a constant reminder to the child's father that it will be brought up in a symbolic language over which she will maintain control:

> Georgina; that was what she was going to call her.
> They'd all call her Gina, but Sharon would call her George. And they'd have to call her George as well. She'd make them. (215)

The absent father is a well established trope in Irish writing but, in making the father a man who commits what is an act of rape while he is drunk, Doyle approaches it in a new way. The novel suggests that Sharon will have control over the child's upbringing but it leaves the reader, as it leaves Sharon, in an in-between state. Even though Doyle's book challenges traditional masculinity and the conventional idea of the father as the indisputable head of the family, and gives voice to the young, urban working class, some readers might feel that it is a more conservative novel than they expected. Despite her disruptive energy, Sharon's destiny is to become a mother; the implications of being an unmarried mother at her age are not pursued; and her own mother, the moral centre of the family, is for the most part marginalized.

This novel is especially disappointing when placed in a wider context of the representation of the mother figure as an icon in Ireland. While the confinement of women to the role of mother is not peculiar to Ireland, as Diane Stubbings says in a study of James Joyce, what is 'of note was the degree to which the mother's role became caught up within Nationalist and religious discourses' (2000: 5). Sharon's role is based on the fact that she decides not to have an abortion even though from a liberal position it would be possible to argue, given the facts of the rape, her age and her economic circumstances, that an abortion would be justified. Given the way that in Ireland nationalist and religious discourses together with economic factors have worked against women's rights, denying women access to birth control and, as enshrined in constitutional amendment in 1982, abortion, the novel treats Sharon's situation and decision to have the child somewhat lightly. The most radical feature of the novel would appear to be its suggestion that if the family unit is to survive, it has to be seen as having several centres and not revolving around one.

To some extent every novel is a product of its own time. One wonders if a novel like *The Snapper* which treats a man forcing his attentions on a woman while she is drunk could have been written following the 1992 'X' case which became the subject of Edna O'Brien's *Down by the River* (1996). The 'X' case involved a 14-year-old Dublin girl, only a few years younger than Sharon, who was made pregnant through rape by a family friend. O'Brien's narrative, which has the girl raped by her father, proffers another version of the father–daughter dyad which haunts Jimmy Sr's relationship with Sharon and of which the text seems at times uncomfortably aware. Indeed, in the sudden introduction of Jimmy's concern with the subject of incest the novel interrupts itself.

The subversive energy of *The Snapper*, despite its failings, seems to emerge from the way behaviour has been policed at many levels, including the state, community and home, in terms of transgression and taboo. It hardly needs pointing out that the symbol of the transgressive woman operates most effectively where, as in Catholic Ireland, there is a close connection between sexual symbolism and questions of order and control. But it is also true that it is in this context that the carnivalesque is most effective, too. Sharon's illegitimate pregnancy turns the Rabbitte household into a site of carnival that challenges other members of the community who are unveiled by their response to Sharon's condition. Significantly, through the introduction of a young puppy, the house itself becomes associated with the scatological elements which Mikhail Bakhtin (1984) celebrated as part of the natural life cycle and which he argued were employed in medieval carnival to mock the spiritual, the ideal and the abstract – the dog vomits, urinates and defecates. The latter, since Jimmy Sr steps in it, serves as a harbinger of the erosion of his traditional role as head of the household. At points in the novel, Sharon herself is associated with vomit and with the toilet bowl. At one level, this reminds us that women's bodies were associated with scatology out of fear of female sexuality and independence. At another, it brings to mind Bakhtin's argument, not fully appreciated by Catholicism's idealization and decorporealizing of the female, that 'in the image of urine and excrement is preserved the essential link with birth, fertility, renewal, welfare' (1984: 148). Thus, the novel challenges Catholicism's failure to celebrate the interleaving of the corporeal and the sacred, and the way this has exaggerated male fear of the female body. This is evident in the scene in the novel where Sharon unnerves the trainee store manager by confronting him with what embarrasses him most – the fact that she has to go to the toilet regularly and the sight of her swollen stomach: 'he blushed, yeh should've seen him. Just cos I said Toilet' (93).

Criminal Desires

In terms of the representation of the maternal and the female, Mary Morrissy's *Mother of Pearl* is a more interrogative text than

The Snapper and more aware of the different social and religious discourses to which women are subjected in Northern Ireland and Ireland. It is Morrissy's first novel and in many respects reflects the fact that she had been a short story writer. For example, Gerry Smyth feels that in this book, Morrissy 'stitches together three interrelated stories which with a little work could probably have stood on their own' (1997: 91). Admittedly, Morrissy seems to like working within episodes carefully defined by geography and/or a particular time span. Her *The Pretender* (2000), the story of a woman who possibly believes she is Anastasia, the surviving daughter of Tsar Nicholas II, moves back in time through periods defined by particular temporal and spatial limits. Thus we move from Virginia, to the Dalldorf Asylum, to Berlin at the time of the First World War, to Borovy Las in Poland and then, once again, briefly, Virginia.

However, there is more coherence in *Mother of Pearl* than critics have generally acknowledged. It consists of four parts, the last one very short, and, although on a cursory reading, it might appear to consist of three fairly self-contained narratives, in fact, it interweaves three perspectives on one crime: the stealing of a newly born child by a woman made childless by an operation to cure tuberculosis. Like Patrick McCabe's *The Butcher Boy* discussed in Chapter 8, *Mother of Pearl* explores the pervasiveness of the origins of a particular crime connected with the mother figure which, albeit in different ways, violates the sacredness with which mothering and motherhood are regarded in Ireland and Northern Ireland. McCabe's novel is concerned with the slaughter of a mother, while Morrissy's text focuses upon how a woman can violate her (supposedly) sisterly bond with other women to take another person's child. In each novel, the consequences and implications of the crime extend well beyond the immediate environs of the crime itself.

The first part of *Mother of Pearl* focuses on Irene, the woman who steals the child; the second part on Rita Spain nee Golden, the child's real mother; and the third part on the return of the child (now named Mary) to her lawful family. Part 4 once again focuses on Irene who stole the child – the novel, like *The Pretender*, returns briefly to the place where it started but acknowledging a temporal shift. The text interleaves a number of ways in which the mother figure may be conceived as an abject presence. First, it introduces in Irene's mother, the mother who excludes her child because she has an illness that at the time was thought to bring shame on the family. The first part of the novel betrays an interest in women incarcerated in an institution through illness and circumstance, which Morrissy repeats, to some extent, in *The Pretender*.

The period in which the first part of the novel is set was one that in Ireland benefited from significant improvements in the treatment of TB sufferers. This was due largely to the new Minister of Health, Dr Noël Browne, appointed in 1948, whose autobiography, *Against the Tide* (1986), became a best-seller just ten years before Morrissy's novel was published. Dr Browne, whose own parents died of TB, himself not only received treatment in an English sanatorium but, on qualifying as a doctor, worked in sanatoriums in England and Ireland. He sought to implement reforms to combat TB contained in the Government White Paper (1946). These proposals coincided with the availability of new drugs that reduced the number of patients needing surgery. The critique of Catholic conservatism and the way in which TB was regarded inside and outside the medical profession in Morrissy's novel, together with the strong feminist line of the criticism, is not surprising since Dr Browne was forced to resign in 1951 when the coalition government of the day failed to support free medical care for women and children that had attracted severe opposition from the Catholic hierarchy.

The way in which TB is conceived in *Mother of Pearl* is very close to that in Susan Sontag's essay 'Illness as Metaphor' which examines the way in which three serious illnesses – TB, Cancer and Aids – have been rendered in figurative language. Sontag recommends an approach to illness that takes it out of the metaphorical language in which it is usually couched. In many respects, this is very similar to the project which Morrissy undertakes in *Mother of Pearl*. But instead of being concerned to take illness and disease out of the metaphorical language in which they are represented, the focus is upon taking women, mothering and motherhood out of the figurative language in which they are represented in Catholicism and Irish and Northern Ireland society in general. Although Morrissy's novel is set in Northern Ireland, the environment is kept vague, and somewhat mythical, so that it could be read as 'somewhere' in Ireland. The novel is not so much concerned with an identifiable, geographical environment, but a larger ideological environment.

In deconstructing the way in which TB was configured in the middle of the twentieth century, Morrissy's focus is very similar to that of Sontag. TB is associated with moral and spiritual failings in the individual, and, in the physical wasting and exhaustion that it causes, with the obverse of capitalist values. Essentially, TB is linked to physical dirt, perceived as analogous of moral impurity: 'She had, by her illness, disgraced the household, her mother believed. It spoke of poverty, a lack of hygiene' (4). In the wider context of the novel, it is ironic that her being sent away to the sanatorium is explained with inferences that she has had to be sent away because she is pregnant, to avoid the stigmatization of the community, whereas later she steals the child because the community bad-mouths her for not bearing children. In this part of the novel, there is the first of a number of women's lifescripts that are not fully developed. Together they interleave to give the reader a sense that women's histories in the mid-twentieth century were located at the intersections of numerous incomplete and partial narratives. Her mother's narrative is anchored in early twentieth-century Ireland, emphasizing how women's identity is not only ideologically but economically determined by the impact of local and global forces:

> She said little, surrendering instead to the venomous interior life that fuelled her. She had hailed from a village further up the estuary now totally abandoned. Famine and emigration had robbed it of its people; Ellen's family had been the last to leave. Like Lot's wife she had looked back on that day and had seen a crumbling jetty and a ramshackle collection of empty houses, some no more than crooked gables already sinking into the bog, and cursed the folly of loyalty and the uselessness of love. (5)

The reference to Lot's wife, like many of the brief, sometimes cryptic allusions to the Bible that pepper this novel, can configure our reading of this passage. Lot, within a Christian culture, has come to signify the dire consequences of a woman's disobedience of her husband and of Patriarchal authority. While Lot's looking back causes her physical death, Ellen gains an insight which destroys her spiritually. But in the circumstances in which she, and by implication, all women are regarded, this is not surprising. As in Lot's case, we are offered only minimal insight into her inner life. Ostensibly a cruel mother figure that turns out her daughter, and never visits her at the sanatorium, she is herself a victim.

The importance attached to motherhood haunts Irene when, not being able to bear children as a result of the operation, she is pressurized by the community into which she moves with her impotent husband. The focus here is 'motherlessness' as a state of ultimate abjection for women. This is especially ironic since the physical realities of pregnancy, as Sharon discovers in *The Snapper*, are themselves regarded as abject. The pregnant woman and the motherless woman are forced to endure a sense of split identity that is like a perverse version of Lacan's mirror stage in child development. In seeing themselves in the way they are objectified, Sharon and Irene enter a problematic relation with the mother figure. Sharon eventually takes advantage of being alone in the house to enter her parents' bedroom:

> She took all her clothes off and locked her parents' bedroom door and looked at herself in the wardrobe mirror and the dressing table mirror. Jesus, she looked terrible. She was white in one mirror and greeny-pink in the other one. Her tits were hanging like a cow's. They weren't anything like that before. A fella she'd gone with – Niall, a creep – once said that she should have been in the army because her tits stood to attention. She looked like a pig. In both the mirrors.   (152)

The two mirrors may be interpreted in a number of different ways, but, at one level, they signify how Sharon, and, in a different sense, Irene, are forced to occupy a space between how they see themselves internally and how they are perceived through external lenses. In *Mother of Pearl*, Irene is regularly confronted by Martha Alward, 'the epitome of Jericho Street – neat, tight-lipped, righteous', who interrogates Irene as to whether she is pregnant. The effect is to hold up a humiliating and distorting mirror to her:

> Irene had lost count of the number of times she had been surveyed in this fashion followed by the same sly inquiries and for Irene the inevitable humiliation of not being able to offer even the smallest of prizes.   (43)

The moment when Irene is forced to lie, she encounters Martha outside the bitterly ironically named 'Monument Dairy', suggesting how women in Ireland and Northern Ireland are cast in a maternal role within a society that values masculine, heroic exploits.

Named after the Virgin Mary, the 'daughter' Irene steals epitomizes the obverse side to legitimate motherhood in Ireland and Northern Ireland – the entrapped mother and the unwanted (not necessarily illegitimate) baby – when she eventually self-aborts her own child:

> [Her husband] searches the rooms for an intruder, a forced lock, rifled drawers, a weapon that could have inflicted such wounds. And finds it in the knitting needle beside the bed. He tries to stem the flow of blood but cannot staunch it. He talks to her through her delirium which has transformed her silence into a kind of exultance of pain. (215–16)

The pregnancy that Mary/Pearl keeps secret from her husband is one of a number of secrets in which her life, like those of many women in the novel, is situated. The fact that she has withheld this knowledge from him, and commits this horrific act, leaves a void within him. Despite their intimacy, he realizes that he had never really known her. At one level, this is because his masculinity is something of a barrier. When he discovers her, asking what she has done, it is 'merely a question'. It is a while before he shows a feminine response: 'Only after the ambulance arrives does he ask again, sorrowfully, the blue light flashing across his face, the scream of a siren drowning out her answer' (216). The abortion becomes a secret which holds the couple apart from their families. As in telling her mother only that she has lost the child, they conceal the truth from her. But there are other secrets encrypted within her life script, including the 'missing' time as Pearl and the way in which she inhabits her mother's memories, including that of her own birth to 'a child conceiving in a rotting house on a summer's evening' (204). She envisages herself haunted by the fact that she has killed her own child:

> I am unfit to be with him, unfit to be with anybody. Cursed, as I am, by a savage reversal of the natural instinct. I have killed his child by my own hand. I struck out and tore away the very stuff of dreams, the cringing flesh and blood, the throbbing pulse. And all for a phantom, a wilful sprite, a demon, perhaps. I will return to our cottage home. Alone. A criminal. (216)

What she has torn out of her, in addition to the foetus, is the socially sanctioned ideal of the good mother. Her home now becomes a site of the 'unhomely'; a locus that is abject and haunted by the unblessed – 'the cries of the creature I expelled there in a mess of a blood and sweat' (217). The aborted foetus signifies the in-between: a biological entity that is not yet a child; removed from the mother's body but, thereafter, constantly haunting it; and in Catholic terms 'unblessed'. But the text shifts the focus from the foetus to the suffering of the mother who is haunted by the abortion and the beyond into which the foetus would have grown as a child. The mother is cast into a state of psychological limbo – a timelag – because, relocated by the experience, she is unable to be sure how she will be inscribed, and will be able to reinscribe herself, in the future: 'Will there be a secret existence hidden there, lurking in the corners of the rooms or hovering airily with promises' (217). The hallucinatory horror which she occupies, and has to work through, is 'other' to the more practical, socio-medical approach: 'Or will there just be the hard, bright, concrete things of the world saying, now, live with us?' (217).

Suffering Women

The numerous references to the Bible and Catholicism in the book provide a framework within which to discuss its perspectives on women. While in *The Snapper* there are few overt references to Catholicism, *Mother of Pearl* is riddled with overt, cryptic, contradictory and ambivalent allusions to the Church. The title of the novel is ambiguous in that it refers to Rita as the mother of Pearl and also invokes the Virgin Mary, as the litanies which sing in her head when Rita attends church after her baby has been stolen remind us: '*Mirror of Justice, Seat of Wisdom, Mystical Rose, Morning Star, Tower of Ivory, Mother of Christ, Mother of Divine Grace, Mother Most Pure, Mother of Pearl...*' (139)

Morrissy's novel reworks various perspectives on the Virgin Mary as, for example, Mater Dolorosa ('Mother of Sorrows') and Mediatrix, able to intercede on behalf of sinners seeking forgiveness from Christ. As studies by scholars such as Jaroslav Pelikan (1996) and Marina Warner (1976) have confirmed, the Virgin Mary is not the fixed referent she is sometimes taken to be.

The origins of her various roles, such as Mater Dolorosa and Mater Gloriosa, are historically specific. Scholars, such as Marina Warner, have pointed out that the Virgin Mary as Lady of Desolation has its antecedents in the ancient world of Mesopotamia and Egypt, but the cult of the mourning mother is a much more recent, thirteenth-century, phenomenon. What makes the figure of the Mater Dolorosa particularly relevant to Morrissy's novel is that it stresses her participation in human kind's pain and suffering. But Morrissy goes further than the Christian tradition associated with Our Lady of Sorrows and identifies the suffering of, specifically, women with her. This is a moot theological point. How could Mary with her knowledge of Christ have identified with his suffering and mourned as inconsolably as Inanna and Isis in their respective situations because she knew that he would rise from the dead? The point is even more complex within the framework of Morrissy's novel. How could a virgin identify with the pains, wounds and tortures of ordinary women? One theological resolution of the former dilemma is that Mary prayed to be granted knowledge of her son's torments. In order to appreciate the framework of Morrissy's novel, we have to assume that she prayed also to experience the sufferings of womankind. Mary's role as Mother of Sorrows is linked to her role as Mediatrix, her capacity to intercede with her son on behalf of suffering humanity, which, like the association of Mary with pain and torment, was crystallized in the Middle Ages.

The novel specifically associates Rita with the Virgin Mary when Imelda queries Rita's choice of the name Mary for the baby: 'Just Mary, plain Mary? Is that because it was a virgin birth? I mean, it was your first time, wasn't it?' (118). But the ambiguity is deeper than this. The title of the novel may be read as descriptive, as referring to Rita, as the biological mother of the child Pearl; to Irene as the temporary fantasy mother; or to the Virgin Mary. Or it may be read, as the litanies imply, as invoking the name of the Virgin Mary, suggesting that the book is addressed to the Virgin Mother on behalf of suffering women. In other words, that the title calls upon the Virgin Mary as a mediatrix on behalf of oppressed women. The trope of female suffering recurs in the text, as it does in Morrissy's subsequent novel that, like *Mother of Pearl*, intertwines the lives of several suffering women.

In *Mother of Pearl*, Irene suffers from tuberculosis; is shamed again by the community because she is childless and, out of desperation, steals Rita's new-born child; and has a relationship with a man who is impotent until he finally rapes her. The child whom Irene steals is the result of an unwanted pregnancy which has subsequent consequences for her state of mind when she is older – which is another way of rewriting the myth of women looking back invoked in the novel's early reference to Lot. Mary/Pearl's father is murdered in a sectarian killing, while the stolen child is returned to her mother when she no longer wants it. The child grows up to have an unwanted pregnancy herself that she self-aborts. Rita Spain's own name might be read as 'Rita's pain'. The effect of the litany, as the procession and the intoxicating smell of incense passes before her, when Rita has had her child stolen, is to make her feel 'blessed and released'. In addressing women's suffering to Mary, is the narrative hoping to exorcise it? Before being invaded by the abjection of what she has done, Mary, having self-aborted her unwanted child, and her past, declares: 'I am a *tabula rasa*, born again, with my history excised, cut out of me. Vacant and bleakly empty, only now am I ready to begin my life' (216).

At one point in the novel, Mary in her imagination compares her biological mother to 'Elizabeth, mother of John the Baptist, grown hopeless with the passing years, for whom a child would be a miraculous favour granted by the message of an angel' (186). This association is significant because from the middle ages to the present day, women who want children but have difficulty in conceiving pray to Mary to help them through intercession with her son. This is in itself ironic because women find themselves praying for help to a woman who supposedly gave birth virginally and without pain. Nevertheless, Mary is associated with the power to bring forth fertility from the earliest accounts of homage paid to her. But the reference to Elizabeth also reminds us that there is a feminist way of reading the Bible, that focuses on the women in the Old and New Testaments rather than upon the men of whom they are normally seen as an adjunct. It also highlights the fact that women who are unable to bear children, and who suffer as a consequence, are one of the Bible's recurring subjects. Yet, it is one that even within the academy is not often considered. The list of women in the Bible whose lives are for a time devastated by their infertility includes Sarah, important in the Old Testament because she is the wife of Abraham; Rachel who is mentioned because she is the wife of Jacob and the mother of

Joseph; and Hannah, known because she is the mother of Samuel, who endured even more 'bitterness of soul' (I Samuel 1: 10) than the others.

Not only are these women, like Morrissy's Irene, shamed because they are unable to bear children but they are further humiliated in having to procure fertile women for their husbands: Sarah gives Abraham her Egyptian maid Hagar while Rachel gives Jacob her maid Bilhah and has to observe Jacob having children by her sister Leah and by Leah's maid Zilpah. The kind of pressure exerted on Irene and Stanley when they set up home together in Jericho Street is redolent of that endured by Hannah which was such that 'she wept, and did not eat' (I Samuel 1: 7).

In invoking these women through the allusion to Elizabeth's infertility, the novel challenges the pressure that the Church and the Bible generally places on childless women. In fact, the Catholic Church teaches that children are a blessing from God, who 'settles the barren woman in her home as a happy mother of children' (Psalm 113: 9). In other words, it is difficult for men and women brought up in a Christian tradition not to 'resort to Biblical Metaphor' (217), to appropriate the words of Morrissy's Mary. Only when Rita and Mel move to Mecklenburgh with their second child, Stella, does she feel they are 'a proper family' (148). But Irene's situation is made doubly ironic because the Catholic Church professes to recognize that 'sterility neither prohibits nor invalidates marriage' (Finnegan, 1997: 247).

That the novel might be read, from a Catholic perspective, as addressed through its title to the Virgin Mary immediately privileges her role in salvation as mediator between Christ and humanity. However, if this is what the title of the novel intends, it is complicated by the ambivalence toward Catholicism and toward Mary which we find in the text itself. This function of bringing relief to the condemned is parodied in the sanatorium in the different kind of 'relief' that Irene brings to men condemned by tuberculosis:

She had her rules. She would never let them penetrate her. If they wanted gratification they must do it themselves. She could touch them, but they must never lay a finger on her. Irene would remain a virgin; she was saving herself. *This* was her calling, she believed, her life's work.   (23–4)

Here Morrissy conflates the Virgin Mary and Mary of Bethany, often mistaken for Mary Magdalene. When Davy Bly, referring to the favours she did the men at the sanatorium, criticizes Irene as 'Miss Holier Than Thou' and then accuses her of being 'nothing but a tramp', and Charlie Piper of being her pimp (25), he not only invokes the Virgin Mary and Mary Magdalene themselves but one of the explanations for the cult of Mary Magdalene as redeemed prostitute: that the Virgin Mary had been too idealized, placed too far beyond human suffering, to be a creditable mediatrix. In fact, the holiness accrued to the Virgin Mary because she gave birth to the Son of God, and the way the Catholic Church consequently encourages women to become brides of Christ, is cryptically parodied in Irene's marriage to 'God' in the name of her husband 'Godwin' – not a surname that has been innocently chosen. Moreover, his story is itself parodic of aspects of Jesus's upbringing, shifting the emphasis from Mary as the vessel of God to Mary as a more independent being:

> A father was never mentioned and Stanley grew up barely believing in him. His mother had seemed to him large and mysterious enough, like a capacious cathedral, to have produced him on her own. He never felt a void in the household, nor was he curious about a man who had never become flesh, who existed only because Stanley knew he must have. (28)

Since Stanley is impotent for much of his life, when Irene steals the child she is a virgin. This is especially ironic given the Catholic Church's interpretation of 'virginity': 'the observance of perpetual sexual abstinence'. And, it proves bitterly ironic in the context of Stanley's eventual rape of Irene; especially given the Church's view of virginity as 'a sign and stimulus of love' (Finnegan, 1997: 260). The latter is doubly ironic given Sontag's observation that 'TB was – still is – thought to produce spells of euphoria, increased appetite, exacerbated sexual desire' (1991: 3).

Irene is further identified with the Virgin Mary when, in the account of her stealing Rita's child, she is welcomed by Mary Blessed to her rooming house with the words 'Plenty of room at the inn!' (56) – an allusion to the fact that in the Bible the pregnant Mary and her husband Joseph are turned away from an inn and have to sleep in a stable where Jesus is born. It is not clear here how much of this is Irene's own illusions. But, at one level, it does not matter. Moreover, the name Mary Blessed when reversed – Blessed Mary – invokes the Magnificat, a song of praise spoken by Mary herself, in the Gospel according to Luke. Here the text highlights, how the Magnificat haunts women in Ireland and Northern Ireland, especially those in Catholic communities:

> And Mary said, My soul doth magnify the Lord.
> And my spirit hath rejoiced in God my saviour.
> For he hath regarded the low estate of his handmaiden; for, behold, from henceforth, all generations shall call me blessed.
> For he that is mighty hath done to me great things; and holy is his name.
> And his mercy is on them that fear him from generation to generation.
> He hath showed strength with his arm; he hath scattered the proud in the imagination of their hearts.
> He hath put down the mighty from their seats, and exalted them of low degree.
> He hath filled the hungry with good things; and the rich he hath sent empty away.
> He hath helped his servant Israel, in remembrance of his mercy;
> As he spake to our fathers, to Abraham, and to his seed forever.
> (Luke 1: 45–55)

In drawing attention to the Magnificat, Morrissy also refers us to its context. The Biblical narrative of Christ's birth, in Matthew (1: 3–6), begins with a genealogy of Christ's name which includes, unusually, the names of women: Tamar, Rahab, Ruth, and Urias's wife. Here Matthew is at pains to include women who were outside the normal bounds of respectability: Tamar had children by her father-in-law; Rahab was a prostitute in Jericho; Ruth was a foreigner, from Moabite and Urias's wife was Bathsheba who committed adultery with David. In their various ways, like the women in Morrissy's novel, they suggest the sufferings of womankind.

One of the better-known details of the Biblical account of the Virgin Birth among Christians is that Joseph 'did as the angel of the Lord had bidden him, and took unto him his wife' (Mark 1: 24). When Irene brings home the child, we are told that 'resignedly, [Stanley] did as he was bid' (74). The echo of 'bidden' in the

English translation of the Gospel is typical of how Morrissy leaves cryptic clues in the text for Christians and others who are familiar with the Bible as to the source material she is reworking. More obvious is the use of the word 'swaddling' which occurs in one of the few, and hence, in Christian churches at Christmas time, the most often intoned, lines in the Bible describing the infant Jesus. We are told that Stanley 'spread out a bath towel and drew back as Irene unswaddled the baby. She lay it out on the towel and free of its encumbrances it kicked and waved its arms, its eyes thrown back, attracted to the shimmering glow of the fire. With a soft shock he realised it was a girl child' (74). This account self-consciously inverts two aspects of the Virgin birth: the baby is a girl and the child is laid out of its 'swaddling' clothes while in the Gospel the baby is 'wrapped in swaddling clothes' (Luke 2: 12). Drawing attention to these details may seem pedantic but the former confirms the feminist dimension of the novel while the latter suggests its overall scheme of 'unwrapping'. By 'unwrapping' I mean the way in which the novel unwraps women from their metaphorical contexts, as Susan Sontag recommended we take illness and disease out of their metaphorical contexts, and also deconstructs women's experiences.

In parodying the Virgin Birth here, and elsewhere, Morrissy reclaims the Virgin Mary from a patriarchal theology. But, feminist theology has had to tackle the dilemma that the Virgin Mary can be a source of inspiration, as she was for powerful women like Joan of Arc. But, in contradistinction to this, Mary can be seen as legitimating the subservience of women to men – since she must kneel before her son – and denying them their own sexuality. Paradox, though, is at the heart of the representation of the Virgin Mother. As Pelikan points out, the titles bestowed on the Virgin Mary, which as I demonstrated above are repeated in the novel, were intended to reflect the 'uniqueness', from a Christian perspective, bestowed upon her (1996: 130). But they were also, as he goes on to argue, an attempt to address the paradox that Mary was the mother of her creator.

This is the position which both Mary/Pearl and the Virgin Mother, after whom she is named, can be said to share. The principal voice of the third part of *Mother of Pearl*, when the different threads of the text are brought together, and hence also of the project as a whole, is Mary/Pearl. Thus, she becomes in effect the mother of the narrative, and thus of Irene herself. If Mary/Pearl is perceived as the mother of the narrative, in that she is its true centre, her nomenclature is significant for the text as a whole. For the importance of Mary/Pearl's name signals the relevance of names in the text as a whole. The deconstruction of these names, from Pearl to Mary to Godwin to Mrs Blessed, which has to form part of the reading process, is an aspect of the way the novel as a whole is concerned with what I called above 'unwrapping'. At one level, unwrapping the relevance of names inverts the process of naming which is generally about construction rather than deconstruction. Naming involves inscribing the child with an identity that is part of a wider web of social and cultural meanings. Thus, the process of unwrapping names can be seen as an aspect of the feminist dimension of this novel, and as part of its deconstruction of the relative status of men and women. Moreover, the selection of names by women in this text is especially important since in Genesis the power of naming is given to Adam. As Shelley Phillips observes, 'naming in Genesis is not only a symbolic act of creativity, but defines women as part of man's flesh, in an inversion of the relationship of mother to child' (1996: 211).

There is an important distinction to be made between the Virgin Mary and Morrissy's Mary. Whereas the Virgin Mother is radiant in her divinity, Pearl is radiant in her womanhood. The Virgin Mary has come to be perceived in Catholic mythology as the way the Saviour came to humanity, and the means by which humanity can come to the Saviour. In Morrissy's novel, Pearl and Irene, both of whom are associated with the Virgin Mary, are the means by which a different view of humanity is broached. Yet, paradoxically, this is a phenomenon, which like the sufferings of barren women, can be linked to the Bible itself. What Morrissy's novel does is to find, hidden in the Bible, an account of suffering women. From this perspective, one of the lines of the Magnificat assumes greater relevance: 'For he hath regarded the low estate of his handmaiden' (Luke 1: 48). Pelikan observes that belief in the unity of the Bible has informed the conviction among generations of scholars that 'the New Testament is hidden in the Old and the Old becomes visible in the New' (1996: 23). Ultimately, *Mother of Pearl* suggests that a new, feminist Bible is hidden in the old.

The association between Pearl and Moses in the novel is relevant to this argument. In the account of Rita waiting to bring her baby home, we learn that 'the Moses basket, which had been

Rita's when she was a baby, stood proudly in the middle of the room' (123). Moses's sister's name, Miryam, was rendered into Greek as Maria and Mireia, both forms occurring in the Gospels (Pelikan, 1996: 28). Thus, etymologically, Miryam is linked to the Marys of the New Testament and also to Miriam, the prophetess and sister of Aaron, who, in Exodus, is said to have led, timbrel in hand, all the women out after her (Exodus 15: 20–1). While Mary is perceived as having wrought reparation for what Eve had done, Pearl and Irene, may be seen as seeking justice for Eve and *Mother of Pearl* may be read as an indictment of what Adam did to Eve.

Thus, *Mother of Pearl* may be said to relocate the Bible, in that it offers a different perspective on it by centring aspects that are often marginalized or not discussed at all. In this sense, the Bible enters a kind of timelag in which it is interrogated but not finally reinscribed. In taking women out of metaphor, especially Biblical and religious metaphor, the text risks relocating them in another set of metaphors, even Biblical ones:

The Garden of Eden. And my first parents. Adam and Eve. Already under threat of expulsion but hanging on to the dream of happiness. Eve, knowing she has stolen her joy, savours it precisely because she knows it will all come to ruin. My first mother, consumed by an illicit love. And Adam, ignorantly happy in the hours before banishment. *My* banishment. I wonder if my Eden still exists? Or has it turned to wilderness without me? You see, I have resorted to biblical metaphor. But it is all I know. And so much more exotic than the literal truth.   (217)

In focusing on the mother figure, *Mother of Pearl* and *The Snapper* are concerned, like *Stir-fry* and *The Maid's Tale* discussed in Chapter 5, with the way in which the condition of being a woman is determined not only by prevailing ideologies but their 'encryptment' within language, and specifically metaphor. In each text, the construction of femininity and motherhood is inseparable from the ways in which masculinity, and fatherhood, is perceived. How gender identity is determined and confined by the available discourses in which it is, and can be, articulated is developed in the next chapter in texts that are also concerned with different forms of violence, and two of them, with mental illness.

8

Limit and Transgression

Roddy Doyle's *The Woman Who Walked Into Doors* (1996), Patrick McCabe's *The Butcher Boy* (1992) and William Trevor's *Felicia's Journey* (1994)

The Woman Who Walked Into Doors, *The Butcher Boy* and *Felicia's Journey* involve violence to women – domestic violence, the murder of a woman who is also a mother by a disturbed child and a serial killer's pursuit of a young woman who becomes an agent in bringing about his suicide. Each of these texts concerns a subject that had previously been marginalized in serious literature. As such, each contributes to the sense of the timelag in which contemporary Ireland finds itself, discussed in Chapter 1. At one level, in giving a voice to previously concealed or half-admitted subjects, these novels present a critique of contemporary Ireland and Northern Ireland; of post-industrial society in Britain as much as Ireland in *Felicia's Journey*; of Americanization and globalization in *The Butcher Boy*. But in the writing itself, there is an element that both attracts and repels the reader, especially in the exposition of sexually related violence. In other words, these texts situate the reader in an in-between position, uncertain for a while at least of what to make of them. This aspect is anchored not only in the choice of subject, but also in an interest in what emerges when we push these kind of subjects to the limit.

Emblematic of the uncertainty, debate and ideological conflict of the 'in-between' space in which Ireland and Northern Ireland are located at the end of the twentieth century, quite apart from that in which groups of people in them are situated, none of the texts come to a resolution. Roddy Doyle's novel leaves us uncertain about the decision which the female victim is about to take;

Patrick McCabe's reveals that its narrator is not the child we have been led to believe but a 40-year-old man frozen in time; and William Trevor's text leaves us with Felicia, between childhood and adolescence, on the streets of London in a state of suspension. Relocated but unable to 'reinscribe' herself:

> She seeks no meaning in the thoughts that occur to her, any more than she searches for one in her purposeless journey, or finds a pattern in the muddle of time and people, but still the thoughts are there. Alone, no longer a child, no longer a girl, with the insistence of the grateful she goes from place to place, from street to street, binding her feet up .... (212)

Indeed, Doyle's victim also finds herself suspended in a muddle of thoughts:

> Do I actually remember that? Is that exactly how it happened? Did my hair *rip*? Did my back *scream*? Did he call me a cunt? Yes, often; all the time. Right then? I don't know. Which time was that anyway? I don't know. How can I separate one time from the lot and describe it? I want to be honest. How can I be sure? (184)

Doyle's Paula Spencer's question – 'How can I separate one time from the lot and describe it?' – is the one asked by all three principal protagonists in these texts as they struggle to make sense of their narratives.

But it is also the problem posed – especially in the two first-person narratives, *The Woman Who Walked Into Doors* and *The Butcher Boy* – by the authors. These two narratives are especially difficult because the account of events given by their protagonists are contradictory, and they do not understand themselves as to what has motivated them. Paula struggles to understand why she denied for so long what was happening to her and Felicia seems, at one level, drawn to a man she instinctively knows is dangerous while he is attracted to a girl whom he suspects will destroy him. At one level, the villains in these texts – the husband who batters his wife, the serial killer and the priests who abuse the children in their care – are very different characters, with different motivations and different socio-cultural contexts to their lives. But each provides not only abuse but also the kindness and affection, even the excitement, that their victims secretly crave.

Like Kathleen Ferguson's *The Maid's Tale* discussed in Chapter 5, Doyle's first-person narrator operates, at times, at a level of false consciousness where the reality becomes a ghost presence that haunts the text: 'It was good to know that you were with him. Watching him, being with him. It was exciting' (191). Like Ferguson's Brigid, Paula enters into a secret dialogue with herself that is an attempt to confront the reality that she distorts or denies. Shortly after having been beaten up by her husband, as he takes her to the hospital in a taxi, she can hardly believe her own duplicity: 'He had just pulled my arm out of its socket, less than an hour before, and I was listening to him; I was actually admiring him, proud of him' (198). In Paula's case, she tells herself that if she could be alone in the hospital with a doctor or nurse she would tell all. But in inventing narratives that justify her inaction, Paula paradoxically inverts the way her husband invents narratives that allow him to lose his temper. As she observes at one point: 'He's making it up as he goes along, making himself believe it; working himself up, building up his excuse' (182).

Each of the texts discussed in this chapter interleaves different modes of behaviour and awareness. Thus not only can Paula Spencer's husband be affectionate and amusing as well as violent but also Hilditch, despite his oppressive creepiness, can offer Felicia the benevolent father figure she secretly desires. Paula's faith in her husband – 'He would have put that anger to use. He wouldn't have been wasted. He'd have been a leader' (191) – and Felicia's mistaken impression of Hilditch as a benevolent father figure become 'ghosts' that they have to exorcise. But these texts also pose problems for their authors at another level. For all the serious purpose we might find in these texts, they are also works of fiction and are designed to provide their readers with a thrilling, intriguing and even, in the case of *The Butcher Boy*, an entertaining story. Thus, although they cannot be accused of trivializing their subject matter, they do fictionalize issues that in many people's lives are an all too abhorrent reality. Thus, at the same time as we might think it is important for literature to tackle subjects such as these, one side of us is bound to be resistant to it. Moreover, readers may be resistant to subjecting what is described in these texts to critical analysis.

The wider context of each of these texts is the way in which violence and abuse have themselves become important subjects in late twentieth-century art, popular culture and the mass media. The point is well made in Patrick McCabe's *Carn*, to which I referred in Chapter 1, in one of the episodes set in the town's Turnpike Inn:

> A pint of beer dripped down John F. Kennedy's smiling face. The video screen went blank and when the picture returned a crazed youth in an asbestos suit was setting a series of young women alight.... They stared open-mouthed as he applied his flame thrower to the feet of a trussed-up girl. (214)

A useful way of approaching this dimension of these texts is through the ideas about 'limit', 'transgression' and 'taboo' proposed by the French philosopher and historian Michel Foucault. In his essay, 'Preface to Transgression', Foucault argues that 'the twentieth century will undoubtedly have discovered the related categories of exhaustion, excess, the limit and transgression – the strange and unyielding form of these irrevocable movements which consume and consummate us' (1977: 49). Here he offers a different way of looking at modernity than the celebratory or triumphalist perspective to which I referred in Chapter 2. Foucault serves to interrupt, the conventional, popular view of history as a linear, progressive continuum. But, more than that, it is important to acknowledge that his ideas are related to 'the death of God' – or, as Foucault thought of God, the perceived presence that gave life its totality and meaning. The absence of what he believed invested life with meaning led, Foucault argued, to a preoccupation in 'modern society' with the limit of thought.

We can see the truth of Foucault's assertion that in the void created by 'the death of God', the twentieth century will become preoccupied with limit *per se* in popular and sensationalist literature and film, especially that which falls into the violent sexploitation category. To an extent, this kind of work haunts *The Woman Who Walked Into Doors* and especially *The Butcher Boy*. However, both writers work within a framework, be it humanist or based on the ideals of Catholicism, which displaces the void that Foucault argued that the end of belief in God created. Thus, in all three texts discussed in this chapter, there is an intriguing tension between assigning limit the kind of sovereignty of which Foucault writes, and which can be found in the more popular genres with which they cross over, and the attempt to recommend a value system which, in the case of Doyle's novel, reinscribes love, marriage and the family as transcendent signifiers, and in respect of *The Butcher Boy*, reclaims positive spiritual values from the failures of Catholicism's principal institutions to abide by its ideals. The corollary of this is the attractiveness and repulsion of limitlessness. A question prompted by the subject matter of these texts, especially *The Butcher Boy*, is whether there is nothing that can not be made manifest within a work of art?

Sexuality and Modernity

For Foucault this concern with limit, and with transcending limitation, was linked to the importance that he believed sexuality had acquired in western culture. Again this provides an appropriate framework within which to approach these texts because each is concerned with straddling the boundaries between the representable and the unrepresentable in terms of sexuality. Foucault argues:

> Perhaps the emergence of sexuality in our culture is an 'event' of multiple values: it is tied to the death of God and to the ontological void which his death fixed at the limit of our thought; it is also tied to the still silent and groping apparition of a form of thought in which the interrogation of the limit replaces the search for totality and the act of transgression replaces the movement of contradictions.   (50)

Here Foucault maintains that modern transgression is impoverished because sexuality is no longer linked as strongly as in previous eras to religion. In other words, 'Sexuality points to nothing beyond itself' (30). This, according to Foucault, had implications for the aestheticization of sexuality in that sexuality invariably offers at best now 'the superficial discourse of a solid and natural animality' (31). Moreover, he argued that 'the death of God does not restore us to a limited and positivistic world, but to a world exposed by the experience of its limits, made and unmade by that excess which transgresses it' (32).

The three texts with which this chapter is concerned explore different dimensions in which the world may be said, in

Foucault's terms, to stand 'exposed by the experience of its limits'. However, *The Woman Who Walked Into Doors* revises Foucault's thesis in that it is concerned not with the void created by the absence of God but by the absence of good. Again though, the absence of good produces, as Foucault said of the absence of God, a concern with limit, since good in itself will impose, like the concept of God in Foucault's argument, a limit to our thoughts and our actions. The way in which the perceived absence of good in Doyle's text produces a concern with limit *per se* is evident in the following passage from the novel:

> He pushed me back into the corner. I felt hair coming away; skin fighting it. And a sharper pain when his shoe bit into my arm, like the cut of a knife. He grunted. He leaned against the wall, over me. I heard the next kick coming; my fingers exploded. Another grunt, and my head was thrown back. My head hit the wall. My chin was split. I felt blood on my neck. Again. Again. I curled away to block the kicks. I closed my eyes. He kicked my back. Again. My back. My back. My back. The same spot again and again. He was breaking through my back. (185)

This passage is structured around the repetition of the violent kicking and emphasizes the resistance of Paula's body as a physical entity in contradistinction to her passivity. His violence becomes a product of his lack of feeling for her. She responds instinctively, as an animal would, adopting, ironically, the foetal position in order to protect the most vulnerable parts of her body. We might see this violence as aberration, yet at the same time it picks up on the more muted violence that accompanies sexual intercourse. The split chin might remind us of the split vagina in the loss of virginity. The repetition echoes the rhythm of penetrative sex. In another context, Paula's expressions of agony might be an articulation of a more pleasurable sense of being violated; especially when she admits: 'The grunting stopped. He was finished; he'd no wind left. I could hear him breathing, slowing down' (185).

Paula's husband's act of violence is one that has been legitimated by popular representations of violence against women. But it is also an extension of the linguistic jeopardy in which young women like Paula, and Sharon in *The Snapper*, find themselves trapped. At one level, Paula and Sharon are constructed and deconstructed by the transgressive excesses of the communities in which they live. As Paula observes: 'If you smiled at more than one [boy] you were a slut; if you didn't smile at all you were a tight bitch' (48). Her first experience of abuse, which on this occasion she could stop, started early when she was fourteen: 'My brother, Roger, called me a slut when I wouldn't let him feel me' (47). The environment in which she grew up is one where young women are taken advantage of but stigmatized by the culture that allows that to happen: 'I was a slut. My daddy said it, fellas said it, other girls said it, men in vans and lorries said it' (47). Coupled with that, her home life with her father is one where she and her sisters are often terrified. But what is especially disturbing about all of this is that it seems to expose the void that Foucault believed was created in any attempt to perceive life in its totality without reference to an external referent that makes sense of it – God in Foucault's case and goodness in Doyle's.

Paula's description of the context in which Carmel grew up – her father burning her sister's blouse, scrubbing her face with a nailbrush, and beating her with his belt – helps us to understand how Charlo enters her life as a spectre rather than a real person. Her appreciation of Charlo is haunted by the absence in her life, as in Francie's in *The Butcher Boy*, of the good father. This is made clear in the frank conversation she has with her sisters, pondering how in the course of their childhood their father changed. This is a family secret which bonds the sisters as the daughters in *Amongst Women*, discussed in Chapter 4, share the secret of their father's punishment of them. When Paula does recall her good father it is in language which, as in *The Butcher Boy*, associates the ideal family with fairy story or a reading primer: 'Once upon a time my life had been good. My parents had loved me. The house was full of laughter. I'd run to school every morning' (56). Not surprisingly, she is unable to see where the so-called heroic violence with which Charlo is associated, and for which he has a reputation, might lead:

But [the name calling] stopped when I started going with Charlo. God, it was great. I could have walked around in my nip with twenty Major in my mouth combing my pubic hair and nobody would have said a word. I was Charlo's girl now and that made me respectable. (49)

Paula doesn't realize at the time that she narrates this, that she projected on to Charlo the consequences of everything which she has had to keep hidden: the violence of her home life; the difficulty of being a young woman in the kind of neighbourhood in which they were living; and anxieties about her sexual identity. The secrecy extended to how she was perceived and to her own bodily functions: 'And then there were periods and keeping them secret and never mentioning them and making sure that no one knew ... .' (48). This kind of secrecy sets the pattern whereby concealment becomes a key part of her sense of self. But the pattern of Paula's life also involves stepping outside herself, which she is able to do as a teenager with Charlo, as her sister managed to step outside the family through becoming pregnant and getting married. With Charlo, Paula experiences a spatial relocation; the status she acquires through being his girlfriend is evident in how she now walks and carries herself. But in reality she enters a kind of timelag in which she unconsciously analyses their relationship and his behaviour – for example, how he fights like a girl in the frenzy of his savagery – but does not realize the full implications of the way she has been reinscribed.

Although the violence inflicted on Paula has little to do with sex *per se*, the account of Paula's early years suggest that in the working-class community in which she lives sexuality had become, as Foucault wryly suggested, 'denatured': 'Since Sade and the death of God, the universe of language has absorbed our sexuality, denatured it, placed it in a void where it establishes its sovereignty and where it incessantly sets up as the Law the limits it transgresses' (50). In Paula's narrative there is plenty of evidence of how language has 'denatured' sexuality: 'Sitting on a wall in the dark would get you a name for yourself. You were looking for trouble, parading yourself, making a show of yourself. Getting yourself a bad name. Dying for it' (48). Foucault is making the point that in the absence of God as the locus of a total meaning of life, sexuality has been relocated but not definitively reinscribed. The significance which sexuality acquired in Ireland, where the Catholic Church had long marginalized it, compounds the sense of confusion and uncertainty of which Foucault writes. However, it also underscores Foucault's point that, although sexuality may attain a newfound sovereignty, it cannot be said to exist within an ideological void. In Doyle's novel, the sovereignty that sexuality has acquired is part of how heterosexual masculinities are defined, normalized and sustained by the way in which female sexuality is defined and stigmatized.

Mental Illness as Taboo

There are various ways of approaching literary representations of mental illness. The most established perspective is to see the cultural construction of the mad person as a signifier. This is the approach followed by Michel Foucault (1961 and 1962) who believed that madness is not a self-evident behavioural or biological fact, but acquires definition and meaning from specific cultural contexts. In this respect, he provides a useful framework in which to explore the representation of madness in the texts discussed in the remainder of this chapter. In art and literature, the mentally ill have come to occupy an ambiguous position. They are perceived as posing a threat to the existing order, and are thus subject to denunciation, while simultaneously, benefiting from a Foucauldian view of madness, may be seen as holding a mirror up to the social order, expressing fundamental, often uncomfortable, truths about it. An obvious example from *The Butcher Boy* is the exposure of paedophilia among Catholic priests, itself an index of the way that the Catholic Church's insistence upon celibacy leads to a distorted sexuality and mental illness:

> Are you all right Francis he'd say. Oh I'm grand Father and dropped my eyelids shyly like Our Lady did. Sit up here he said and slapped his knees. So up I went. What does Tiddly do then only take out his micky and start rubbing it up and down and jogging me on his knee. (79)

More recently than Foucault's work, postmodern theories of space have provided further ways of interpreting mental illness. By postmodern theories of space in this context, I mean those in which space is perceived as constructed in a dialectical relation with what occupies it, as opposed to theories in which space is conceived as an inert, given context of what occurs within it. As far as the mentally ill are concerned, postmodern thinking about space has led to a focus upon the way 'mad identities' are constituted in particular spatial contexts. This has led in turn to a focus upon people being labelled 'mad' or 'mentally ill' through their experience of sites where their circumstances, lifestyles, experiences and problems become an issue.

Hester Parr and Chris Philo (1995) argue:

> In the chaos of psychosis certain delusions ('unrealities') can become the metaphorical or imagined place for an accepted internal identity, be this only a temporary place 'to settle', but at the same time there may be a need to find some more worldly place (an ordinary 'reality') where it will be safe to express something to other people of what happens in the middle of the private delusional geographies. (222)

The narrative can be viewed as Francie's attempt to construct a 'place "to settle".' Its focus, though, is upon 'what happens in the middle of the private delusional geographies' in which Francie occupies a no-person's land. Parr and Philo have suggested that 'the "place" or "placelessness" of the mentally distressed person lies at several intersections of internal and external reality' (222). This concept of a multilayered intersection of the private and the public is useful to our understanding of the text. The narrative of *The Butcher Boy* runs through spaces where characters, their location and social processes interact in a context which is only partially anchored, and where there is an opportunity for a lot of creative cross cutting. These intersections provide McCabe, as they provide Doyle in *The Woman Who Walked Into Doors*, with the opportunity to pursue social critiques. But the possibilities of doing so are greater in McCabe's text than in Doyle's because the spaces and the social processes negotiated by the mentally ill interact on many levels. In other words, what Parr and Philo label 'private delusional geographies' provides fiction with a space that is itself something of a fiction. This is exemplified in the incident when Francie requests 'corned beef' in a shop:

> I says to the shopgirl I wanted corned beef. You must be going to make a fair few sandwiches says the shopgirl no I said no! I'm not making any sandwiches. What are you talking about – *sandwiches?*, I said. The shopgirl was red and she said I was only saying you don't have to shout at me. It made me all nervy and I dropped the corned beef on the way out of the shop. What were they all looking at? Mrs Connolly was

pretending not to but I could see her turning away at the last
minute pretending to squeeze a pan loaf saying is this
fresh? What are you looking at Connolly I wanted to say to
her .... (130)

As throughout the novel, there are clues here as to what is psychologically wrong with Francie. The way he over reacts to someone turning away from him and his obsession with Mrs Nugent's
breasts – 'Then slowly she unbuttoned her blouse and took out
her breast Then she said: This is for you Francis' (60) – suggest a
child locked in what psychologists such as Melanie Klein (1991)
identified as the mental condition of a child who has been unable
to progress to adult subjectivity.

But *The Butcher Boy's* first-person narrator, like that of *The
Woman Who Walked Into Doors*, exists within a void where limit
and transgression are privileged. The monstrous child was a
recurring trope in the mid-twentieth century, featuring in films
that included Mervyn LeRoy's *The Bad* Seed (1956), Joseph
Losey's *The Damned* (1961) and Roman Polanski's *Rosemary's
Baby* (1968) and novels such as William Golding's *Lord of the Flies*
(1954) and John Wyndham's *The Midwich Cuckoos* (1957) (Petley,
1999: 87–107). But the question has to be asked, in what context
do they exist? Often the principal feature of their ideological location is the absence of God. Without an external referent that
makes sense of the totality of life, to adapt Foucault's argument,
madness becomes a limit and a site of transgression *per se*. At one
level, Francie Brady as a mentally disturbed child is a cultural signifier, a vehicle for the type of disturbing social truths mentioned
earlier. But, at another level, he represents the mentally disturbed
child as limit.

Jo-Ann Wallace (1995) provides a further gloss on the way
McCabe approaches the mentally disturbed child as limit within
wider notions of 'madness' as cultural signifier, and the way in
which such children are often constructed in sites where madness
is perceived as an issue. Wallace departs from those perspectives
on childhood grounded exclusively in 'an essentially biologistic
and universal paradigm of childhood "based on the idea of natural growth"' (289). Following the work of figures such as Philippe
Ariès, and bringing the child as a subject-position out from the
margins of social theory, Wallace finds herself in a situation akin
to Bhabha's 'timelag', admitting that 'it is difficult at this stage to

imagine how a theory of the child-subject might proceed' (203). However, what makes her work especially appropriate to our understanding of *The Butcher Boy* is her thesis that, in the late twentieth century, the child became a site of anxiety.

Thus, the concern with limit in *The Butcher Boy* is evident also in the way his perceived mental illness is constructed through contexts where he is rendered a pariah figure. At one point in the novel, he enters a shop where the respectable members of the community are going about their daily business. The concern with the mentally disturbed constructed in terms of limit, rather than their illness *per se*, is evident from the way the emphasis falls not upon his behaviour but the responses of the others to him: '... off I went out the door as I went by the window I could see Mrs Connolly saying something and the other women nodding then raising their eyes to heaven' (16).

As I indicated earlier, at the end of the novel we realize that *The Butcher Boy* is supposedly a narrative written or related in some way by an institutionalized adult who is frozen in his childhood. As such, it brings to mind the interest, which can be traced back to the eighteenth century, in the writing, visual art and sculpture that came out of psychiatric hospitals, prisons and asylums. This work was sometimes encouraged and sometimes discouraged by them. While many of the discourses about this work from the nineteenth century, by prominent figures such as Lombroso, Noyes and Simon, are outmoded by today's ideas and interests, this early activity is pertinent to our appreciation of McCabe's novel for two reasons. The novel demonstrates how many of the ideas in circulation through the work of people like Lombroso (MacGregor, 1989) are still in circulation in the twentieth and twenty-first century through popular mythology. Second, they are important as the first people who did what many novelists, such as McCabe in *The Butcher Boy* and William Trevor in *Felicia's Journey*, are trying to do, confront the often chaotic, seemingly meaningless, and at times bizarre and frightening, manifestations of mental disturbance. In other words, mental disturbance as limit.

The *Butcher Boy* encourages us to ask where Francie's hospital narrative comes from. Is it an expression of his insanity, causing us to think of the pioneering, nineteenth-century work on the art of the insane? Or, is it the expression of Francie's last hold on sanity? Wittingly or unwittingly, *The Butcher Boy* demonstrates many of the ideas and myths around the art of the insane that developed in the work of figures such as Cesare Lombroso (1835–1909). Lombroso was in his day an influential anthropologist, criminologist and psychiatrist, preoccupied, like the Victorians generally, with diagnosis and classification. Francie Brady's narrative demonstrates many of the characteristics that Lombroso claimed to have found in the art of the insane, ideas that then passed into the public domain and are still invoked in popular renditions of the behaviour of the insane, in for example, the work of Stephen King. What makes the links between McCabe's novel and the nineteenth century's ideas about madness is their shared interest in madness as limit. This is evident in the characteristics of the art produced by people suffering from mental illness which the nineteenth century chose to emphasize and which McCabe, probably unwittingly, follows.

The features of the art of the insane which Lombroso and his contemporaries stressed included obscenity that, in the work of male patients, was often linked to perverse ideas about women, especially women who appear to be from the 'respectable classes'. The latter is very much a feature of Francie's fantasies about humiliating and dominating Mrs Nugent:

> And now you Mrs Nugent. I don't think you're putting enough effort into it. Down you get now and no slacking. So Mrs Nugent got down and she looked every inch the best pig in the farmyard with the pink rump cocked in the air. Mrs Nugent, I said, astonished, that is absolutely wonderful. (61)

The movement from Mrs Nugent's initial remark about Francie being a pig, to Francie's internalization of himself as a pig and its association with something dirty and abhorrent, to the construction of himself as a pig-man and then a butcher, to his fantasies about Mrs Nugent and Phillip as pigs illustrates, as Clare Wallace (1998) says, 'the substitutive structure of Francie's logic' (161). But it also suggests how this substitutive logic is locked into a chain of thought about obscenity and perversity.

The emphasis upon defecation and the lower parts of the body in Francie's punishment of what he perceives as Mrs Nugent's snobbery overturn some of Bakhtin's ideas about the canivalesque mentioned in the discussion of *The Snapper* in the previous chapter:

> Yes, pigs are forever doing poo all over the farmyard, they
> have the poor farmer's heart broken. They'll tell yu that pigs
> are the cleanest animals going. Don't believe a word of it. Ask
> any farmer! Yes, pigs are poo animals I'm afraid and they sim-
> ply will cover the place in it no matter what you do. So then,
> who's going to be the best pig in the pig school and show us
> what we're talking about then, hmm?   (61–2)

Whereas Doyle responds to the subversive, mischievous and celebratory elements of the carnivalesque, which Bakhtin (1984)
believed had its roots in the medieval carnivals that allowed a
temporary space for misrule and letting off steam, McCabe develops its darker aspects. For all its celebration of the body and the
profane, Bakhtin also realized there were violent undertones and
misogynistic connotations to medieval carnival. It is these violent
and misogynistic undertones in the art of the insane that mark the
concern with limit in nineteenth-century thought about mental illness and betrays McCabe's concern with limit in *The Butcher Boy*.

The compulsive involvement with minutiae, and the use of
symbols in an allegorical way, which the nineteenth century identified with madness are also characteristics of Francie's behaviour. Lombroso noticed that the mentally ill tended to use strange
materials in their art, again betraying an interest in mental illnesses' limit, and this may be mirrored to an extent in the way
Francie creates his ideal 'home', ironically around the corpse of
his father and a smashed television set. But more significantly,
like the work that Lombroso discussed, *The Butcher Boy* becomes
grotesque through its concentration upon detail:

> When I got home there wasn't a whisper in the house only for
> the flies, nothing only da in the armchair by the radio....
> I gave his shoulder a bit of a shake and when the hankie fell
> out of his pocket I saw that it was all dried blood.... I pulled
> his chair into the fire and said sit there da go on now. I built it
> up good and high I used everything I could find in the yard it
> was the first time there had been a fire in the house for as long
> as I could remember. It was good, flickering away there and
> the shadows swarming all over the ceiling. I rooted about and
> found bread and toasted it on a fork then we had tea all we did

was just sit there that was all we wanted to do. Da looked at me and when I seen those eyes so sad and hurt I wanted to say: I love you da.   (118–19)

Lombroso's work suggested that mental illness took the subject back in time. In *The Butcher Boy*, this is evident in Francie's condition, frozen in time as a child, and in his frequent allusions to the comic world of the child. Most significant of all is the way in which the narrative as a whole conflates the 'artistic faculty', which Francie clearly possess in order to produce this narrative, and 'moral insanity'.

Thus, the echoes of nineteenth-century perceptions of the art of the insane in McCabe's work is indicative of how that art has been perceived as existing at what Foucault would call the 'limit'. But it also betrays McCabe's interest in exploring 'limit', evident also in how the mother–child relationship is pursued in *The Butcher Boy*.

Reading Psychoanalytically

In *The Butcher Boy* and *Felicia's Journey*, the focus is upon the consequences of early childhood experiences, especially a child's relationship with its mother. Although this area of personality development has been mercilessly parodied and treated, quite rightly in some respects, with scepticism, each of these texts ask us to consider the proposition that our early experiences influence us and help make us what we are, including how we respond to others of the same as well as those of a different gender, and the way that we make love. But these two novels appear to be less interested in the psychology of the mother–child relationship but the relationship taken to a grotesque limit.

The Butcher Boy and *Felicia's Journey* deal with characters that have been influenced by their early experiences in extreme ways. Even on a cursory reading, we can see that the child's primordial experience at their mother's breasts is invoked in McCabe and Trevor's novels. Melanie Klein's theories (1991) are especially relevant to *The Butcher Boy* and *Felicia's Journey* because each concerns a protagonist who has strong feelings of guilt, anxiety and anger arising from their early relationship with their mother. Klein found that a child's anxieties were more likely to be caused by the child's own sense of guilt. One of the sources of anxiety that Klein identified was feeding at the mother's breast, an experience embedded in the subconscious. Klein argued that while our mother's breasts offer our first experience of warmth, security and comfort, it is at our mother's breasts that we first experience rejection when they are withdrawn. According to Klein we also experience greed and self-indulgence for the first time at our mother's breasts. It hardly needs pointing out that the child is capable of abusing the breast that is offered. Klein's psychoanalytical study of children revealed that a child can desire the mother's breast – can want to feed at the mother's breast – but can feel guilty about damaging it. In later life, whether an adult feels comfortable or not with his/her own appetites can have been determined by his/her experience at the mother's breast. The lasting influence of these early experiences is the basis of a school of psychoanalytic thought called 'object relations theory'.

Melanie Klein's observations of children at play and her psychoanalysis of children led her to conclude that there is a stage in child development when the child thinks in terms of a good breast and a bad breast. The breast that is offered the child is seen as 'good' but the breast that is withdrawn is seen as 'bad'. Part of acquiring 'maturity' for Klein was recognizing that there isn't a 'good' breast and a 'bad' breast but that the breast is both 'good' and 'bad'. In other words, the child transcends the restrictive 'good' and 'bad' binarism and learns to recognize that no object, including his mother, is either entirely good or bad. However, this maturity is not always fully acquired and splitting, which Klein thought of as an attack upon reality, can lead to a psychotic state. It is this psychotic state, at its most extreme, that marks the preoccupation with limit in both McCabe's and Trevor's novel. The way individuals, like Francie and Hilditch, see the world in terms of black and white mirrors in very sinister ways how a child thinks of a 'good' and a 'bad' breast rather than in terms of a breast (person) that can be 'good' and 'bad'. McCabe gives this argument an interesting twist by drawing attention to the way in which in the Cold War the communists were frequently presented within a simplistic East/West and Capitalism/Communism binary.

Klein argues that loving phantasies derived from the relationship with the breast as an object of desire and affection. According to Kleinian thought, the child then projects its love phantasies on others. Other people are experienced as a source of love and comfort. The object of love and comfort becomes in Klein's language an 'imago'. S/he is then internalized as a fantasy figure. In this situation, the protagonist sees the heroine as a part object – as a good breast. In Kleinian theory adult subjectivity is rooted in recognizing whole objects, in which characteristics felt to be good and loved coexist with characteristics felt to be bad, hated and feared.

The fact that Francie has failed to make the transition from thinking in terms of simple good–bad binarism is the reason he is so at home in the rigid binarism of children's stories and comics. Unfortunately, Mrs Nugent represents the 'good mother', frequently the absent present in fairy stories, which Francie desires. His mother, whom he loves, is for him the 'bad mother', eventually withdrawing permanently from him through her suicide for which he blames himself. Mrs Nugent, as the 'good mother', comes between Francie and his real mother because she reminds him of the way his own mother failed him, and probably how he thinks of himself as having failed her. Within this context, the ostensibly gruesome details of her murder become highly symbolic because in cutting open her front, Francie seems to signify a desire to re-enter the womb. At the opening of the novel, he purports to speak to us from a womb-like place in which he feels safe – 'a hole under a tangle of briars .... You could see plenty from the inside but no one could see you' (1).

From Madness to Transgression

Particularly important to a discussion of the 1980s and 1990s Irish novel is the shift in focus in Foucault's work from 'madness' to transgression. This shift actually occurs in *The Butcher Boy* because it is so much a novel about limit. It is not, though, simply a literary artistic manoeuvre; it is a way of exploring the inconsistencies and chaos in identity. 'Transgression' is distinguished in Foucauldian terms from 'taboo'. For Foucault (1977), taboo exists in a dialectical relation to limit, and at one level, it can be said to reaffirm limit. But transgression, in Foucault's view, 'is not related to the limit as black to white' (35). The role of transgression is 'to measure the excessive distance that it opens at the heart of the limit' (35). It would be possible to argue that in selecting an unmarried woman who is having a child by a man old enough to be her father and is the father of one of her friends as the key protagonist of *The Snapper*, Doyle is deliberately seeking to enter 'the excessive distance…at the heart of the limit'. This is certainly true for the conclusion of *The Butcher Boy*; the killing of a woman who is a mother is in Catholic terms a sin that cannot be forgiven. As a reminder of this, when Francie wheels Mrs Nugent's body in a wheel barrow, he passes another barrow carrying a statue of the Virgin Mary to whom the villagers now pray for her to intervene and save them from the impending apocalypse. This juxtaposition of Mrs Nugent's corpse and the statue of the Virgin Mary, both treated in different ways with profanity, opens up a moral apocalypse – a signifier of what lies in Foucaldian terms at 'the heart of the limit'. In killing a mother figure, Francie has effectively murdered the Virgin Mary. Thus, in Francie's killing, to appropriate Foucault's thesis, 'the limit opens violently onto the limitless, finds itself suddenly carried away by the content it had rejected and fulfilled by this alien plenitude which invades it to the core of its being' (34). Foucault sees transgression as a singular moment of contestation. The very gravity of what Francie has done, and the implied apocalyptic consequences, highlights the singularity of the murder:

> She stumbled trying to get to the phone or the door and when I smelt the scones and seen Phillip's picture I started to shake and kicked her I don't know how many times. She groaned and said please I didn't care if she groaned or said please or what she said. I caught her round the neck and I said: You did two bad things Mrs Nugent. You made me turn my back on my ma and you took Joe away from me. Why did you do that Mrs Nugent? She didn't answer I didn't want to hear any answer I smacked her against the wall a few times there was a smear of blood at the corner of her mouth and her hand was reaching out trying to touch me when I cocked the captive bolt. I lifted her off the floor with one hand and shot the bolt right into her head *thlok* was the sound it made, like a goldfish dropping into a bowl. If you ask anyone how to kill a pig they will tell you cut its throat across but you don't you do it longways. Then she just lay there with her chin sticking up and I opened her then I stuck my hand in her stomach and wrote PIGS all over the walls of the upstairs room. (195)

This passage begins with the kind of male violence exposed in *The Woman Who Walked Into Doors*. But it is interrupted by a reference to the smell of scones, signifying an idealized domestic environment. The word 'please' is one that might be used between two people making love; here, of course, Mrs Nugent is begging for mercy. The word 'groan' is an appropriate one for the author to have chosen to convey the victim's pain, but McCabe has selected a word that in another context can suggest pleasure. The word 'touch', too, can have tender connotations – McCabe might have used words that in this context might have better conveyed the violence of the struggle. What we have here is language that, as Foucault says, is sometimes 'immobilized in scenes we customarily call "erotic" '. But the language is, to employ Foucault's words, 'suddenly volatised in a philosophical turbulence, when it seems to lose its very basis' (39). This loss of the conventional basis of language is reinforced by *thlok* which interrupts the text and reminds us of the blurred boundary between graphic realism and fantasy in a child's comic.

What kind of language, Foucault (1977) asks, arises from the death of God? Foucault's answer, and it is borne out by the last part of *The Butcher Boy*, is that it will be a language 'chased … from its original dialectics' (39). There is a very strong sense of void at the end of the novel. The bonfire that Francie makes betrays the complex eclecticism of his life, of what has gone into making his identity. At one level, the burning of the Sacred Heart suggests that this once revered Catholic icon has now become one more sign among many others. But another way of reading the burning of this icon is that Francie has rejected the ideals with which it is associated, including the blessedness of the family:

> There was one [picture] of da pressing the mouthpiece [of his trumpet] to his lips. On you go, I says. Then the Sacred Heart with his two fingers up and the thorny heart burning outside his chest. Do you remember all the prayers we used to say in the old days Francie? He says. Oh now Sacred Heart I says, will I ever forget them? May the curse of Christ light upon you this night you rotten cunting bitch – do you remember that one?   (207)

The ambiguity that it acquires in Francie's eyes is part of the critique of Catholic hypocrisy in the text as a whole. All the Catholic institutions that should have offered him help and guidance fail

Francie. But these institutions can be separated from the ideals and principles of Catholicism that they may be seen as betraying.

It is also significant to a reading of the murder of Mrs Nugent as opening up what Foucault calls the 'excessive distance ... at the heart of the limit', that *The Butcher Boy* closes by transgressing the respect normally assigned to the corpse as the body of a person. The sacred respect with which the corpse is normally viewed acts as a kind of compensatory symbolism. This, though, is in turn haunted by the corpse as, in Julia Kristeva's terms, the ultimate signifier of the 'abject':

> The corpse (or cadaver: *cadere*, to fall), that which has irre-demiably come a cropper, is cesspool, and death; it upsets even more violently the one who confronts it as fragile and falla-cious chance. A wound with blood and pus, or the sickly, acrid smell of sweat, of decay, does not *signify* death. In the presence of signified death – a flat encephalograph, for instance – I would understand, react, or accept. No, as in true theatre, without makeup or masks, refuse and corpses *show me* what I permanently thrust aside in order to live. These body fluids, this defilement, this shit, are what life withstands, hardly and with difficulty on the part of death. There, I am at the border of my condition as a living being. My body extricates itself, as being alive, from that border. Such wastes drop so that I might live, until, from loss to loss, nothing remains in me and my entire body falls beyond the limit – *cadere*, cadaver. If dung sig-nifies the other side of the border, the place where I am not and which permits me to be, the corpse, the most sickening of wastes, is a border that has encroached upon everything.
>
> [....]
>
> Deprived of world, therefore, I fall *in a faint*. In that com-pelling, raw, insolent thing in the morgue's full sunlight, in that thing that no longer matches and therefore no longer signifies anything, I behold the breaking down of a world that has erased its borders, fainting away. The corpse, seen without God and out-side of science, is the utmost of abjection ... imaginary uncanni-ness and real threat, it beckons to us and ends up engulfing us. (1982: 3–4)

The corpse, deprived of its compensatory symbolism, itself opens what is at the heart of limit.

Between Art and Madness

The notion of a space which is opened when art and madness are joined together, constituting a sense of what Foucault called 'perpetual rupture', is central to William Trevor's *Felicia's Journey*. In elaborating on his concept of 'perpetual rupture', Foucault defined it further as the 'breaking point': 'The dissolution of a work in madness, this void to which poetic speech is drawn as to its self-destruction, is what authorizes the text of a language common to both [poetic and psychological structures]' (1977: 85). In the killing of Mrs Nugent and the chaos which brings *The Butcher Boy* to its conclusion, there is evidence of what Foucault describes: dissolution; the way in which the language of the text is drawn, almost, to its self-destruction; and the overwhelming sense of a void in which this occurs. In *Felicia's Journey*, the text once again appears to be drawn to self-destruction, and to a void created by the death of God. This time it is because the psychopath Hilditch, who presents himself throughout as a Father figure and as a benevolent being who watches over children who stray from the straight and narrow, is all the time drawing them to their deaths. Presenting himself as the 'good father', he is secretly the evil father of the Gothic horror tale.

The British Mental Health Act (1959) describes the psychopath as a 'persistent disorder or disability of mind … that results in abnormally aggressive or seriously irresponsible conduct'. One school of thought is that the concept of the psychopath developed from an eighteenth- and nineteenth-century category of criminal known as a 'moral imbecile'. These imbeciles were perceived as suffering from an 'illness of morality'. Whether this is to be trusted or not, it is one view of a type of criminality that has grabbed the literary and popular imagination. However, the psychopath in literature and film is often as much the subject of popular discourses about 'monstrosity' as medico-legal analysis. The origins of the monstrous demon that haunts the representation of extreme criminality in western literature can be traced back through the Bible to ancient literatures. At one level, it gives expression to our most deep-rooted fears and anxieties as humans, but, at another level, it 'others' the extreme depravity, 'at the heart of the limit', that men particularly but not exclusively are depicted as capable of. Thus, there is often a tension in modern writing between the representation of monstrous criminality as something innate or absolute, or as something removed from normal human behaviour, and as something relative, the product of psychological or environmental factors.

However, if the monstrous demon figure provides a way of conceptualizing almost unimaginable criminality, it is itself a relative rather than an absolute configuration. It depends upon changing concepts of what constitutes the most serious and worrying crimes at particular times and is interleaved with the projection of cultural anxieties and phobias on to other, and 'othered', peoples and physiological types. Even the depravity with which particular demonized criminals are associated is not absolute. At different times equally appalling acts will be invested with a greater cultural significance than at others.

Felicia's Journey is a mixture of genres: exile narrative, innocent abroad narrative, psychological thriller and serial killer narrative. Serial killer narratives usually focus on the killer and a number of victims, or a single victim who turns out to be one of many, who fall prey to him early in the text or before the point where the story begins. In this novel, the main protagonist is not killed and the attempted murder is delayed until the end of the narrative. Serial killer narratives are often structured around the life story of the killer interconnecting with the life histories of his victims. *Felicia's Journey* interleaves the life histories of Hilditch and Felicia. In serial killer narratives, coincidence is the key. The murder(s) can be traced back to a single coincidence, such as the victim having the kind of hair about which the killer has a particular fetish. Part of that coincidence is often a chance meeting – an element of fate that joins two otherwise very disparate lives. The single moment of time that triggers the events of Trevor's novel is the meeting between Felicia and Hilditch at his place of work when she asks him about the whereabouts of the lawnmower factory.

In joining, in Foucault's terms, 'art' and 'madness', Trevor organizes the text around the implications of interleaving two narratives. Felicia is the subject of one narrative – her quest to find Johnny that turns into a journey for an abortion. But she is the object of another – Hilditch's – without realizing it. Although he plans, without perhaps fully recognizing it, to kill her, he creates fictional narratives around her. Some of them are secret, such as pretending to the woman serving in Buddy's cafe, out of Felicia's earshot, that she is his girlfriend. Other fictions are in what he tells

Felicia, for example, that he has talked to his hospitalized wife about her predicament whereas in reality he has no wife and has no one he must visit in hospital. Thus, many of the episodes in which Felicia and Hilditch are brought together operate on several levels. For example, in the episode in Buddy's café, Felicia is made to believe by Hilditch that he is upset because his wife has just undergone an emergency operation and is poorly. She is also made to think that his wife is concerned for her welfare, even though all his wife apparently knows about Felicia is what Hilditch has told her. This pretence has the effect of further convincing Felicia that Hilditch, like his wife, is an exceptionally kind person. The reality, of which she is not aware, is that Hilditch is trying to manipulate the scene so that the staff working there admires him because he has a girlfriend young enough to be his daughter. In his own imaginings, he also thinks of her as 'Beth', thereby blurring the boundaries between the various girls he has killed.

While Felicia thinks she lives in one kind of universe, as it were, all the time she is living in another. Hilditch tricks her into visiting factories with him and steals her bank notes so that she is more likely to become dependent upon him. While she thinks she is making a decision of her own free will in going to his house for help, she has in reality become a pawn in his game with her:

> He recalls as a child trying to entice a mouse into a trap that was made like a cage. You put the cheese down and then go away. Every day you put the cheese down a little closer to the metal wire and in the end the mouse goes in of its own accord, confident that it knows what's what.   (111)

Hilditch's control of Felicia casts him as a kind of author, manipulating the details of his narrative, and inventing lives in which the subjects have no agency themselves. Hilditch increasingly reduces Felicia to a character in his fictive narrative. In fact, this has resonance for the whole of her life. Throughout the novel, she is not the subject of her own history; others control her, sometimes subtly, and on other occasions quite openly. Johnny manipulates her into having sex with him by lying to her. Her father named her after a woman, who manned the barricades in the Easter Rising, an action that places her in his version of reality. In this larger context, the account of Felicia's feelings for Declan Fetrick become more important than the amount of space devoted to them in the novel might suggest:

> When she was twelve Felicia had been in love with Declan
> Fetrick. He was older, already employed on the ready-meats
> counter of the Centra foodstore…. She never spoke to Declan
> Fetrick, a scrawny boy who was trying to grow a moustache, and
> she never told anyone else about how she felt, not even Carmel
> or Rose or Connie Jo, but every day and every night for nearly a
> year she thought about him, imagining his arms tightening
> around her, and the soft bristles of his boy's moustache.   (27)

Felicia conceives of her destiny as that of most women in Catholic
Ireland – to fall in love and marry. Declan is not simply a real person but a symbolic presence in her life. As in Paula and her sister's
case in *The Woman Who Walked Into Doors*, a man is seen as providing the means of escape from her restricted and restrictive family
life. His arms 'tightening around her' signify the sense of protection she, like Paula, desires. In other words, in Kleinian terms,
Declan in *Felicia's Journey* and Charlo in *The Woman Who Walked Into
Doors* are imagos. Declan's symbolic status in Felicia's life is
enhanced by the fact that he is on the threshold of adulthood. But
if we return to this passage having read more of the novel, the dark
undertones become more obvious. The fact that Declan works on a
'ready-meats' counter not only suggests the way in which men
regard women as 'meat', seeing them in terms of their flesh, but
Hilditch's murder of them, and more specifically the ham which
Felicia notices hanging ominously in his kitchen when she enters it.
The fantasy of Declan's arms 'tightening around her' is double-
edged, suggesting the violence which many women endure at the
hands of men, as well as Hilditch's plans to kill her.

The meat image in relation to sexual relations is a recurring
trope in contemporary Irish fiction. Here we might compare
what is implied in this account of Felicia's fantasies with Rita
and Mel's first sex in Morrissy's *Mother of Pearl*, discussed in
Chapter 7. They take a journey over a stagnant river, through
cobbled alleys, and waste ground. But the detail which is most
stressed is McMahon's butcher's shop: 'the word VICTUALLER
set in brown and beige tiles below the window. Glimpse of the
chopping block like the rump of a fossilised mammal and the
sheen of the circular slicer' (96). The allusions to meat, butchery
and dismemberment are echoed in the account of the derelict

house on, the appropriately named, 'Rutland Street': 'A woman was said to have been murdered there, done in with a hatchet' (97). Unlike the cryptic ambiguity in the account of Felicia's fantasies, the ambivalence here is unmistaken. The couple have entered what is described as 'forbidden territory. Haunted'. The word 'haunted', standing alone in its own sentence, stresses the connection between the murdered woman and Rita's loss of virginity. In effect, Rita Golden is murdered, and with her the innocence and wonder of her life as a young woman:

> Now Rita was here, but with a man (Mel, being four years older), which made it safe .... And being stroked, his fingers in the crook of her neck, a hand on her bare thigh where he'd pushed up her skirt, murmuring words that sounded both venomous and sacred. He gasped when he touched her, as if it wounded him. And then ... and then, it stopped being safe. Wan light drained from a mauve sky. Above, the rafters gaped .... (97)

The language here is both figurative and, as in the final image of the gaping rafters, monstrous. Like Felicia, in her fantasy, Rita is attracted to an older man because, like Paula Spencer, she, too craves protection. But, of course, Felicia's fantasy with Declan never becomes reality, except with Johnny. And there, to judge from her fantasy about Declan, what she initially might have conceived of as safe, stops being so.

The way in which Felicia, unwittingly, like many Irish women at the time of the Anglo-Irish war, is a character in other people's, usually men's, stories anchors a larger concern in the book with the boundary between fiction and reality. Hilditch constructs his regimental past – all the portraits in the hallway he has purchased. Felicia's father constructs a narrative of Ireland with which Felicia finds it hard to identify. Like Hilditch's imagined past, it is masculinist, based on patriotism, heroism and sacrifice, and ultimately becomes more central to his life than his own family, certainly his daughter.

The plot line, based on the intersection of Felicia and Hilditch's life stories, is one to which we, as readers, must retain a critical detachment because what is going on can hardly ever be taken for granted. But the story is also 'othered' in another way. It is based on the intersection not only of two life stories but of two 'outlawed' narratives: Felicia's history as a Catholic girl who is exiled by sectarianism and her Catholic environment because she has had a relationship with an Irishman serving in the British army; and Hilditch's narrative which is that of a murderer. In other words, the text brings together a naive girl who has transgressed the laws of home, community and church, and a man who has failed to grow beyond his relationship with his mother and lives alone in a large house that connotes his 'detached' life. Thus, the principal narrative is located on the edges of ordinary experience, which is reflected in the choice of locations that are themselves 'on the edge' such as factories on industrial estates and motorway cafes. The latter, particularly, signify the text's concern with limit, themselves opening up on 'excessive distances', literally and, as places of abduction of young females, metaphorically.

At one level, Hilditch's activities parody the Catholic notion of a benevolent and merciful Father who seeks out those who sin. But, like Francie Brady, his behaviour is related to the primary orality associated with infants at their mother's breast. Not coincidentally, Hilditch's pursuit of young girls is linked to his obsession with food, and when he secretly creates a metaphor for the game he is playing with Felicia, he chooses one involving cheese. Both his eating habits and his preying on young girls involve meticulous planning, and he has clear ground rules. For example, he always watches the girls for some time to learn as much as he can about them and their patterns of behaviour, and never picks them up near his home or place of work. Intriguingly, these are rules that he breaks in the case of Felicia. We learn that 'he likes to look at something tasty before he takes the initial bite' (72). This dates from the age of six and at the time was observed by his mother. This pattern of behaviour seems to inform the way he waits before raping and then killing the girls. The litany of girls' names – Elsie, Beth, Gaye, Sharon, Jakki (51) – parallel the variety of biscuits in his biscuit barrel: raspberry creams, coffee creams, chocolate digestives, fig rolls, kit-kats (52).

In Hilditch's case, as in Francie's, it seems pertinent to recall that Klein linked primary orality, which Hilditch seems never to have outgrown, with the way in which the child divides the world into 'good' and 'bad' mirroring the 'offered' or 'good' breast and the 'withdrawn' or bad breast. Hilditch's mother is actually seen by him in these starkly simplistic terms. The bad mother is the sexual mother who is only fully revealed at the end of the novel who went with men and preyed on him as a child:

> Had she always foreseen, when he was six and eight and ten,
> when he sat beside her watching *Dumbo* and *Bambi*, when first
> he practised his signature, when he wrote down *Major Hilditch*:
> had she always known that she would turn to him when there
> was no one else? When the insurance-man winked and said no
> time for anything today, did she foresee – already – what
> would happen in this house? (195)

As with *The Butcher Boy*, there are two absent presences: the child
who has never had access to what is conventionally thought of as
a childhood in a loving and caring family, and the good mother.
In Hilditch's case, the good mother, the self-sacrificing, supportive mother enshrined in the Irish constitution, disappears very
quickly from his life. Remembered especially from his sixth year,
she occasionally interrupts the narrative, breaking into it as she
does his consciousness. For example, at one point he is collecting
his food at the canteen: ' "Oh, what a timid one you are!" his mother
used to say when he was six. He smiles again, pleased that the
remark has come back to him' (126). Thus, the text encourages us
to ask whether Hilditch's preference for girls who are 'pre-sexual'
or relatively inexperienced, is a means by which he is endlessly
renogiating, within his own mind, his relationship with his
mother. The pattern of his involvement with them is invariably
the same. He eventually accuses them of coming on to him, and
then kills them. In other words, they become in Kleinian terms
imagos, but unlike Felicia's Declan and Paula's Charlo they are
negative imagos. Nevertheless, these phantasies projected on to
the girls are then internalized:

> You could see Beth thinking it; you could see her searching her
> thoughts and finding it. And Elsie Covington, then the others;
> they broke in somehow. They trespassed on his privacy
> even though he took them to places and lavished a bit on them
> in their time of need, the Irish girl too. You could tell, from the
> way she stood there in her nightdress, that she respected nei-
> ther his house nor himself because she knew.   (196)

Is he, we might legitimately ask, killing the 'bad' mother? Felicia
effectively signs her death warrant in a single moment of time;

when she comes downstairs in his house in her nightgown, her coat thrown over her, and her feet bare. He sees her as teasing him.

In some respects, the novel is a version of the 'Red Riding Hood' story with Hildtitch as the big bad wolf. When Felicia arrives at the factory she is wearing a red coat and headscarf. At the moment when she comes down the stairs in her nightgown, it is her red coat she has thrown over herself. But the wilderness which in the story of Red Riding Hood is associated with the forest is here brought into a domestic setting, as is apparent in the account of Felicia's entry into Hilditch's kitchen:

> The kitchen is enormous, the biggest Felicia has ever been in. Its wooden ceiling is stained with the vapours of generations, a single ham hook all that remains of the row there must once have been. Two dressers are crowded with china; a long deal table occupies the central area; pairs of tights hang from drying-rails on a pulley. There are four upright chairs, a step-ladder against one wall, an old sewing machine in a corner, a mangle. The refrigerator and an electric stove seem out of place.   (114)

The opening sentence invokes Red Riding Hood's response to the wolf's large eyes and teeth when she enters her grandmother's bedroom. The stain suggests the past that has left Hilditch psychically handicapped, as well as the blood of his young victims. The latter is also suggested by the detail of the one ham left hanging which also suggestively prefigures Hilditch's own suicide. The split life that Hilditch lives is reflected in the temporal duality of the kitchen – the modern refrigerator and stove standing in contradistinction to the old sewing machine and the mangle. This duality is analogous also of the division of his mother into a good and bad figure. The 'pairs of tights', perhaps suggest the latter, and her sexuality.

The invocation of fairy tales in this novel is highly appropriate. After all, they were conceived, as Jack Zipes has argued in his book-length study of the subject (1988), as warning tales addressed to young women – cautioning of the dangers in straying from the straight and narrow. But fairy tales, Zipes maintains, also have a liberating power because they can present us with a means by which the idealized home may be reclaimed. The opposed protagonists, he argues, learn to free themselves from the conflicts that prevent them from attaining their idealized home. Given that Felicia runs away from ideological conflicts that render her home oppressive, in search of a man she believes will provide her with an ideal home, and takes the kind of dangerous paths which traditional stories, at one level, warned us of, the novel appears especially ironic when read through Zipes's perspectives on fairy stories.

Hilditch himself is at pains to establish Felicia's vulnerability – that she has run away from home, and does not come from a secure family – from behind a mask of seeming concern. In effect, he establishes her as the female victim in a fairy story. But the fact that Hilditch strays is as important as Felicia's transgression. Hilditch's fastidiousness and the way he barricades himself into his house at the end betrays the importance to his identity of boundaries. His existence has been based on maintaining discrete boundaries between his private life and work, between fantasy and reality.

The enigma at the heart of the novel from his point of view is why he chooses to depart from his customary practices. Why did he break the rules of not picking up girls near his home or place of work and of not bringing the girls to his home afterwards? Early in the novel he appreciates the dangers for himself in breaking his rules but finds the transgression exciting. There is a further enigma: the stress on the fact that Felicia is different from the others. Does he, like many serial killers, want to be caught? Does he realize that Felicia is the one who will release him from what has become the burden of 'seriality'? At one point he tries to explain that often people want to do something that doesn't appear to be in their best interests (149). Felicia's search for Johnny and Hilditch's pursuit of Felicia determine the structure of the narrative, and the reader looks forward to the space which will be opened when these narratives reach their limit. Like *The Butcher Boy*, this is a novel about the sovereignty of 'limit', and the collusion of literature and the reader in that sovereignty.

Exploring subjects that have been marginalized – at least as far as serious literature is concerned – these novels are also dealing with topics that have been silenced. What they also have in common is their preoccupation with what Foucault called limit and with the 'distance' that opens up at the point of limit. The preoccupation with limit focuses a wider concern with the cultural significance of transgression, which again may be read through Foucault's thesis that the twentieth century will become increasingly concerned with sexuality as limit, devoid of any larger meaningful point of reference. These texts confirm what Foucault says but their preoccupation is with sexually tinged violence as limit.

9

Return to Silence and Beyond

Speculative Narrative in Bernard
MacLaverty's *Grace Notes* (1997) and
John Banville's *Birchwood* (1973)

Grace Notes and *Birchwood* represent different poles in contemporary speculative fiction. The former, a version of the exile narrative, concerns a young composer and unmarried mother, suffering from clinical depression, who returns to Northern Ireland from Scotland on her father's death. The latter is more of a modernist, surrealist work that appropriates the Big House narrative and is set in Ireland around the time of the Great Famine. In a different context, each has at its centre the relationship between an adult and their parents. But, although *Grace Notes*, despite its to-and-fro movement between different periods in the central protagonist's life, is a more traditional novel than the highly allusive *Birchwood*, they are both speculative narratives concerned, in their different ways, with the return of what has been secret or suppressed. But what separates the engagement with what Freud labelled Nachträglichkeit, introduced in Chapter 3, in these texts from the novels discussed previously, is their emphasis upon exploring the possibility of transcendence.

While many of the novels that we have looked at so far involve the movement out of silence, *Grace Notes* moves into silence and the significance of the gaps between sound which the novel redefines as 'appropriate noise'. It awakens us, as the novel's principal protagonist Catherine is awakened in the text, to the significance of what is often concealed by our attention to sound rather than silence that MacLaverty relates to the innovative

198

concept of pre-hearing. The concept of pre-hearing is linked to a further concept, 'inner hearing', derived from the influence of a significant female ancestor, and associated with female cultural and corporeal identity. Thus, while the text moves toward silence, it, ostensibly paradoxically, brings a female voice and consciousness out of the margins where it has been silenced.

Many of the texts that we have discussed up until now have explored the possibility of moving out of an 'in-between' location or timelag, as well as examining what it means to occupy such a physical or temporal space within different specific political and historical contexts, *Birchwood* enters a philosophical space that is in-between conventional representations of good and evil and temporal spaces that are outside of linear, and even cyclical, notions of time.

Pre-hearing

Grace Notes, like *Birchwood*, is an interruptive narrative; it is concerned to disrupt the world in which most of us, who are not musicians, live by defamiliarizing it. As a musician, the central protagonist, Catherine, lives with, and through, a heightened sense of sound that develops into a greater awareness of the gaps between sounds. Indeed, whereas in Seamus Deane's modernist novel *Reading in the Dark*, the fear is of being struck dumb, in *Grace Notes* the fear is of being struck deaf. Indeed, this is what happened to Catherine's great grandfather when a Loyalist bullet ricocheted off a wall close to his right ear. When Anna is born, one of the first parts of her body that Catherine scrutinizes is her ear. Not surprisingly, Catherine remembers her childhood enjoyment of the playground slide as being different from that of other children because of her appreciation of the sounds her body made in contact with it:

> Catherine had loved the slide. *Ding dang dung ding dong.* Ascending notes as she'd run up the iron steps – *sleeth* – she'd slide down the shute and then race back to climb the steps. *Ding dang dung ding dong* running up, *sleeth*, down again. She must have been the only child in the town who liked running up the steps better than sliding down the shute.   (176)

Grace Notes, though, is not simply intent upon opening its readers' ears as well as their eyes. It is a philosophical text concerned to take us back to what is presented as a human faculty that we have temporarily lost. Whereas McGahern's *Amongst Women*, which we discussed in Chapter 4, is concerned with pre-verbal, or pre-symbolic sound, *Grace Notes* explores the notion of 'pre-hearing'. At one point, beside the sea, with her baby, Catherine compares the silence, or what she would rather call 'appropriate noise', with the yelling of the children at break-time in the school where she taught. This passage associates the pre-hearing with the rhythmic and the feminine as European psychoanalytic theory links the pre-verbal with them:

> All was quiet except for the sliding in of the sea, the rhythmic unfurling of small waves and sometimes the metallic screeching of a gull... Here there was such silence. Not silence, but appropriate noise. Catherine sat there by the sea, lost in her ears. *Pre-hearing*. (213)

As I suggested earlier, pre-hearing is in turn linked in the novel to 'inner-hearing', which has its origins in Catherine being taught to think of her name in terms of its rhythm. This in itself presents a feminine way of appropriating the masculine tradition of 'naming'. Indeed, Catherine comes to see her female family lineage as nested like Russian dolls – her daughter inside herself, herself inside her mother and her mother inside her grandmother (171). This is a view of history which has been marginalized, especially in post-Treaty Ireland, by emphasis upon the masculine line, legitimated by the celebration of the men who led, and those who were killed in, the Easter Rising, as evidenced in Felicia's father's nationalist scrapbook in *Felicia's Journey* discussed in Chapter 1.

When we first encounter her, Catherine is undertaking a geographical movement but this is analogous of larger and more profound shifts in her life. The most important of these is the way in which she has brought her own musical composition from the margins of her life, giving up her teaching job in order to become unemployed and devote herself full time to her own creativity. In the novel, pre-hearing itself is embedded in marginal spaces as diverse as the beach and the kitchen but they are all spaces associated with women.

Like the association of the pre-symbolic with the feminine, the concept of pre-hearing, through what the novel describes as 'inner hearing', veers toward an essentialist notion of female identity oriented upon motherhood and the domestic. This is suggested in Catherine's memories of one of the formative presences in her life, Granny Boyd. The grandmother stands in contradistinction to Catherine's mother between whom there is a rift. The rift is forged in two stages – the first when she learns that Catherine has given up her job and the second when she learns that she has a child and has been using birth control. Her mother is incredulous that Catherine has given up her job and is writing for herself because having an employer is 'the way the world works' (88), and her attitude towards her daughter's pregnancy betrays how far her Catholicism is a part of her sense of self. Yet when her daughter leaves, she buys her a wheaten loaf – 'It's good bread. Do you for your breakfast' (119). Her explanation gives the purchase a kind of logic but, of course, the bread works symbolically as well as pragmatically within the narrative. Bread is the archetypal symbol of the visible and manifest life – the materiality we all share. In turning conciliatory towards her daughter, although not entirely forgiving, Mrs McKenna acknowledges the flesh that she and Catherine, and her granddaughter Anna, share. It is especially symbolic that Mrs McKenna buys a wheaten loaf because bread when broken and shared represents a shared and united life.

Catherine's grandmother's influence on her granddaughter is very different from that which Felicia's nationalist and oppressive grandmother had on her. Indeed, Catherine thinks of the set of variations for string orchestra on which she is working as 'stitching small segments together the way Granny Boyd had made quilts' (144). The older woman teaches her 'catches' which she sings along to the rhythm of her sewing machine. The objects that define Granny Boyd – especially the sewing machine – are associated with domesticity and conventional assumptions about the role of the mother. But Granny Boyd serves to 'de-scribe' rather than 'inscribe' the mother or grandmother figure. The pun on the manufacturer's name – 'Singer' – dislodges the sewing machine from its normal restricted associations and links it to the pre-symbolic and to pre-hearing, in turn closely connected to the instinctual and spontaneous life of the female freed from the constrictions of patriarchal symbolism.

The allusion to Granny Boyd's quilt is highly significant, for the quilt is not only a female art form. It brings women of different generations and families together in a lineage that lies outside the materiality that traditionally serves to constrain, silence or, at best displace, female community. The allusions to the quilt and to what Granny Boyd calls 'rounds of the kitchen' are important to Catherine in realizing her own compositions because the female corporeal identity signified by them becomes a creative resource. Thus, while Catherine is drawn toward 'silence', or 'appropriate noise' at one level, this is associated with a female identity and lineage that has been silenced by conventional nationalist history and patriarchal culture.

In helping her grandmother in the kitchen, Catherine learns what her Granny Boyd calls 'the rounds of the kitchen'. In working with and alongside her, Catherine acquires a heightened sense of hearing: 'Catherine's tongue would disappear and she would listen to the whisper of her grandmother's thread being drawn through the material and to her own scissor noise as she cut out the papers' (185). When, at the end of the novel, Catherine attends the first performance of her composition, the orchestra becomes, in her mind, 'a stitching machine' (276). Like 'an optical illusion in sound', akin to drawings where the same picture can be an old woman or a child, Catherine and her grandmother are brought together: 'The mind flicked. Grandmother? Girl? Girl. Grandmother' (275). The second movement is a celebration, in somewhat essentialist terms, of the woman's body: 'Visceral music. Sound shaking the blood from the walls of her womb. The rhythm of a woman's life is synchronised with the moon and the moon is synchronised with the sea, ergo – a woman is synchronised with the tides' (274).

Catherine's own political persuasions are also very much the product of her grandmother's influence, and very different from the political convictions represented by Felicia's grandmother in William Trevor's novel. In *Grace Notes*, the map of Northern Ireland is haunted by another map constructed out of what Catherine calls 'the geography of the places of death' (127). Again these become an important aspect of cultural identity for both men and women, in Ireland and Northern Ireland. But Catherine insists, ignoring the part that female freedom fighters and paramilitaries have played in the Troubles and in the Anglo-Irish wars, let alone the part played by a female British prime minister, 'it was a map which would not exist if women made the decisions' (127). Nevertheless, the way in which the European musical heritage has been shaped by the predominance of male composers is not gainsaid in the text. Thus, it stresses that, although there is plenty of music celebrating the 'God-part' of the birth of Christ, there is little celebrating birth as a phenomenon, or even the 'man-part' of Christ's birth. The narrative suggests that this subject, like the female presence in music, has been dormant waiting to erupt and interrupt. In this, it conflates the movement in the text toward silence with its concern to bring female corporeal and cultural identity out of the narratives that have silenced it. From the silence that Catherine redefines as 'appropriate noise' there is a female-oriented music that has been dormant, waiting to interrupt.

Grace Notes is located in a timelag that is largely anchored in the gestation of Catherine's composition which is itself compared to a spore weighting to germinate. The time that it takes to compose music must include the space in which one is waiting for inner-music to materialize, to begin to take shape. What is important to the novel is how one views intervals such as this, invoking at one point Stravinsky's thesis that 'rhythm was intervals of a certain duration' (128). The novel interrupts the concept of time as linear, shifting the emphasis to the gaps within linearity. Catherine's view of time, which comes to inform her wider worldview, is borrowed from her Chinese mentor Huang Xai Gang, that music derives not from notes but the space between notes. These spaces are called 'grace notes' and it is the ambivalence of the term that the novel enters and tries to open up.

The term 'grace notes' stresses the importance of the dormant as much as the 'in-between', as does the narrative itself, evident in the image of the Rose of Jericho, a desert plant that can lie dormant until hot water is poured over it, when it erupts and interrupts the period of inactivity to which it has been confined. The novel also highlights how music can be seen as 'the grace of God'. In the Kiev monastery that Catherine visits, the two meanings of the term are brought together, for in the 'interval' represented by communism in Russia, when religion was not allowed, music became 'a way of praying' and of 'receiving God's grace' (125). The conflation of these two meanings of 'grace' provides the basis for Catherine's composition.

At one level, Catherine's composition marks her liberation. The culmination of one of her movements is anchored in her

perception of her pregnant body as a drum: 'On this accumulating wave the drumming has a fierce joy about it' (276). But the
composition presents us with more than just Catherine's release.
The direct reference to the music coming to 'its climax' highlights
the way in which Catherine has rendered the experience of the
female orgasm in music, conveyed in words such as 'a carillon of
bells', 'cascade', 'bells yell the melody', 'accumulating wave',
'fierce joy' and 'jigging and sawing'. Employing religious
imagery – tabernacle, transubstantiation and joy – the novel
works from and through a space that lies outside of the symbolic,
and ultimately of discourse itself:

> At the moment when the music comes to its climax, a carillon
> of bells and brass, the Lambegs make another entry at maxi-
> mum volume. The effect this time is not one of terror or depres-
> sion but the opposite. Like scalloped curtains being raised, like
> a cascade of suffocation being drawn back to the point it came
> from and lights reappearing. The great drone bell sets the beat
> and the treble bells yell the melody. The whole church rever-
> berates. The Lambegs have been stripped of their bigotry and
> have become pure sound. The black sea withdraws. So too the
> trappings of the church – they have nothing to do with belief
> and exist as colour and form. It is infectious. On this accumu-
> lating wave the drumming has a fierce joy about it. Exhilaration
> comes from nowhere. The bell-beat, the slabs of brass, the
> whooping of the horns, the battering of the drums. Sheer fuck-
> ing unadulterated joy. Passion and pattern. An orchestra at full
> tilt – going fortissimo – the bows, up and down, jigging and
> sawing in parallel – the cellos and basses sideways ... A joy that
> celebrates being human. A joy that celebrates its own reflection,
> its own ability to make joy. To reproduce.   (275–6)

Ostensibly, the inclusion of the Lambeg drums, associated with
Loyalist fanaticism, the provocative aspect of the Orange parades
and with men rather than women, is controversial. Initially, the
inclusion of the drums is haunted by their political connotations,
and by the way in which they function as key objects in the
cultural and corporeal identity of the Portadown loyalists.
However, Catherine selects them because she sees that they can
be loosened from the set of meanings that confines them. In other
words, she recognizes that the drums are haunted by their

potential as musical instruments 'to make joy' rather than by the political materiality that the drums and the Orangemen share. And what she does, in effect, is to bring the joyful potential of the Lambeg drum out of the margins where it has been silenced by its political employment. This is made evident to us by the account of an event that is a musical equivalent of the concept of 'transubstantiation'. When they are first employed, the drums convey Fascist-like aggression, 'a brutalising of the body, the spirit, humanity' (273). When they next appear, they are designed to convey the opposite. At one level, the problem is how they can mean two things at once. At another level, it is to recognize that the ability of the drums to communicate human joy haunts the drums' ability to express 'depression and darkness' and not the other way around.

The shift in the cultural significance of the drums – people and musical instruments being part of a metaphysical, transcendent reality rather than a political materiality – involves dislodging them from one set of associations and integrating them with another. But in itself, this process of moving from one set of connotations to another is part of a larger pattern that recurs throughout the text, and not always as positively as this. For example, despite its celebration of the maternal body, there is also a dark undercurrent in the novel associated with motherhood, evident in the songs concerned with infanticide and the dangers to children posed by paedophiles. However, rather than challenge the novel's positive approach to the maternal and to motherhood, these dark moments are, in fact, haunted by the celebratory sense of joy encapsulated, for example, in Catherine's composition. This is the opposite of the way in which we might normally think. Thinking of the joy of birth as haunting the darker aspects of life is one of the discoveries toward which the narrative progresses, through the verbal equivalent of musical movement and counter-movement. In other words, the view implied by the university teacher that the songs of infanticide cast a dark shadow across the lullabies associated with mothering is reversed so that the latter casts a shadow across the former.

Catherine's Music

In the first part of Catherine's composition, the instruments of the orchestra carry the brutalizing violence of sectarianism, Fascism and of her own alcoholic partner. The music in the initial movements is haunted by Dave's violent attack upon Catherine when he almost slams the piano lid down on her fingers. The way in which the instrument and the music is suddenly made discordant – 'The bang of the lid was like a gunshot. Every string in the piano vibrated for a long time' (240) – is incorporated into the first movement. Like the Lambeg drums, his interruption is violent and disintegrating. Like the 'tormented orchestra', she tries to keep her head, not wanting to wake the baby. For a while he attacks her, eventually falling away, leaving her alone. This, too, is incorporated in her orchestral piece: 'Eventually, after an intense struggle, the orchestra falls away section by section until only the drums are left pulsing' (272). Catherine encapsulates the way in which women who are the victims of violence are constantly haunted by it, as the different parts of the orchestra seem to be looking over their shoulders waiting for the re-entry of the Lambeg drums. In the first movements, the Lambeg drums intrude as strangers but they render the orchestra strange to itself: 'Annoyance has crept in. The orchestra is angry and shrill now as it has a post-mortem on the intervention and what can be done if it happens again' (272).

The drums initially silence the female values and corporeality which Catherine discovered through her grandmother. Within this violent, alienating language, the mother as singer – exemplified by Granny Boyd – becomes the woman as bitch. But, later, we realize that female values and perspectives are not so much silenced as lying dormant. In Catherine's composition, the woman as singer is encapsulated in the ordinary, simple yet mysterious opening. It brings to mind Catherine by the beach, formulating the concept of pre-hearing.

However, Catherine's composition suggests that even this sympathetic association of women with nature needs to be subjected to scrutiny in a society that tries to restrict women's shared corporeal identity. The wispy, barely audible nature of the opening, encapsulates the disempowerment of female being and desire in a male-dominated society. The silence that follows the first intervention of the Lambeg drums is like that 'induced by a slap in the face or the roarings of a drunk' (271). It is a musical metaphor for the way in which what was a haunting presence – masculinist violence – at the outset becomes even more aggressive and dominating. But it is also the silence that follows their intervention that is significant for in it, we are made conscious of what is lying dormant waiting to erupt and interrupt. The violent and aggressive first movement is haunted by the potential joy that emerges, explosively, in the second movement. When the Lambeg drums re-enter in this context, they have been changed, feminised, by the fortissimo: 'The orchestra soars in conjunction with the Lambegs, and the Lambegs roar in response to the orchestra ...' (276).

The wider political and ideological implications of this musical metaphor perhaps bring to mind John McGahern's concern with the feminization of traditional masculinity in *Amongst Women*. What separates this movement from the wispy opening of the piece is that it is empowering while the former in its frailty was suggestive of disempowerment. In fact, it serves to critique the diffidence with which the composition opened. While at the out-set there is the suggestion of female desire being displaced on to nature – particularly the wind driven waves of the beach – here there is the unmistakeable suggestion that the *jouissance* emanates from the female body as an expression of the mystery that lies within and outside it. The way in which the orchestra explodes into life in the final section of Catherine's composition is analogous not only of the female orgasm but the way in which what has laid dormant in the Rose of Jericho is suddenly enlivened when boiling water is poured onto it.

The Nature of God's Heart

Turning to John Banville's *Birchwood* at this stage in the chapter might appear to be an interruption comparable to the Lambeg drum in Catherine's composition. *Grace Notes* and *Birchwood* are very different texts. *Birchwood* appropriates the Big House narra-tive and the tropes associated with it: insularity, decay and crisis. It is also set in a surreal version of the nineteenth century, around about the time of the Great Famine, a period during which the author could not have possibly lived. However, the two novels share a concern with the nature of art.

There isn't the same singular sense as in some Irish texts, for example, Seamus Deane's *Reading in the Dark*, that the narrator is engaged in an almost Faustian quest. Yet Banville's protagonist's narrative is haunted by thoughts of his 'father grinning in his grave at the notion of his paltry son fiddling with this, with *his*, baroque madhouse' (31). Admittedly, there is a strong suggestion throughout that this is a narrative based on questions that Gabriel should really not be asking. However, this suggestion of the artist as a kind of Faust figure is only one of several ways in which the artist is conceived in this novel. In fact, the different locations with which Gabriel Godkin is associated provide different perspectives on the role of the artist: the 'attic' suggests art for its own sake, and removed from the real world; the cellar signifies a journey into the crypt, the hidden, and the inaccessible; and the wood invokes what is primitive, wild and outside the accepted norms of civilization. Thus, the novel interleaves, and to a certain extent plays off against each other, various perspectives on the role of art in relation to Irish history and culture. But, while MacLaverty's novel overtly moves the reader toward, and into, a female corporeal space associated with nature, Banville seems, ostensibly, to take us into a 'crypt' that, rooted in the primitive and the wild, is potentially destructive. This 'crypt' is not located only in the external world but within individual and familial pasts.

Like other modernist contemporary texts, again Seamus Deane's novel is an example, *Birchwood* is based on fragmentary information from written or oral sources. Thus, unlike *Grace Notes*, in addition to being concerned with the revelation of what is hidden, it is concerned to bring order and coherence to what is fragmentary and silenced. In piecing together fragments, the spaces between the fragments are important. Here there is silenced information waiting dormant and having the potential to erupt and disrupt when the fragments begin to cohere. Whereas in *Grace Notes* what lies dormant and waiting to erupt is perceived as generally positive, in *Birchwood* there are more suggestions that what will emerge may be negative and destructive.

This impression is given initially by the space, or gap, in the novel between order and chaos. The binarism of order and chaos is implicit in the names of the rival families, the Godkins and Lawless. In entering this space, the narrator finds himself situated, as many of the protagonists we have encountered in the texts discussed in previous chapters, between 'relocation' and 'reinscription':

I feel that if I could understand it I might then begin to understand the creatures that inhabit it. But I do not understand it.

> I find the world always odd, but odder still, I suppose, is the
> fact that I find it so ...   (175)

It is not surprising that Gabriel should feel this way, since his
predicament is that of art faced with horrendous suffering and
death. A member of the Godkin family, named after God's special
messenger in the Bible, he is confronted by a family history that,
in his own words, amounts only to a 'glorious record of death and
treachery' (15). It hardly needs pointing out that the connotations
in the names refer to the way in which the Ascendancy in the
nineteenth century thought of itself and the Catholic people,
mainly peasantry, that were forming themselves into agricultural
secret societies in order to win rights for themselves and entitle-
ment to their lands. Nor does it need underscoring that in the
description of the families, and their feuds, we have a veiled
perspective on the Anglo-Irish war that is akin to Moran's
hindsight in McGahern's novel.

However, in the name Godkin, there is another layer of meaning that is waiting to erupt and interrupt the text. The connotations in the family name suggest that the novel might also be seen
as a way of looking at the Old Testament. The names of the families in *Birchwood* highlight one of the principal binarisms of the
Old Testament: law and lawlessness. One of its key themes is the
bringing of the Law that separates God's chosen people (in effect,
God's kin) whom he leads out of slavery in Egypt from those who
are without Law (the Lawless). The covenants and treaties that
God makes with Abraham, Isaac and Jacob are eventually
extended, through the laws inscribed by Moses, to the entire
nation. In this respect, there are interesting parallels with the Irish
nation and America for both nations were created in accord with
prevailing ideologies for which they served as a blue print. In the
novel, Gabriel's great, great grandfather takes over the house
from the Lawless family and the demise of the Lawless dynasty is
assured when the narrator's father marries Beatrice Lawless. The
treachery and licentious behaviour within the family echoes the
treachery around inheritance and the licentious behaviour of
some of the Patriarchs in the Old Testament. In other words, the
novel draws our attention, like *Mother of Pearl* which we discussed in Chapter 7, to aspects of the Bible that have been marginalized. Indeed, what is implicitly revealed about the Bible
through this novel might be seen as a crypt within it. Beatrice is

unable to have children reminding us of the barren wives in the Bible who gave their maids and sisters to their husbands to compensate for their weakness, again an aspect of the Bible discussed earlier in Chapter 7.

That the history of Israel as encapsulated in the Old Testament is not dissimilar, in many respects, from that of the families in this novel is important to the text. We might take the example of David, described in the Bible as 'a man after God's own heart'. He gets Bethsheba, the wife of one of his soldiers pregnant, and in order to marry her, he sends her husband to the front line where he is certain to be killed. Even allowing for the fact that David expressed regret for all that he had done, and was forgiven by God, his story begs questions about the nature of God's heart.

However, Gabriel's narrative also enters another, equally disconcerting, conceptual space: the space between David's behaviour and the beautiful psalms he was able to compose. How, then, do we convincingly put together these two dimensions of 'a man after God's own heart'? How do we put together the various perspectives that are possible on the family's histories – indeed on Irish history itself? The dilemma is centred in the text on the nature of the Godkins. Gabriel's father has an incestuous relationship with his sister which resulted in a deal that Gabriel would become the temporary heir apparent but that the property would pass eventually to his secret twin, Michael, brought up by his Aunt. As she anticipates, Joseph Godkin reneges upon the deal. The travelling circus, too, mirrors the lawlessness that haunts familial relations and desire. The mother of Angel and Silas's twins turns out to be Sybil, while Silas desires to have sex with Ada and Ida simultaneously. Ada is in fact the mother of the haunted Sophie from a brief relationship with Mario. Thus, whereas the patriarchal in *Grace Notes* is haunted by female values and corporeality, in *Birchwood* it is haunted by lawlessness.

In different ways, both novels suggest an alternative to the conventional modes of thinking. *Grace Notes* argues that we should pay attention to silence, to the gaps between sounds, as much as the sounds or musical notes themselves. *Birchwood* suggests that the problem lies not in how we reconcile the opposites of, for example, good and evil or beauty and ugliness, but in our thinking along these lines to begin with. This notion of duality enters the texts through the names of the two families; the duality in Gabriel's behaviour mirroring the duality we can find in the

Old Testament; the opposition and confusion of dream and reality; and the presence of twins. Twins have traditionally represented what is perceived in European thought as the two sides of
human nature, and of nature itself as well as the contemplative
tradition in opposition to action, the spiritual as opposed to the
physical and the sacred as opposed to the profane.

Not surprisingly, the Godkin family, like the Old Testament itself,
is haunted by the murkiness of its past, of which the wood in the
novel would seem to be analogous – 'the trees grew wicked
and deformed, some of them so terribly twisted that they crawled
horizontally across the hill' (31) – as it is of aspects of human kind
generally, of aspects of Irish history and of the subconscious. But it
is this notion of being haunted by evil that becomes the subject of
this book – a subject that, as we shall see in the next section, is
turned on its head. And, there is a parallel here to the way in which
Grace Notes sees violent masculinity as haunted by the feminine.

The Haunting of Evil

We normally think of our world being haunted by evil. This is as
generally accepted as the paradox that at the same time as we
find evil repulsive, we are also attracted to it. Thus, there appears
to be nothing unusual or exceptional in Godkin's response to one
of the sets of twins that he encounters at the travelling circus that
he temporarily joins. Despite, or because, Ada is 'sullen, given to
incoherent rages, dark laughter, careless cruelty', he finds that she
displays a 'certain vicious splendour' (121–2). And we probably
don't find it unusual, or off putting, that Gabriel is attracted to the
darkest, gloomiest parts of the wood and sees them as constituting ' a hideous, secretive and exciting place' (31). This is, after all,
a novel indebted to the Gothic, and this is what readers generally
read the Gothic for. But the dilemma around which the text turns
is that the wood is not seen as haunted by what is 'hideous' and
'secretive'. Attracted, as he is, to the 'hideous, secretive and
exciting' wood, what haunts Gabriel is the 'other' wood, the
'eponymous patch of birches' that 'lift the spirits'. This 'other'
wood is associated with the pre-verbal and the feminine.

This does not mean that the novel is grounded in a romantic
moral idealism based on a return to nature. In a sense the
travelling circus takes Gabriel and the reader back to nature. But

the nature that it takes us to is one of savagery and violence, exemplified in the account of Angel preparing a meal:

> Angel took the still warm furry dead brutes and slit their bellies. The vivid entrails spilled across the table, magenta and purple polyps, tender pink cords, bright knots of blood, giving off a nutty brown odour. She hacked off the paws, chopping through bone, lopped off the head, peeled the skin. Into the big black pot it went, that painfully nude flesh, the turnip too, sliced carrots, parsnip, thyme and other aromatic things. Silas, beating the strop with the razor, lifted his head and sniffed, the wings of his red nose fluttering delicately.   (134)

The violent reality of eating meat is normally hidden within the art of the cook pot. Here it is emphasized in the first part of the passage. But eventually, the tables are turned, and in a way that poses some pertinent questions. Is the pleasure of preparing and eating such a meal haunted by the savagery that goes into it? Or is the savagery haunted by the delicate aromatic smell?

For the nomadic Israelites, it was important to welcome fellow travellers to their tent for a meal. In the above passage, Gabriel is offered the hospitality that was shown by caravan dwellers in the Old Testament to strangers. But strangers were only expected to stay for as long as it took to prepare and eat a meal. Their presence, like Gabriel's visit with the travelling circus, is temporary – an interruption in all their lives. The episode with the travelling circus is an interruption not only in Gabriel's life but also in the narrative. And if the emphasis upon the blood and guts in the preceding passage appears to be an interruption, it may be because in the Bible God's kin inherited strict laws concerning the preparation of food. Indeed, partly through poverty and partly through religious recommendations, meat was eaten normally only on special occasions. The laws concerning the preparation of meat, such as those preventing the draining of blood or boiling a kid in its mother's milk, drew boundaries around food and eating outside of which were the possibility of cruel practices.

At one level, the circus is identified with the birch wood for it is something that lifts the spirits:

> The exotic, once experienced, becomes commonplace, that is a great drawback of this world. One touches the gold and it

turns to dross. It was not so with Prospero's band. I travelled
with them for a year, borne onward always amid an always new
and splendid oddness which sprang not merely from the excitement of new sights and sites, a new sea of faces every night, but
was the essence of these fickle things joined with something
more, a sense of strange and infinite possibilities.   (125)

However, this does not square with the 'reality' of the circus
which, at another level, is a ramshackle affair:

The caravans were garish ramshackle affairs daubed with rain-
bows of peeling paint, with stovepipe chimneys and poky little windows and halfdoors at the front. Grasses and moss,
even a primrose or two, sprouted between the warped boars of
the barrel-shaped roofs. The horses, starved bony brutes, stood
about the field with dropping heads, spancelled, apparently
asleep. The tent was crooked, and sagged ominously. A woman
unseen began to sing.   (105)

Again, the question arises as to whether the power of the circus to
present 'a sense of strange and infinite possibilities' is haunted, if
not undermined by, the reality. However, this passage is much more
complex than it seems. It actually puts doubt into doubt. For the
account of the caravans' threadbare nature – its garishness, peeling
paint, starved animals and crooked tent – is haunted by the image
of the rainbow, the reference to the primroses and the unseen
woman's song. The latter brings to mind the 'music, palpable and
tender, which [Gabriel discovers] a wood in summer makes' (31).
'Tender' here, in turn, links the music of the summer wood and
Gabriel's mother's voice when she calls him from his solitary wan-
dering in the dark wood: 'She leaned over me, enfolding me in a
tender weight of love and concern, murmuring incoherently into
my ear, warm round words, swollen like kisses' (32). The wood's
music, the unseen woman's song and his mother are linked. Gabriel
is left pondering the defamiliarizing power in this connection:
'I perceived in my familiar kingdom the subtle strains of this new
music' (33).

As in *Grace Notes*, the pre-verbal, or non-verbal, interrupts the
symbolic. Here Gabriel's father is left pacing impatiently, smoking a cigar and kicking leaves. But the feminine and the maternal
at this point is associated with instability – Gabriel's mother's
words are incoherent, words are confused with kisses, and

hearing and touch are somehow conflated. What is communicated is sound – murmuring, rhythms – rather than the understanding associated with symbolic language of the father. Gabriel is called not by recognizing his name or even words but by sound – 'hallooing' and a 'cry'. In his mother's tears, Gabriel believes that he has encountered something important, related to what at this point in the text he calls 'harmony' although he does not pretend to believe that he fully understands it.

The above description of the travelling circus or theatre is also interesting in that what undermines the sense of promise associated with the circus is present within it. Once again there are allusions to the Old Testament: the rainbow – in Genesis the symbol that God would never again destroy the earth – and the Tabernacle that the nomadic Israelites erected to pray to God. Each, in Christian thought, is a symbol of the meeting of God and humankind, heaven and earth and the visible and invisible. Even the wider context of the Great Famine has Biblical echoes, for in the Old Testament famine and similar pestilences were a means by which the faith of God's chosen people were tested. The passage suggests that instead of thinking of the exotic side of the circus being haunted by the disarming 'reality', we ought to think of its dilapidation and decay as haunted by its beauty.

Similarly, the problem from Gabriel's viewpoint is that his family might be seen as haunted as God's kin by the fact that they are linguistically linked to God – as the Patriarchs in the Old Testament can be seen as haunted by the promise of a glory which is not delivered. The 'glory' that haunts the evil behaviour, though, is not a stable referent. It reveals itself in moments of interruption, and at best is intimated rather than fully revealed:

> Listen, listen, if I know my world, which is doubtful, but if I do, I know it is chaotic, mean and vicious, with laws cast in the wrong moulds, a fair conception gone awry, in short an awful place, and yet, and yet a place capable of glory in those rare moments when a little light breaks forth, and something is not explained, not forgiven, but merely illuminated. (33)

Thus, the novel turns on its head the notion of good being haunted by evil, and focuses upon evil being haunted by 'good', however defined and fleetingly intimated. In this respect, the novel presents us with a different ontological perspective from the novels that we discussed in the previous chapter, which are primarily concerned with the absence of good, and with the way limit is privileged within the void created by this loss.

Fleeting Insights

In the novel, the birch woods that lift the spirits are analogous of Ida, for whom it was 'the continuing oddity of things that fascinated her' and who refused to call 'ordinary the complex and exquisite ciphers among which her life so tenuously hovered' (122). She might be seen, the novel suggests, as haunting her darker sister Ada rather than haunted by her more menacing sister, which would accord with the more familiar Gothic version. However, there is an ambivalence around Ida, and may be around the birch wood itself. Ida is said to have 'tenuously hovered', a point reinforced by her violent, nonsensical and sudden death. Indeed, hers is the kind of tragedy that fuels a determinist, diabolical reading of the universe, and sees what is 'good' as constantly haunted by the stronger presence of evil.

Throughout the text, there is the suggestion that good is a tenuous spectrality – it is never defined as stable. This is especially pronounced in Part Three of the novel which is named after John Donne's poem 'Aire and Angels' which introduces a phantom love, without face or name, that is compared to the apparition of angels. Having been first aroused by the ethereality of the phantom's spiritual loveliness, the narrator of the poem seeks for it to be made physically manifest. The poem provides a useful framework within which to discuss Rose and Ida within the novel's wider concern with spectrality. At one level, Ida might be seen as the manifestation, albeit unexpected manifestation, of Rose – the long lost, secret sister that Gabriel invents, subconsciously, to distract attention from the fact that Michael is his secret, mad twin brother. In other words, the imagined Rose in the course of the narrative turns into Ida. But, as Ida, Gabriel's imagined, secret sister becomes the object of her brother's desires. The ghost of incestuous desire that is a family spectre haunts the relationship between Godkin and Ida at some deep level. All this begs the question, what happens to Rose after Ida's death. Then she is replaced by Michael – who up until then is the secret mad brother that Gabriel tries not to admit to. Michael exorcises Rose. Rose is an imaginative, romantic construction whereas Michael signifies the given 'reality'.

In a sense all this is prefigured in Gabriel's brief, secret sexual liaison with the peasant girl Rose, who with legs with 'rich red scratches, crescents of blood-beads' (66), anticipates Ida's violent death. The account of this peasant girl seems to be the opposite of the phantom love in Donne's poem. The episode introduces Rose as an overtly physical presence: 'She had short dark hair rolled into hideous sausage curls. A saddle of freckles sat on her nose. She wore sandals and a dress with daisies on it. She was pretty, a sturdy sunburnt creature' (65). Although Gabriel and Rose have a physical relationship, they part. She remains a virgin which perhaps makes it easier for Gabriel to remember her as a phantom, 'an iridescent ideal' (68). She becomes an object, an 'imago' on which he projects his phantasies. But what worries Gabriel is the way he splits Rose as an ideal from Rose as 'a tawdry thing' (68).

Eventually, Gabriel reveals to the reader, and himself, that he is a fantasist – forced to admit that there never was a Prospero leading him to a 'rosy grail' (172), and again for a narrator who thinks of narrative in terms of echoes and coincidences this allusion to *The Tempest* is significant. Both texts challenge belief in a physical purity and spiritual ideal that can be separated from the more tawdry aspects of life. But more than that, it is sceptical of seeing revelation as the manifestation of any simple or determinable presence. This is an important distinction between Banville's novel and *Grace Notes*. Thus, the spectrality of Ida is not a given of her weakness compared with Ada. It is a signifier of a faith that not only hovers but also must hover at the limit of representation and language. In the last paragraph of his narrative, Gabriel suggests: 'Intimations abound, but they are felt only, and words fail to transfix them' (175). Otherwise intimations become knowledge that by definition is inevitability grounded in an empirical moment.

Thus, *Birchwood* underscores the spectrality of 'intimations' as a necessity. As such, intimations can be seen as belonging to what might be called a 'third space' that is itself a kind of spectrality. As much as the novel interweaves its way between given binarisms – spiritual and physical, beauty and ugliness, order and chaos, law and lawlessness, fact and fiction – it tries to occupy a place outside binarisms. The Molly Maguires who eventually besiege the estate are hermaphrodites and neither Godkin nor Lawless. As Michael's membership of the band suggests, they signify those in

Ireland who have been born, like Michael, of an incestuous relationship, and who occupy a space outside the categories of 'legitimate' and 'illegitimate'. Michael and Gabriel stand in a relationship that is outside the normal brother dyad. Rose, too, outside of binarisms and outside of time, occupies a spectral space as does the travelling circus.

Stepping outside time is crucial to the narrative that in its chronological confusion is not faithful to time. Gabriel himself, on joining the circus, becomes a spectral presence – Johann Livelb. At the end of the novel, he declares that he is not his father and different from him: 'I shall stay here, alone, and live a life different from any the house has ever known' (174). 'Justinette' signifies this third space – the third being or term created from Justin and Juliette. This way of looking at these twins, whom Gabriel admits frighten him, was conceived by the person in the narrative who most haunts the narrator: 'I realize that of all the creatures I have lost I miss most his valiant and fastidious spirit' (120). Magnus alone has the ability to cast a spell with his music and storytelling and bring the troupe out of its 'cocoon of melancholy' (120). In that respect, he and not Silas is the true Prospero. Within the philosophical theme of the novel, Silas's desire to sleep with both Ada and Ida is analogous of aesthetically balancing what each represents. What Magnus offers is an alternative that is literally outside time.

The unified, comprehensive meaning for which Gabriel strives throughout much of the novel appears to be more solid than the fragmentary insights with which he works. But the text offers in contradistinction to this a reciprocal experience rooted in a series of discontinuous events. They have the effect of rendering as spectre the wider sense of the unequivocal of which they partake while never eschewing their own spectrality. At the end of the book, it is the equivocal in its spectrality that Gabriel accepts: 'There is no form, no order, only echoes and coincidences, sleight of hand, dark laughter' (174). He discovers what he knew at the outset of the narrative – that intimation depends upon the subject's ability to eschew the stabilizing referent:

> I looked down on the broken fountain, at last year's leaves sunk in the dead water. The windows of the house were blinded with light. Shadow and sunshine swept the garden, a bird whistled suddenly, piercingly, and in the surface of the pool below me a white cloud sailed into a blue bowl of sky. (12)

The focus here is on how intimation has been figured in terms of light, colour, movement and penetration. These are all unstable referents. Essentially intimation depends upon the capacity to allow for interruption. In the course of the novel, many of the moments of interruption to which Gabriel responds are essentially feminine, from the chora, and he feels addressed by them, such as his mother's voice beckoning him from the woods, and the unseen woman's song from the circus 'rising through the still spring morning' which he says 'called to me' (105). The interruption is often linked, in turn, to an instability which enables the perception of beauty, as when the cloth which his mother is carrying slips from under her arm, and 'opened like an ungainly flower, and from out of its centre staggered a bruised blue butterfly' (33). Here the intimation of beauty is associated with traditional icons of the feminine – the flower, and the butterfly. They are also symbols of the transitory and fleeting moment. But in this context, the unstable signifiers of beauty produce a reaction in Gabriel's mother that betrays her feeling about what has happened – she begins to cry. This bodily response interrupts his father's self-contained masculinity – ' "Jesus," said Papa, without any particular emotion, and walked away from us' (33).

Thus, although, *Grace Notes* and *Birchwood* are very different kinds of texts and are situated at different poles in contemporary speculative fiction, they differ from the novels discussed previously in their emphasis upon the possibility of transcendence. Unlike many of the novels that we have discussed, concerned with the movement out of silence, *Grace Notes* stresses a re-visioning of silence and the gaps between sounds as the basis of bringing an essentialist understanding of female cultural and corporeal identity out of the histories and narratives that have silenced them. Its redefinition of silence is dependent upon recognizing the dormant, what is waiting to erupt and interrupt. *Birchwood* is similarly concerned with what is dormant and waiting to erupt. But it is situated in the spaces between the fragments of information that the narrator is seeing to put together and in the gaps between the binarisms that determine conventional ideas about good and evil, and beauty and ugliness. In suggesting that evil is haunted by good, instead of good being haunted by evil, *Birchwood* discovers, like *Grace Notes*, a goodness, or sense of beauty, associated with the pre-verbal and the female. Insight into this pre-verbal reality is less certain and sure in *Birchwood* than the pre-hearing which *Grace Notes* champions.

Afterword

I have chosen to provide an 'Afterword' at this point rather than a 'Conclusion'. Throughout, I have argued that the late twentieth-century novel in Northern Ireland and Ireland might be usefully read through Homi Bhabha's work on what happens when the previously marginalized or silenced emerge from the margins and through Jacques Derrida's ideas about concealment. I see this book as part of an ongoing engagement on both my part and the reader's with Irish fiction. If, as I have tried to argue, the late twentieth-century novel in Ireland and Northern Ireland occupies an in-between cultural and intellectual space, then, it almost goes without saying, that space is marked by uncertainty and ideological conflict. However, it is important to separate the postmodern novel in Ireland and Northern Ireland from the Anglo-American postmodern novel. Generally speaking, the latter is often much more committed than many contemporary Irish novels to an all-pervading scepticism as to whether representation can ever be anything more than the product of, and the disseminator of, preconceptions. To adapt Bhabha's terms, it is on the side of 'relocation', perhaps at times endlessly so, rather than 'reinscription'. More often than not, it is the reverse that is true of the Irish novel.

However, the in-between space occupied by the contemporary Irish novel, characterized by continuity and disruption, is a place of intervention in the here and now. The encounters with the late modern or postmodern in some of the texts that I have discussed invariably share an abiding scepticism of the brash, new consumer-oriented society evident in the public faces of many late twentieth-century cities, especially the way in which they hide, in their spatial organization, for example, what challenges or undermines postmodern society's celebration of itself. The emphasis in these novels does not fall solely upon exposing the postmodern as 'no-place spaces'. They are as, if not more interested, in the capacity of the postmodern to seduce, to redefine and, even, to hide the processes by which cultures are being, to employ Featherstone's terms once again, 'decontextualised, simulated [and] reduplicated'.

Revealing not only what is hidden but also exposing the processes of concealing is a recurring trope in contemporary Irish fiction. Elleke Boehmer's argument that women's writing can interrupt 'the language of official nationalist discourse and litera-ture with a woman's vocality' begs a number of questions, as far as Irish writing is concerned, about that vocality – not least the extent to which it is part of an in-between space, and emerges from margins, that have been shrouded in secrecy. Not only do many Irish women writers 'remap', or 'map' rather than 'trace' in the language of postmodern geography, the geographies and his-tories that have marginalized them, but they also confront the dominant discourses and frames of reference that have deter-mined their cultural and corporeal identity and/or silenced them in their sexuality and desires. How gender identity is determined and confined by the available discourses in which it is, and can be, articulated is developed in some of the novels discussed, through the mother figure, and the cultural construction of mater-nity, and in others through the exploration of secret, female desires and fantasies. Numerous texts pursue how the latter are silenced even within the marginalizing discourses of femininity and womanhood.

But, although the texts discussed in this book are different from each other, they each read history through the interconnec-tion, which is sometimes concealed in authoritative discourse, of power, obedience and subversion. Some of them are linked in their preoccupation with 'mimicry' and its role, paradoxically, in both the maintenance and the secret subversion of authority. Others interleave an exploration of what is secret and hidden in the various communities within Ireland and Northern Ireland, with what is 'encrypted' in language and discourse, determining, for example, the status afforded women and the behaviour of men towards them, and the nature of masculinity. While, as the French philosopher Jacques Derrida said, we normally think of what is hidden as separate from what conceals it, many of these novels usefully refocus our attention upon the close relationship between what is hidden and the individual or national consciousness in which it is concealed.

Those novels that I have suggested might be profitably read through specific psychoanalytic frameworks, concerning, for example, self-harm or fetishism, provide a further basis for developing Derrida's ideas about what is secret and 'encrypted'.

For, frequently, the contemporary Irish novel envisages what is concealed both as a secret removed from the public face which the protagonists and/or the nation present and, also as affecting, often negatively, the wider sense of that person and/or nation's sense of being and identity.

Exploring subjects that have been marginalized – at least as far as serious literature is concerned – some of these novels, too, share a preoccupation with what Foucault called limit and with the rupture that opens up at the point of limit. The preoccupation with limit focuses a wider concern with the cultural significance of transgression. In a broad based understanding of transgression, some of the novels discussed explore the twentieth century's increasing concern with sexuality as limit, a concept usefully read through Foucault's work, especially how he links this to the loss of God, and to the loss of a larger meaningful point of reference.

What emerges from some of the novels concerned with violence, especially sexually related violence as limit, is the difficulty of transcendence. But, generally speaking, in their commitment to 'reinscription', many of these novels eschew the kind of 'excessive distances', or indeed even void, which Foucault thinks of as opening up at the heart of limit. In bringing what has been silenced out of silence, and what has been marginalized out of the margins, the Irish novel finds itself in a space of anxiety, uncertainty and of redefinition rather than definition, not least because of the emergence of what has been previously 'encrypted' or silent. For some, it can be a place of radical openness but not all embrace it wholeheartedly. However, the interrogative opportunities it provides invariably lead back to what has been hidden, to the secrets, and the impact – often the trauma – of keeping those secrets, in national, local, domestic and personal life. The political and the cultural interleave not only in private and public discourse, albeit where the 'encrypted' is as relevant as what is overtly articulated, but also in the silences. Indeed, in one of the final texts discussed, silence itslf is redefined as a positive space – an in-between space in which what will erupt and disrupt is lying dormant.

Appendix: Time Chart

A comprehensive time chart of the social and political history of Ireland and Northern Ireland is beyond the scope of this book. This select chart is intended to help readers new to Irish literature to begin to place the novels discussed in a wider context and to understand more fully the historical and political allusions in the critical discussion.

Key Novels and Concomitant Political and Cultural Events

1916
Easter Rising.
James Joyce, *A Portrait of the Artist as a Young Man*.

1918
After its election victory Sinn Féin sets up the Dáil (Assembly) in Dublin.

1919–21
War of Independence. Britain initiates changes in the Royal Irish Constabulary (RIC), the force against which much of the IRA campaign has been directed, to boost morale and to increase its effectiveness by equipping it with rockets, bombs and shotguns.

1920
British Government launches a recruitment drive to attract ex-soldiers to a new force in Ireland, nicknamed the Black and Tans because of their distinctive uniform. Generally speaking, they prove to be ill disciplined, poorly trained and ignorant of Ireland where they arouse considerable animosity. In July, a second force, the Auxiliaries, is established in 15 heavily armed, mobile divisions. Although better trained than the Black and Tans, they are unprepared for guerrilla warfare. In November, recruitment begins to the Ulster Special Constabulary intended to perform a peacekeeping role in the communities from which they were recruited. At this time there are three classes of constables: A class are full-timers; B constables are part-timers; and the C class is a reserve of, mainly, elderly men. But 1920 also sees the Government of Ireland Act, creating two governments, with limited devolved powers, one in Belfast and one in Dublin. Whilst this is acceptable to the Unionists, it is opposed by Irish nationalists who generally support the IRA campaign.

1921
On 11 July, a truce is declared in the Anglo-Irish War. Negotiations between Sinn Féin leaders, led by Michael Collins and Arthur Griffith, and the British Government, led by Prime Minister Lloyd George, begins in October. Eventually the Anglo-Irish Treaty is agreed on 6 December.

Under the Treaty, Southern Ireland is to become the Irish Free State, a self-governing dominion with complete freedom in domestic affairs. This causes deep divisions among nationalists, some of whom reject it because it fails to deliver a republic. Others argue for it on the grounds that it should provide the freedom to achieve nationhood in the future. The Treaty causes a rift between Michael Collins and fellow Sinn Féin leader, Eamon de Valera.

1922

James Joyce, *Ulysses.*

The Irish Free State is formed. The RIC is disbanded and replaced, in February, by the Garda Siochana in the Irish Free State and, in June, by the Royal Ulster Constabulary in Northern Ireland.

1925

The Ulster Special Constabulary is reorganized, retaining only a reduced number of B Specials intended to undertake security work and support the Royal Ulster Constabulary.

1927

Fianna Fáil enters the Dáil.

1932

Fianna Fáil wins the General Election in a coalition with Labour.

1935

The Criminal Law Amendment Act (Section 17) makes it illegal to sell or import contraceptives.

1936

The Ulster Society for Historical Studies is founded.

1937

The Irish Constitution (Bunreacht na hÉireann). The Constitution stipulates: 'No law shall be enacted providing for the grant of a dissolution of marriage.' The Irish Historical Society is formed.

1938

Fianna Fáil elected with overall majority. Anglo-Irish Treaty.

1939

James Joyce, *Finnegan's Wake.*

Outbreak of World War II. IRA bombing campaign in England. Offences Against the State Act passed in June in the Free State. De Valera involved in anti-partition regulations.

1946

Health and Insurance Acts 1946–8 extend the welfare state to Northern Ireland.

1947

Butler Education Act of 1944 extended to Ulster.

1948

Republic of Ireland declared. Dr Noël Browne, a doctor with experience of working with TB, is appointed Health Minister (in February). He seeks to implement the 1946 White Paper. (See, Mary Morrissy's novel, *Mother of Pearl*, 1996.) The Health Services (Northern Ireland) Act.

1951

Dr Browne resigns as the Republic's Health Minister in April after the Government fails to support a scheme that promised to provide free medical care for mothers and children that had attracted considerable opposition from the Catholic Church hierarchy. In Northern Ireland, Ian Paisley initiates the Free Presbyterian Church. Paisley, whose Unionist political persuasions are inseparable from his religious beliefs, proves a dominant presence in Northern Ireland politics over the next half-century and more.

1953

Queen Elizabeth visits Belfast; Catholic councillors are excluded from the official lunch.

1954

Public Order Acts passed in Northern Ireland. Flags and Emblems Act gives special protection to the Unionist flag. Liam Kelly becomes leader of an IRA splinter group.

1955

Brian Moore, *Judith Hearne*.

1956

IRA Campaign of Resistance to British Occupation launched in Northern Ireland in December (1956–62). An attempt to bomb Brookeborough police barracks on New Year's eve kills Sean South and Fergal O'Hanlon from the Irish Republic.

1957

Catholic bishops condemn IRA campaign. Internment without trial is re-introduced in Northern Ireland. Death of a Royal Ulster Constabulary (RUC) constable in County Armagh in July creates outrage. De Valera re-introduces internment in the Republic – arrests of IRA men in the South.

1958

White paper on economic development of Ireland published in Dublin. First programme of economic expansion in Ireland. Ardmore Film Studios opened.

1959

Judith Hearne published as *The Lonely Passion of Judith Hearne*.

Seán Lemass (Fianna Fáil) succeeds Eamon de Valera as Taoiseach (Prime Minister) of Ireland. De Valera has been Taoiseach 1932–48, 1951–4, 1957–9. This is seen by some as the end of one era and the beginning of another. De Valera is linked to a rural petit bourgeoisie and a vision imposed upon Ireland that privileged an isolationist, traditionally moral and rural-based society.

1960

Brian Moore, *The Luck of Ginger Coffey*; Edna O'Brien, *The Country Girls*. The Irish government sets up the Irish Film Finance Corporation to help induce foreign filmmakers to Ireland.

1961

Ireland applies for membership of the European Economic Community (EEC). Votes in Ireland appear to reject political extremism with Fine Gael and the Labour Party increasing their seats in the Dáil. New Year's Eve, the newly established Irish television station, Radio Telefís Éireann, comes on air. President de Valera feeds the ambivalence with which the mass media is regarded by conservative forces in Ireland, acknowledging that it might serve to build the nation's character but may lead to decadence and dissolution. The new generation, exemplified by Seán Lemass, thinks of it as opening up Ireland to the wider world. (See, Patrick McCabe's novel, *The Dead School*, 1995.)

1962

Edna O'Brien, *The Lonely Girl*.

Radio Telefís Éireann established in Ireland. IRA calls off campaign in Northern Ireland. Cuban missile crisis brings the United States and Russia to the brink of war. (See, Patrick McCabe's novel, *The Butcher Boy*, 1992.)

1963

John McGahern, *The Barracks*.

Second programme of economic expansion in Ireland (1963–4). The Beatles play the Adelphi cinema in Dublin. Show band craze in Ireland with over 400 new-style ballrooms. American President John F. Kennedy visits Ireland in June. America thinks of Ireland in transition because of its younger generation of politicians and the growing awareness that Ireland's destiny lay within a wider European context. Kennedy's visit underlines the view of many at the time that the 1960s is a watershed for modern Ireland because of his support of social reform and free enterprise. On 22 November, Kennedy is assassinated in Dallas. These events preoccupy a number of Irish writers in the late 1980s and early 1990s who grew up in this period. See, for example, Roddy Doyle's novel, *The Commitments* (1989), Patrick McCabe's *Carn* (1989) and *The Butcher Boy* (1992). In Northern Ireland, Ian Paisley leads a protest march against the lowering of the Union flag at Belfast City Hall to mark the death of the Pope.

1964

Edna O'Brien, *Girls in their Married Bliss*; William Trevor, *The Old Boys*.

Liberalization of film censorship. In Ireland, the number of television licences has risen from 201 095 the year before to 258 988 while the number of radio licences has decreased from 336 939 to 292 899. The television presenter becomes a new cultural icon in Ireland, especially those fronting 'chat shows' such as Gay Byrne. This cultural development is one of the subjects of Patrick McCabe's novel, *The Dead School* (1995).

1965

John McGahern, *The Dark*; Edna O'Brien, *August is a Wicked Month*.

Seán Lemass discusses economics matters with the Prime Minister of Northern Ireland, Terence O'Neill, at Stormont. McGahern's new novel, *The Dark*, about adolescence, which includes a reference to masturbation, is seized by Customs Officers. In October, he is sacked from his job as a primary school teacher in Dublin. In the United States, Malcolm X is assassinated and Martin Luther King leads a civil rights march in Montgomery. The widespread publicity that civil rights movements are acquiring in America invigorates the civil rights movement in Northern Ireland.

1966
The fiftieth anniversary of the Easter Rising. Lemass, after years of industrial unrest and critical, independent reporting of Ireland's economic policies, argues that the national television station has a responsibility to the government. He retires and Jack Lynch (Fianna Fáil) becomes Taoiseach. De Valera secures a further term as President. The Anglo-Irish Free Trade Area Agreement comes into being furthering Ireland's participation in international economic competition. St Patrick's College, Maynooth, opens the door to lay students. The Ulster Volunteer Force (UVF), formed in 1912, is reconstituted as an anti-Catholic organization and declares war on the IRA, planting a bomb in County Down. In Ireland, an explosion marks the fiftieth anniversary of the Easter Rising, destroying the upper part of Nelson's Pillar in Dublin that had been erected to commemorate the Battle of Trafalgar (foundation stone laid in 1808). The head, recovered from the rubble, is now in the Dublin Museum. On the arts front, the rebuilt Abbey Theatre opens in Dublin.

1967
The Northern Ireland Civil Rights Association (NICRA) is formed to demand removal of anomalies that discriminate against Catholics. The Association argues for one person one vote in local elections to replace the property/company vote, the disbanding of the B Specials, a reform of the system by which public housing is allocated and the repeal of the Special Powers Act. The founding of the Association is indicative of the political context but also of the voice that a new generation, benefiting from the 1940s Education Acts, is acquiring. Ireland's second application to enter the EEC is unsuccessful. On the Arts front, the Cork opera house is opened. New legislation provides for the unbanning of books after 12 years. In Tralee, following protests led by the parish priest, a public appearance by Jayne Mansfield is cancelled.

1968
In Northern Ireland, on 5 October, a civil rights march is held in Derry, organized by the Derry Housing Action Committee. On 9 October, a student march in Belfast, in protest at police brutality, is blocked by a counter demonstration organized by Ian Paisley. Formation of Derry Citizen's Action Committee. On 16 October, a People's Democracy march is held in Belfast. On 17 November, the Nationalist Party adopts a policy of civil disobedience. Attacks on Catholic homes 1968–9 recalls the IRA into existence. On November 22, Terence O'Neill, Northern Ireland Prime Minister, announces a package of reforms which include the allocation of houses by local authorities on the basis of need and a proposal that the powers of the Londonderry Corporation be taken over by a Development Commission.

In Ireland, the encyclical Humanae Vitae is published in newspapers on 30 July, reaffirming past papal condemnations of every artificial method of birth control. The Higher Education Authority (HEA) is established to co-ordinate the planning and finance of higher education. Civil Rights demonstration in Dublin.

1969

Northern Ireland: the year opens with the start on 1 January of the four-day People's Democracy March from Belfast to Derry. It proves to be a magnet for sectarian violence. Terence O'Neill resigns in April after six years as Premier of Northern Ireland, faced with escalating violence and civil unrest. Major James Chichester-Clark replaces him. In the summer, tensions between the Catholic community in Londonderry and the RUC are running high following the death of Sammy Devenney in his own home at the hands of the RUC. What came to be known as the Battle of the Bogside, Londonderry, begins on 13 August. On the 14 August, the Prince of Wales Own Regiment relieves the police. The Report of the Cameron Commission, September, finds that claims of discrimination made against Catholics are substantiated. It is critical of Stormont and the police in its assessment of sectarian conflict. The Hume report, October, recommends that the RUC becomes an unarmed force and that the B Specials are disbanded. A few days after the publication of the Hume Report, James Callaghan, Home Secretary, makes a two-day visit to Northern Ireland, agreeing proposals for reforms to the RUC and the central housing authority. Also in 1969, Bernadette Devlin is elected to the Westminster Parliament and in her maiden speech warns of the violence with which British troops entering Northern Ireland will be met. Third programme of economic expansion in Ireland. Also in Ireland, Charles Haughey's budget frees writers, composers, painters and sculptors from income tax from earnings from works judged to be of cultural merit. Samuel Beckett is awarded the Nobel prize.

1970

Edna O'Brien, *A Pagan Place*.

Provisional Sinn Féin is formed. Ian Paisley, an opponent of reforming unionism, is elected to Stormont and Westminster. The Social Democratic and Labour Party (SDLP) is formed, incorporating nationalist and Labour Party groups. The leader is Gerry Fitt, and John Hume the Deputy Leader. The SDLP proves to be the nationalist voice until Sinn Féin begins to contest elections in the 1980s. The first open battle between nationalists and British troops occurs in the Ballymurphy area of Belfast. The army uses tear gas and a curfew is imposed. Following the recommendations of the Hunt Report, the multi-sectarian Ulster Defence Regiment replaces the B Specials. However, disillusionment of Catholics with the new force develops quickly as it is realized that the commanders and many of its members are former B Specials. In Ireland, the ban on Catholic students attending Trinity College, Dublin, is lifted.

1971

John Banville, *Nightspawn*.

1971 is a significant year in the Troubles, not least because internment without trial is reintroduced in Northern Ireland, and 1500 people are interned before the year is out. The introduction of internment sparks off numerous protests. Apart from street protests, the SDLP announces from 15 August a campaign of civil disobedience in which an estimated 16 000 householders withhold their rents and rates for their council homes. On the 19 October, five MPs, including John Hume and Bernadette Devlin, begin a 48-hour hunger strike. The Ulster Defence Association, an umbrella organization for loyalist groups, is formed. Ian Paisley's Democratic Unionist Party is founded. Dedicated to terrorist acts against Catholics, the UVF, re-formed in 1966, kills 15 people in a bomb explosion at McGuirk's bar on North Queen Street. Although the UVF claims responsibility, the Loyalist News blames the atrocity on the IRA. Ruairi O Bradaigh is elected President of Sinn Féin. The Women's Liberation Movement holds its first public meeting in Dublin. Faced with the prospect of increased terrorist activity, the Dáil bans the holding or purchase of arms for use outside the Republic. Radio Telefis Éireann bans patriotic ballads.

1972
Jennifer Johnston, *The Captain and the King*.
Bloody Sunday, 30 January, in Derry, on which 13 Civil Rights marchers are shot dead by British Army paratroopers and as many are injured. What exactly happened on the day is hotly contested. The report of a British enquiry, led by Lord Widgery, does not condemn the soldiers but does accuse them of behaviour that 'bordered on the reckless'. The city coroner, Hubert O'Neill, describes what happened as 'unadulterated murder'. The IRA is accused of pursuing its ends through indiscriminate murder. Subsequently, the army moves into the Bogside area of Derry that has become a no-go area. Bloody Friday, 21 July, on which IRA bombs kill nine people and maim 130 in Belfast, the majority of whom are shoppers at the targeted bus station and in the city centre. The Unionist controlled Parliament refuses to agree to Prime Minister Edward Heath's demands that Westminster take over control for security. Stormont is suspended and direct rule imposed on 28 March. The same month, two women are killed and 136 people injured in a bomb explosion at the Abercorn restaurant, Belfast. The Heath Government proposes an Irish Assembly elected by proportional representation as a solution to the Northern Ireland problem. There are bomb explosions in Dublin and the Northern Ireland conflict clearly enters domestic politics in Ireland. The Kevin Street office of Provisional Sinn Féin is closed down. The Special Criminal Court, which allowed for juryless courts and army officers to act as judges, is reintroduced. The special constitutional position of the Catholic Church in Ireland is removed. Ireland signs a treaty joining the EEC, but in the 1970s it faces increased domestic terrorism and a high rate of inflation. The Dáil requires the surrender of all firearms. Section 31 of the Broadcasting Act bans representatives of the northern republican movement or their apologists from broadcasting. 1972 also sees the publication of *The Future of Northern Ireland: A Paper for Discussion* produced by the Darlington Conference in October, attended only by the unionists, the Alliance party of Northern Ireland and the Labour Party.

1973
John Banville, *Birchwood*; Jennifer Johnston, *The Gates*.
Ireland enters the EEC (1 January). Liam Cosgrave (Fine Gael) is elected Taoiseach on a narrow majority in a coalition of Fine Gael and Labour

parties, after Lynch calls elections in February hoping to strengthen his position. In this year, too, in Ireland, the Council for the Status of Women is established. The Misuse of Drugs Bill is passed reflecting public anxiety about the increasing use of heroin and cocaine among young people, especially in Dublin. In Northern Ireland, 1973 sees the creation of the Northern Ireland Assembly and a power-sharing executive is agreed. But Ian Paisley vehemently opposes the Sunningdale Agreement, named after the conference centre in Buckinghamshire where the Treaty was signed on 9 December, which brings the Assembly into being. He proves to be a key player in the Ulster Workers' Strike that is largely responsible for the collapse of this short-lived assembly (see next). One person is killed and 250 injured in the IRA London bomb explosion (March). Gerry Adams, former Provisional Commander in Anderstown, becomes Provisional IRA Chief of Staff.

1974
Jennifer Johnston, *How many Miles to Babylon?* John McGahern, *Leavetaking*.
In April, the Secretary State for Northern Ireland, announces he will remove the illegal status of the UVF and Sinn Féin. As expected from Paisley's opposition, the Ulster Unionist Council rejects the Sunningdale Agreement and the power-sharing executive. The Ulster Workers' Strike of 14–28 May 1974 brings Northern Ireland to a standstill. Brian Faulkner, the Chief Executive, resigns after the Secretary of State for Ireland, Merlyn Rees, refuses to meet with representatives of the Ulster Workers' Council. Faulkner's Unionist colleagues also resign which brings the Northern Ireland Executive to an end. Thus, direct rule from Westminster is reimposed in the same month. In Ireland, the Anti-Discrimination (Pay) Act is passed, giving women doing a similar job as men with the same or associated employer the right to equal pay. Guildford and Birmingham pub bombings (November and December). Ireland's status as a nation is enhanced when it takes over the Presidency of the EEC.

1975
Edna O'Brien, *Mother Ireland*.
The so-called 'Birmingham Six' are jailed for life at Lancaster Crown Court for their part in the Birmingham bombings. The 'Guildford Four' are tried for the pub bombings in Guildford and Woolwich. Internment without trial is suspended in December in Northern Ireland. De Valera dies at the age of 92 and is honoured with a State Funeral.

1976
John Banville, *Doctor Copernicus*; William Trevor, *The Children of Dynmouth*.
In February, IRA prisoner Frank Stagg dies in Wakefield Prison, England, after 61 days on hunger strike. The Northern Ireland convention, convened the previous year, collapses. Merlyn Rees, the Secretary of State for Northern Ireland, announces, in March, that paramilitary prisoners convicted of terrorist offences will no longer be entitled to special category status which enables prisoners to enjoy free association, to do no prison

work and allows them not to wear prison uniforms. Paramilitary prisoners argue that they are entitled to special category status as 'prisoners of war'. The 'blanket protest' begins in September in the new 'H-blocks' of the Maze Prison where IRA prisoners refuse to wear the prison uniform. The New Women's Peace Movement is started in Northern Ireland. In 1976, also, the British ambassador in Dublin is killed.

1977

Jennifer Johnston, *Shadows on Our Skin*.
In Ireland, Jack Lynch (Fianna Fáil) becomes Taoiseach. The Employment Equality Act is passed and the Employment Equality Agency is established. The first McDonalds fast food outlet opens in Dublin marking the cultural change which has occurred in Dublin in the 1970s and which is reflected, for example, in the Barrytown novels of Roddy Doyle and the work of Dermot Bolger. Northern Ireland's peace women – Mairead Corrigan and Betty Williams – are awarded the Nobel Peace Prize.

1978

The Family Planning Act is passed in Ireland legally entitling married women in the Republic to fertility control available through chemist shops on prescription. With reference to Northern Ireland, the European Court of Human Rights in Strasbourg finds that the interrogation techniques used on internees in 1971 were 'inhuman and degrading'. The Amnesty International Report on the alleged ill-treatment of people by the RUC at the Castlereagh Interrogation Centre is published. The Standing Committee of Bishops condemns the violence in Northern Ireland. The Maze prisoners, in the face of no favourable response from the British Government on their political status, begin what came to be known as the 'Dirty Protests' (1978–80) in which the paramilitary prisoners refuse to clean their cells and smear excrement over the walls.

1979

Jennifer Johnston, *The Old Jest*; John McGahern, *The Pornographer*; Brian Moore, *The Mangan Inheritance*.
The People's Peace Movement collapses after running out of funds. Margaret Thatcher becomes Britain's first woman prime minister and promises to pursue a tough security policy in Northern Ireland. Airey Neave, the Conservative spokesman on Northern Ireland, is killed by a car bomb planted by the Irish National Liberation association. Lord Mountbatten and three relatives are killed in a bomb explosion on his boat off Co. Sligo. Thatcher is involved with Dublin in talks about greater cross-border co-operation. Ian Paisley is elected to the European Parliament. In Ireland, Charles Haughey (Fianna Fáil) becomes Taoiseach. Máire Geoghegan-Quinn, Minister for the Gaeltacht, is the first woman to hold ministerial office since the formation of the Republic. The first elections to the European Parliament are held in Ireland. Pope John Paul II visits Ireland, warning against violence and reaffirming traditional family values. The first popular radio channel in Ireland is introduced as a result of pressure from pirate radio stations.

1980
Bernard MacLaverty, *Lamb*.
In April, it is announced that paramilitary prisoners will not be entitled to special category status, regardless of the offences that they have committed. In May, Charles Haughey and Margaret Thatcher pledge greater co-operation between their governments. The Anglo-Irish summit at Dublin Castle results in acknowledgement that the economic and political interests of the people of Great Britain, Northern Ireland and Ireland are linked and pledges of developing the relationship between the two countries. In October, in protest at the ending of special category status, IRA prisoners in 'H-block' in the Maze Prison begin a hunger strike campaign that lasts until the 18 December. Internment in Northern Ireland is abolished. In Ireland, the first female High Court judge is appointed.

1981
John Banville, *Kepler*, Jennifer Johnston, *The Christmas Tree*.
Amid high inflation and rising unemployment in Ireland, Garret Fitzgerald (Fine Gael) becomes Taoiseach. Eileen Desmond becomes Minister for Health and Social Welfare, the first woman to hold a senior government post in Ireland. Forty-eight young people are killed and 128 injured in a fire at the Stardust ballroom in north Dublin. A special day of mourning is declared and the Dáil is closed as a mark of respect. This serves to focus public attention on the Dublin youth, especially the Northsiders featured later in Doyle's Barrytown trilogy. In Northern Ireland, in January, prisoners agree to clean their cells. The strike is resumed when prison authorities refuse to pass on clean clothes from the prisoners' relatives. In March, the imprisoned leader of the IRA army, Bobby Sands, begins a new hunger strike on the fifth anniversary of the removal of special category status from paramilitary prisoners. He dies 66 days later. Haughey tries to persuade the British Government to find a way of ending the hunger strikes. The hunger strike is finally called off on 3 October 1981. Anglo-Irish relations are deteriorating.

1982
John Banville, *The Newton Letter*.
In Ireland, Charles Haughey (Fianna Fáil) succeeds Fitzgerald as Taoiseach, but Fitzgerald regains power the same year. In July, the IRA London Park bombs kill 11 soldiers. In the same month in Ireland, a young nurse, Bridie Gargan, is brutally murdered in Phoenix Park, Dublin, by Malcolm Macarthur, son of a well-connected family. His association with the Irish Attorney-General creates a scandal for the Haughey Government. In October, the American entrepreneur John De Lorean, who had received grants from the British Government to relocate his car factory to Northern Ireland, is arrested for his part in a plan to smuggle cocaine into the United States.

1983
Nuala Archer (ed.), *Woman's Part: An Anthology of Short Fiction by and about Irish Women 1890–1960*; Bernard MacLaverty, *Cal*; Brian Moore, *Cold Heaven*; William Trevor, *Fools of Fortune*.

New Ireland, or All Ireland Forum, results from meetings between Garret Fitzgerald's government and the SDLP and the Alliance Party. Fitzgerald fails to consult the Unionists who reject the idea, as does Margaret Thatcher. The Forum argues that there are three solutions to the Northern Ireland problem: a united Ireland, a federal settlement or a joint Irish–British administration. Although it comes to nothing, the Forum signals the need to address Northern Ireland within a wider constitutional context, involving Ireland. Gerry Adams is elected President of Sinn Féin and MP for West Belfast. On 17 December, five people are killed and 91 injured by an IRA bomb in Harrods in London during the Christmas shopping rush. In Ireland, in the Kerry Babies case, a single mother, who buried her dead baby on her farm, finds herself accused of the murder of a baby whose body is washed up on White Strand Beach, Cahirciveen. Fianna Fáil is pushed by pro-life pressure groups to call an anti-abortion referendum. (Abortion is prohibited in Ireland under the 1861 Offences Against the Persons Act.)

1984

Linda Anderson, *To Stay Alive*; Jennifer Johnston, *The Railway Station Man*; Neil MacCafferty, *A Woman to Blame* [an account of the Kerry Babies case]; Ruth Hooley (ed.), *The Female Line* [a collection of writings by Northern Irish women].

President Reagan visits Ireland. British citizens living in Ireland are allowed to vote in general elections in Ireland. An IRA bomb explodes at the Grand Hotel, Brighton, during the Conservative Party conference on 12 October. Five people are killed and 30 injured. The bomb is probably intended to assassinate Margaret Thatcher.

1985

Dermot Bolger, *Night-Shift*; Mary Leland, *The Killeen*.

The Anglo-Irish Agreement, also known as the Hillsborough Agreement, which attempts to involve the Dublin government in a solution to Northern Ireland, is signed on 15 November and provokes outrage among Unionists. In Ireland, the Family Planning Bill is passed. It sets the age for buying contraceptives at 18, removes the need for a prescription and drops the bona fide family planning stipulation. Contraceptives will be available from chemist shops, doctors' surgeries, health centres and family planning clinics. The Interim Radio Commission is established to advise on the future control of broadcasting. The National Newspapers of Ireland pressure group is established.

1986

John Banville, *Mefisto*; Deirdre Madden, *Hidden Symptoms*; Patrick McCabe, *Music on Clinton Street*.

An attempt to remove constitutional prohibition on divorce in the Republic is defeated. The first purpose built refuge for battered wives is opened in Dublin. (The subject of domestic violence against women is explored in Roddy Doyle's *The Woman Who Walked Into Doors*, 1996, discussed in Chapter 8.) At the Old Bailey in London, Patrick Magee is given eight life sentences for his part in the Brighton bombing in 1984.

1987

Mary Beckett, *Give Them Stones*; Maude Casey, *Over the Water*; Jennifer Johnston, *Fool's Sanctuary*.

In Ireland, Charles Haughey (Fianna Fáil) becomes Taoiseach. In the Hamilton Judgement the High Court places injunctions on the Well Women Centre and on Open-Line Counselling prohibiting the operation of non-directive counselling services. In Northern Ireland, 11 people are killed in the Enniskillen bombing.

1988

Linda Anderson, *Cuckoo*; John Banville, *The Book of Evidence*; Roddy Doyle, *The Commitments*; Patrick McCabe, *Carn*; Edna O'Brien, *The High Road*; Glenn Patterson, *Burning Your Own*; Elizabeth Shannon, *I am of Ireland: Woman of the North Speak Out*; William Trevor, *The Silence in the Garden*.

The Independent Radio and Television Commission in Ireland is charged with establishing a network of local and regional stations and for awarding a franchise for a second, private television network. The Irish football team reaches the quarter-finals in the European Championships.

1989

John Banville, *The Book of Evidence*; Dermot Bolger (ed.), *Invisible Cities: the New Dubliners: a Journey Through Unofficial Dublin*; Louise DeSalvo, Kathleen Walsh D'Arcy and Katherine Hogan (eds), *Territories of the Voice: Contemporary Stories by Irish Women Writers*; Patrick McCabe, *Carn*; Robert McLiam Wilson, *Ripley Bogle*.

The Guildford Four are declared innocent of the crimes for which they have served 14 years in prison. The national alternative to RTE radio, Century Radio, is established. The alternative to RTE television, TV3, is awarded a franchise although it is not to come on air until 1998. The Minister of Communications in the republic is forced to back down over proposals to reorganize broadcasting which mean, among other things, that Century Radio will cease to be a privatized service. The first local radio station, in Dublin, is established. The Society for the Protection of the Unborn Child wins an injunction prohibiting students at Trinity College, Dublin, disseminating information about abortion to first-year students resulting in four students who continue to do so being charged with contempt of court. Mary Robinson, who is to be elected President the following year, represents them.

1990

Dermot Bolger, *The Journey Home*; Roddy Doyle, *The Snapper*; John McGahern, *Amongst Women*; Brian Moore, *Lies of Silence*; Joseph O'Connor, *Cowboys and Indians*; *The Field Day Anthology of Irish Writing* (introduction, Seamus Deane); Joseph O'Connor, *True Believers*.

Mary Robinson (born 1944) is elected President of the Republic (1990–7). She is a feminist lawyer, educated at Dublin University, Trinity College Dublin, and Harvard University. On taking up her post, she talks of women having been 'outside of history' in Ireland – a phrase borrowed from the poet Eavan Boland – and of women now being written back into it. This provides a useful framework within which to consider many contemporary novels. Other significant events in women's history include the prosecution of the Irish Family Planning Association for selling condoms in a Virgin megastore and the formation of the Dublin Abortion Information Campaign in November. The country's morale is boosted when the Irish football team reaches the quarter-finals in the World Cup.

1991

Roddy Doyle, *The Van*; Jennifer Johnston, *The Invisible Worm*.

This is not a year that dispels public disillusion with politicians and the judiciary. ITV's exposure in 'World in Action' of the Goodman Meat Empire confirms public disillusionment with corruption and favour in Irish politics. (On attitudes towards politicians, especially among the young people of Ireland, see Dermot Bolger, *The Journey Home*, 1990.) On a positive note, Roddy Doyle's *The Van* is shortlisted for the Booker Prize.

1992

An important event in Ireland highlighting the progress that still had to be made in equal opportunities for young girls and women in Ireland is what came to be known as the 'X' case. This case in which her friend's father allegedly raped a 14-year-old girl, receives widespread publicity not least because she is prevented from travelling to England for an abortion. The Dublin Abortion group distributes information, defying the law that made even providing the phone numbers of British clinics to pregnant women illegal. The X case mobilizes liberal public opinion, resulting in the Government dropping its ban on gay sex and introducing an age of equal consent. Subsequent reforms to the Constitution guarantee a right to travel and to information. The Government's opposition to court judgements that, effectively, makes abortion legal in cases where there is a threat to the health or life of the mother, is withdrawn. However, legislation in favour of abortion in these cases is not forthcoming.

Charles Haughey resigns following allegations that in 1982 he knew that the telephones of two journalists were being tapped. Not universally welcomed, Albert Reynolds, finance minister and former dance hall owner, takes over as Taoiseach. Irish voters ratify a treaty strengthening monetary and political integration within the European Community. Repeal of the Eighth Amendment Campaign (REAC) is formed in early March, and primarily based in Dublin and the large towns. Fianna Fáil loosens ties with the 'pro-life' campaign in order to win liberal ground associated with the Labour Parties and Fine Gael. Formerly relying upon rural support, it is now more dependent on support from the urban areas. Patrick McCabe's, *The Butcher Boy* is shortlisted for the Booker Prize.

In Northern Ireland, the Ulster Defence Association, formed in the 1970s, is banned for terrorist activities.

1993

John Banville, *Ghosts*; Emma Donoghue, *Passions Between Women: British Lesbian Culture 1668–1801*; Roddy Doyle, *Paddy Clarke Ha Ha Ha*; Brian Moore, *No Other Life*; Mary Morrissy, *A Lazy Eye* (short stories).

In March, an IRA bomb in Warrington, near Liverpool, kills two children. First IRA cease-fire. The McKittrick Report on segregation in Northern Ireland is published (50 per cent of its residents live in areas which are

90 per cent one religion). The Report of the Opsahl Commission finds evidence of self-imposed segregation in working-class areas and communal pressure deterring people from selling property to those of another religion. In October, a bomb in a Shankill Road shop kills 10 people. John Hume, leader of the Socialist Democratic Labour Party, tries to revive with Gerry Adams, the Irish Peace Initiative. This leads to the Downing Street Declaration by John Major and Albert Reynolds (15 December), and the Joint Framework initiative. The British Government declares that it has no 'selfish strategic or economic interest in Northern Ireland' and will 'encourage' a political settlement in Northern Ireland based on the people of Northern Ireland and Ireland to 'exercise the right of self-determination on the basis of consent'. The Declaration is welcomed by the SDLP but Sinn Féin is disappointed that it does not draw more effectively on the Adams/Hume agreement. Ian Paisley denounces the Declaration as a betrayal of Ulster. In Ireland, President Mary Robinson and Queen Elizabeth II become the first Irish and British heads of state to meet for 71 years.

1994
Emma Donoghue, *Stir-fry*; Kathleen Ferguson, *The Maid's Tale*; Joseph O'Connor, *Desperadoes*; William Trevor, *Felicia's Journey*.
The IRA announces 'a complete cessation of military operations' on 31 August. The spirit if not the letter of the move is generally welcomed. Shortly afterwards, in October, Loyalist paramilitaries, too, declare a cease-fire. Ulster Volunteer Force leader, Gusty Spence, talks of their 'abject and true remorse' for the suffering that their violence has caused. 36 per cent of the workforce in Ireland is now made up of women, the majority married. In the early days of the Republic this was discouraged and legislated against. However, many of the women are in low-paid jobs. Ireland has a new Taoiseach, John Bruton (Fine Gael), Albert Reynolds having been embarrassed and forced to resign when it was revealed that the Attorney General had appointed a President of the High Court who had mishandled the extradition of a Roman Catholic paedophile priest. The optimism of the year is checked when the Court of Criminal Appeal reduces the sentence of the man convicted of raping the 14-year-old-girl in the X case (see 1991).

1995
John Banville, *Athena*; Seamus Deane, *Reading in the Dark*; Emma Donoghue, *Hood*; Jennifer Johnston, *The Illusionist*; Patrick McCabe, *The Dead School*; Brian Moore, *The Statement*; Mary Morrissy, *Mother of Pearl*; Kate O'Riordan, *Involved*; Glenn Patterson, *Black Night on Black Thunder Mountain*.
Disillusionment with many aspects of public life in Ireland in the late 1980s and 1990s, especially concerns over corruption and the increasing power and influence of large companies, is reflected in the establishment of the Commission on the Newspaper Industry. Specifically, it is brought about by widespread concern over the large share that The Independent Group has acquired in the newspapers in Ireland. But continuing cynicism about public life in Ireland is not alone in driving the public agenda

in the mid-1990s. The wider political future is also kept to the front of the public mind. Interest in the future of Ireland and Northern Ireland as one island is reflected in The Idea of the Union in which contributors to debates about cementing Ireland and Northern Ireland argue rationally and, largely on economic grounds, for the Union. Disillusionment with public institutions in Ireland is dispelled temporarily by the results of the Divorce Referendum. The vote to change the provisions of the 1937 Constitution on marriage is carried by 50.3 per cent of the votes cast. The result reflects the changing social attitudes and demography of Ireland with considerable support from the working-class areas of Dublin and the twenty–thirty age group.

1996
Roddy Doyle, *The Woman Who Walked into Doors*; Deirdre Madden, *One by One in the Darkness*; Frank McCourt, *Angela's Ashes*; Robert McLiam Wilson, *Eureka Street* Edna O'Brien, *Down By the River*.
The mood of optimism that has generally prevailed in the previous 12 months, despite not inconsiderable scepticism in some quarters, comes to an end. The Irish Peace Process collapses in February with accusations of Unionist intransigence and Sinn Féin duplicity. There is some renewed hope when US Senator George Mitchell reports on the prospects of decommissioning paramilitary weapons. He advises that all-party talks should start so that decommissioning can begin. However, Prime Minister John Major is not in agreement with him and is insistent upon prior decommissioning. Depressingly for the optimists, the cease-fire agreement ends with two people killed in the Canary Wharf (London Docklands) bombing.

1997
John Banville, *The Untouchable*; Dermot Bolger, *Father's Music*; Emma Donoghue, *Kissing the Witch*; Bernard MacLaverty, *Grace Notes*; Brian Moore, *The Magician's Wife*.
In Britain, the Labour Party wins the General Election. As a result, the Irish Peace Process is invigorated and the cease-fire is restored. Ireland has a new Taoiseach – Bertie Ahern (Fianna Fáil) – and a new President. Professor Mary McAleese succeeds Mary Robinson. Formerly Pro Vice-Chancellor of Queen's University Belfast, she is a Northern Ireland nationalist, who attended secondary school on the Falls Road in the fiercely republican part of Belfast. Married with three children, she has personal experience of the Northern Ireland conflict – her parents lost their home and business in sectarian violence in Belfast. In the wake of McAleese's election, and the way the Presidential campaign brought to the fore debates about nationalism, the Ireland Institute is established by Declan Kiberd, among others, to address the perceived Revisionist (anti-nationalist) stance of the media. The different attitude towards Ireland displayed by the New Labour Government compared with the Major and Thatcher administrations is perhaps evident when Prime Minister Tony Blair publicly acknowledges that the British Government of the day could have done more to prevent the Irish Famine that began in 1845. This does not convince everyone and some media commentators find it gimmicky.

1998

Jennifer Johnston, *Two Moons*; Patrick McCabe, *Breakfast on Pluto*; Joseph O'Connor, *The Salesman*.

The renewed efforts of the New Labour Government results in The Good Friday (Belfast) Agreement (April) between the Dublin and London governments and the main Northern Ireland parties to share power. The agreement provides for North–South and British–Irish representative bodies. One of its suggestions is that a statement that all who live on the island share a common identity replaces the existing constitutional claim that all 32 Counties belong to the same nation. However, the new mood of optimism shared by many inside and outside Ireland is shattered by the Omagh Bomb explosion. It is carried out by the Real IRA, a splinter group, in response to the Good Friday Agreement and kills 28 people and injures 310.

1999

Roddy Doyle, *A Star Called Henry*; Patrick McCabe, *Mondo Desperado* (short stories).

To mixed media reaction, but generally welcomed, devolved government is established in Northern Ireland and ministerial powers returned to Stormont after 27 years. It is proposed that David Trimble, the Ulster Unionist leader, will be Northern Ireland's First Minister, Seamus Mallon deputy first minister and Brid Rogers, a founding member of the SDLP, a fluent Irish speaker who has lived in Northern Ireland since 1960, minister of agriculture and rural development. Martin McGuiness, former IRA chief of staff, is to become minister of education, and Sinn Féin's Bairbre de Brun minister of health, social services and public safety. The Patten report on policing in Northern Ireland (September) recommends the setting up of a Northern Ireland Police Service. The 175 recommendations include a new badge, oath of allegiance and uniform, and a positive recruitment policy towards Catholics. The report fails to meet nationalist demands for a disbandment of the RUC and angers Unionists broadly supportive of the constabulary. The Ulster Unionist Party sees the proposed changes to the name, badge and flag as a 'gratuitous insult' to the force. 1999 also sees, in Ireland, another major scandal around the anti-abortion laws. The founder of the Adam's Pregnancy Advice Centre is alleged to have unlawfully adopted a four-day-old baby from a college student who had sought advice on her pregnancy from the agency.

2000

Emma Donoghue, *Slammerkin*; Jennifer Johnston, *The Gingerbread Woman*.

Devolved government returns to Northern Ireland at midnight on Monday, 29 May, after its suspension in February following the failure of the Ulster Unionists and Sinn Féin to reach agreement over the decommissioning of IRA weapons. In May, the Ulster Unionist Council votes to support its leader David Trimble and rejoin Sinn Féin in a power-sharing executive, accepting the IRA's offer to put its arms 'beyond use'. In January, Peter Mandelson, the Northern Ireland Secretary, confirms that the government intends to dismantle the 78-year-old traditions of the

RUC. Its draft proposals include scaling the force down from 13 500 officers to about 7500, dependent upon the security situation, and recruiting
from a 50–50 pool of Protestants and Catholics. The name will change to
the Police Service of Northern Ireland and the cap badge, a crown, too,
will change. Gerry Adams rejects the terms of the new policing bill, argu-
ing that the original proposals of the Pattern bill had been watered down.
The SDLP is also critical of the bill.

2002

Emma Donoghue, *The Woman Who Gave Birth to Rabbits* (short stories).
The IRA issues a statement in July ahead of the thirtieth anniversary of
Bloody Friday. It expresses the 'sincere apologies and condolences' of the
IRA to all non-combatants, killed or injured by them in their thirty-year
campaign. The IRA reiterates that it is 'committed unequivocally to the
search for freedom, justice and peace in Ireland' and 'to the peace process
and to dealing with the challenges and difficulties which this presents'.
Three hundred people march in Dublin to mark the tenth anniversary of
the X case and to support a NO vote in the latest anti-abortion referendum.

Select Bibliography

Abraham, N., 'Notes on the Phantom', in N. Abraham and M. Torok, *The Shell and the Kernal: Renewals of Pyschoanalysis* trans. N. T. Rand (Chicago: Chicago University Press, 1994).

Bakhtin, M., *The Dialogic Imagination: Four Essays* trans. C. Emerson and M. Holquist (Austin: Texas University Press, 1981).

——, *Rabelais and His World* trans. H. Iswolsky (Bloomington: Indiana University Press, 1984).

Baudrillard, J., *Symbolic Exchange and Death* ed. M. Gane, trans. I. Grant (1973; London: Sage, 1993).

Belsey, C. and Moore, J., *The Feminist Reader* (London: Macmillan, 1997).

Bew, P. and Gillespie, G., *Northern Ireland: A Chronology of the Troubles* (Dublin: Gill and Macmillan, 1993).

——, *The Northern Ireland Peace Process 1993–1996* (London: Serif, 1996).

Bhabha, H. K., 'Of Mimicry and Man: The Ambivalence of Colonial Discourse', Modern Language Association Convention, October 1983, rpt. in *Modern Literary Theory* ed. P. Rice and P. Waugh (London: Arnold, 2001), pp. 380–7.

——, *Nation and Narration* (London and New York: Routledge, 1990).

——, 'Postcolonial Authority and Postmodern Guilt', in *Cultural Studies* ed. L. Grossberg, C. Nelson and P. Treicher (London and New York: Routledge, 1992).

Boehmer, E., 'Stories of Women and Mothers: Gender and Nationalism in the Early Fiction of Flora Nwapa', in *Motherlands: Black Women's Writing from Africa, the Caribbean and South Asia* (London: The Women's Press, 1991).

Buse, P. and Stott, A. (eds), *Ghosts, Deconstruction, Psychoanalysis, History* (Basingstoke: Macmillan, 1998).

Cahalan, J. M., *The Irish Novel* (Dublin: Gill and Macmillan, 1988).

Cairns, D. and Richards, S., *Writing Ireland: Colonialism, Nationalism and Culture* (Manchester: Manchester University Press, 1990).

Carlson, J. (ed.), *Banned in Ireland: Censorship and the Irish Novel* (London and New York: Routledge, 1990).

Castle, T., *The Apparitional Lesbian: Female Homosexuality and Modern Culture* (New York: Columbia University Press, 1993).

Cleary, J., 'Modernization and Aesthetic Ideology in Contemporary Irish Culture' in *Writing the Irish Republic: Literature, Culture, Politics* ed. R. Ryan (Basingstoke: Macmillan, 2000).

Cronin, M., *A History of Ireland* (Basingstoke: Palgrave, 2001).

Cronin, M. and Regan, J. M., *Ireland: The Politics of Independence, 1922–49* (Basingstoke: Macmillan, 2000).

Deane, S., *Nationalism, Colonialism and Literature* (Minneapolis: University of Minnesota Press, 1990).

——, A *Short History of Irish Literature* (London: Hutchinson, 1996).

Derrida, J., *Of Grammatology* trans. G. Spivak (Baltimore, MD, and London: John Hopkins University Press, 1976).

——, 'Foreword', *The Wolf Man's Magic Word: A Cryptonym* trans. N. Rand (Minneapolis: University of Minnesota Press, 1986).

——, 'Marx c'est quelqu' un', in J. Derrida, M. Guillame, and J-P Vincent (eds), *Marx en Jeu* (Paris: Descartes & Cie, 1997).

Dixon, P., *Northern Ireland: The Politics of War and Peace* (Basingstoke: Palgrave, 2001).

Elliott, M., *The Catholics of Ulster* (London: Penguin, 2000).

Featherstone, M., *Consumer Culture and Postmodernism* (1991; rpt. London: Sage, 1996).

Finnegan, S., *The Essential Catholic Handbook: A Summary of Beliefs, Practices and Prayers* (Norwich: Canterbury Press, 1997).

Foucault, M., *Madness and Civilization: A History of Insanity in the Age of Reason* (1961) trans. R. Howard (London: Tavistock, 1965).

——, *Mental Illness and Psychology* (1962) trans. A. M. Sheridan-Smith (New York: Harper and Row, 1976).

——, *Language, Counter-memory, Practice: Selected Essays and Interviews* ed. D. F. Bouchard, trans. D. F. Bouchard and Sherry Simon (Ithaca, New York: Columbia University Press, 1977).

Gąsiorek, A., *Post-war British Fiction: Realism and After* (London: Arnold, 1995).

Gibbons, L., *Transformations in Irish Culture* (Cork: Cork University Press, 1996).

Grant, P., *Breaking Enmities: Religion, Literature and Culture in Northern Ireland, 1967–1997* (Basingstoke: Macmillan, 1999).

Gray, T., *Ireland this Century* (1994; rpt. London: Warner Books, 1999).

Harmon, M. (ed.), *The Irish Writer and the City* (Gerrards Cross: Colin Smythe, 1984).

Harte, L. and Parker, M. (eds), *Contemporary Irish Fiction: Themes, Tropes, Theories* (Basingstoke: Macmillan, 2000).

Harte, L. and Pettit, L. 'States of Dislocation: William Trevor's *Felicia's Journey* and Maurice Leitch's *Gilchrist*' in *Comparing Postcolonial Literatures* ed. A. Bery and P. Murray (London: Macmillan, 2000).

Hennessey, T., *A History of Northern Ireland, 1920–1996* (Basingstoke: Macmillan, 1997).

Herron, T., 'ContamiNation: Patrick McCabe and Colm Toíbín's Pathographies of the Republic', in *Contemporary Irish Fiction: Themes, Tropes and Theories* ed. L. Harte and M. Parker (Basingstoke: Macmillan, 2000), pp. 168–91.

Holland, S., 'Re-citing the Rosary: Women, Catholicism and Agency in Brian Moore's *Cold Heaven* and John McGahern's *Amongst Women*', in *Contemporary Irish Fiction: Themes, Tropes and Theories* ed. L. Hatre and M. Parker (Basingstoke: Macmillan, 2000), pp. 56–78.

Hughes, E. (ed.), *Culture and Politics in Northern Ireland 1960–1990* (Buckhingham: Open University Press, 1991).

Humphreys, A. J., *New Dubliners: Urbanization and the Irish Family* (London: Routledge and Kegan Paul, 1966).

Imhof, R., *John Banville: A Critical Introduction* (Dublin: Wolfhound, 1997).

Jameson, F., 'Marx's Purloined Letter', in *Ghostly Demarcations: A Symposium on Jacques Derrida's* Specters of Marx (London: Verso, 1999).

Keith, M. and Pile, S., *Place and the Politics of Identity* (London and New York: Routledge, 1993).

Keogh, D., *Twentieth-Century Ireland: Nation and State* (Dublin: Gill and Macmillan, 1994).

Kiberd, D., *Inventing Ireland: The Literature of the Modern Nation* (1995; rpt. London: Vintage, 1996).

Kirkland, R., *Literature and Culture in Northern Ireland Since 1965: Moments of Danger* (London and New York: Longman, 1996).

Klein, M., *The Selected Writings of Melanie Klein* ed. J. Mitchell (Harmondsworth: Penguin, 1991).

Kristeva, J., *Powers of Horror: An Essay on Abjection* trans. L. S. Roudiez (1941; trans. New York: Columbia University Press, 1982).

——, *Strangers to Ourselves* trans. L. Roudiez (New York: Columbia University Press, 1984a).

——, *Revolution in Poetic Language* (New York: Columbia University Press, 1984b).

Lloyd, D., *Automated States: Irish Writing and the Post-Colonial Moment* (Dublin: Lilliput, 1993).

MacGregor, J., *The Discovery of the Art of the Insane* (Princeton, NJ: Princeton Unversity Press, 1989).

Mahony, C. H., *Contemporary Irish Literature: Transforming Tradition* (Basingstoke: Macmillan, 1999).

Marshall, A. and Sammells, N., *Irish Encounters: Poetry, Politics and Prose* (Bath: Sulis Press, 1998).

McCarthy, C., *Modernization: Crisis and Culture in Ireland 1969–1992* (Dublin: Four Courts Press, 2000).

McMinn, J., *The Supreme Fictions of John Banville* (Manchester: Manchester University Press, 1999).

——, 'Versions of Banville: Versions of Modernism', in *Contemporary Irish Fiction: Themes, Tropes and Theories* ed. L. Harte and M. Parker (Basingstoke: Macmillan, 2000), pp. 79–99.

McNay, L., *Foucault: A Critical Introduction* (Cambridge: Polity Press, 1994).

Meaney, G., *Sex and Nation: Women in Irish Culture and Politics* (Dublin: Attic Press, 1991).

Merleau-Ponty, M., *The Visible and the Invisible* (Evanston: Northwestern University Press, 1968).

Miller, D., *Women Who Hurt Themselves: A Book of Hope and Understanding* (New York: Harper Collins, 1994).

O'Brien, E., *Seamus Heaney: Creating Irelands of the Mind* (Dublin: The Liffey Press, 2002).

O'Brien, G. 'The Aesthetics of Exile', in *Contemporary Irish Fiction: Themes, Tropes and Theories* ed. L. Harte and M. Parker (Basingstoke: Macmillan, 2000), pp. 35–55.

O'Connor, P., *Emerging Voices: Women in Contemporary Irish Society* (Dublin: Institute of Public Administration, 1998).

Parr, H. and C. Philo, 'Mapping "Mad" Identities', in *Mapping the Subject: Geographies of Cultural Transformation* ed. S. Pile and N. Thrift (London and New York: Routledge, 1995).

Pelaschiar, L., *Writing the North: The Contemporary Novel in Northern Ireland* (Trieste: Edizioni Parnso, 1998).

Pelikan, J., *Mary Through The Centuries: Her Place in the History of Culture* (New Haven and London: Yale University Press, 1996).

Petley, J., 'The Monstrous Child', in *The Body's Perilous Pleasures: Dangerous Desires and Contemporary Culture* ed. M. Aaron (Edinburgh: Edinburgh University Press, 1999).

Phillips, S., *Beyond the Myths: Mother–Daughter Relationships in Psychology, History, Literature and Everyday Life* (Harmondsworth: Penguin, 1996).

Pile, S. and N. Thrift, *Mapping the Subject: Geographies of Cultural Transformation* (London and New York: Routledge, 1995).

Ricouer, P., 'Mimesis and Representation', *A Ricouer Reader: Reflection and Imagination* ed. M. J. Valdes (Hemel Hempstead: Harvester Wheatsheaf, 1991).

Rose, G., *Feminism and Geography: The Limits of Geographical Knowledge* (Cambridge: Polity Press, 1993).

Ryan, R., *Writing in the Irish Republic: Literature, Culture, Politics* (Basingstoke: Macmillan, 2000).

Soja, E. W., *Postmodern Geographies: The Reassertion of Space in Critical Social Theory* (London: Verso, 1989).

Smyth, A., *The Abortion Papers Ireland* (Dublin: Attic Press, 1992).

Smyth, G., *The Novel and Nation: Studies in the New Irish Fiction* (London: Pluto Press, 1997).

Steele, V., *Fetish: Fashion, Sex and Power* (Oxford: Oxford University Press, 1996).

St. Peter, C., *Changing Ireland: Strategies in Contemporary Women's Fiction* (Basingstoke: Macmillan, 2000).

Stubbings, D., *Modernism and the Representation of the Maternal: The Mother-Figure in Anglo-Irish Literature, 1882–1939* (Basingstoke: Macmillan, 2000).

Sweetman, R., *On Our Backs: Sexual Attitudes in a Changing Ireland* (London: Pan, 1979).

Wallace, C., 'Running Amuck: Manic Logic in Patrick McCabe's *The Butcher Boy*', *Irish Studies Review* 6 (2), 1998, 157–63.

Wallace, J-A., 'De-scribing *The Water-babies*', in *De-scribing Empire* ed. C. Tiffin and A. Lawson (London and New York: Routledge, 1994).

Wallace, J-A., 'Technologies of "the child": towards a theory of the child-subject', *Textual Practice* 9 (2), 1995, 285–302.

Warner, M., *Alone of All Her Sex: The Myth and Cult of the Virgin Mary* (1976; rpt. London: Pan, 1990).

Walshe, E. (ed.), *Sex, Nation and Dissent in Irish Writing* (Cork: Cork University Press, 1997).

Weekes, A., *Irish Women Writers: An Uncharted Tradition* (Lexington, KY: University of Kentucky Press, 1990).

Wolfreys, J., *Victorian Hauntings: Spectrality, Gothic, the Uncanny and Literature* (Basingstoke and New York: Palgrave, 2002).

Zipes, J., *Fairy Tales and the Art of Subversion* (London and New York: Routledge, 1988).

Index